ROTH FAMILY FOUNDATION

Imprint in Music

Michael P. Roth
and Sukey Garcetti
have endowed this
imprint to honor the
memory of their parents,
Julia and Harry Roth,
whose deep love of music
they wish to share
with others.

The publisher and the University of California Press Foundation gratefully acknowledge the generous support of the Roth Family Foundation Imprint in Music, established by a major gift from Sukey and Gil Garcetti and Michael P. Roth.

Terrible Freedom

The publisher gratefully acknowledges the General Publications Fund of the American Musicological Society, supported in part by the National Endowment for the Humanities and the Andrew W. Mellon Foundation.

Terrible Freedom

THE LIFE AND WORK OF
LUCIA DLUGOSZEWSKI

Amy C. Beal

UNIVERSITY OF CALIFORNIA PRESS

University of California Press
Oakland, California

© 2022 by Amy C. Beal
First Paperback Printing 2024, ISBN 9780520401273 (pbk)
Library of Congress Cataloging-in-Publication Data

Names: Beal, Amy C., author.
Title: Terrible freedom : the life and work of Lucia Dlugoszewski / Amy C. Beal.
Other titles: California studies in 20th-century music ; 31.
Description: Oakland : University of California Press, [2022] | Series: California studies in 20th-century music ; 31 | Includes bibliographical references and index.
Identifiers: LCCN 2021057666 (print) | LCCN 2021057667 (ebook) | ISBN 9780520386655 (cloth) | ISBN 9780520386662 (epub)
Subjects: LCSH: Dlugoszewski, Lucia, 1925–2000. | Composers—United States—Biography. | Music—United States—20th century—History and criticism. | Modern dance music—United States—20th century—History and criticism. | Erick Hawkins Dance Company | BISAC: MUSIC / Individual Composer & Musician | MUSIC / Genres & Styles / Dance
Classification: LCC ML410.D6815 B43 2022 (print) | LCC ML410.D6815 (ebook) | DDC 780.92 [B]—dc23
LC record available at https://lccn.loc.gov/2021057666
LC ebook record available at https://lccn.loc.gov/2021057667

31 30 29 28 27 26 25 24 23 22
10 9   8   7   6   5   4   3   2   1

for Paul Tai

I suppose the most important thing, the heaviest single factor in one's life, is whether one's born male or female. In most societies it determines one's expectations, activities, outlook, ethics, manners—almost everything.... [Women] don't often seem to turn up mathematicians, or composers of music, or inventors, or abstract thinkers. But it isn't that they're stupid.

    URSULA K. LE GUIN, *The Left Hand of Darkness* (1969)

I have two gifted pupils: one is Polish and the other was born in France, the son of a German who used to play with Paul Klee in the evenings (violin and piano). The son is called Christian Wolff. I don't know the Pole's name, it is too difficult.

    JOHN CAGE, letter to Pierre Boulez, 5 June 1950

CONTENTS

List of Illustrations   xi
Acknowledgments   xiii

Margins, Shadows, and Footnotes: An Introduction   1

1 · Lucille in Detroit (1925–48)   10

2 · Letters from New York (1949–51)   28

3 · New York Beginnings: A Broader View (1950–53)   45

4 · Expanding Creativity and Collaboration (1953–60)   63

5 · The Disparate Element (1960–70)   82

6 · Aesthetic Immediacy (1970–80)   108

7 · Rage (1980–87)   131

8 · Losses (1988–2000)   147

Out from the Shadows: A Conclusion   162

Appendix 1: Selected Works List   167
Appendix 2: Lucia Dlugoszewski–Erick Hawkins Collaborations   173
Appendix 3: Discography   174
Notes   177
Sources and Bibliography   209
Index   219

FIGURES

Figures follow page 62

1. Baby book photographs, ca. 1931.
2. Dlugoszewski family portrait, ca. 1931.
3. The young Lucille at the piano in the *Detroit News*, 1939.
4. School portrait, ca. 1939.
5. "Officers' Club" high school photograph, ca. 1941.
6. Lucille relaxing under a tree (date unknown).
7. Lucille posing for the camera (date unknown).
8. Dlugoszewski's Wayne State University transcripts, page 1.
9 and 10. Publicity portraits of Dlugoszewski with her invented percussion instruments (ca. 1962).
11. Dlugoszewski posing with instruments (date unknown; ca. 1960).
12. Dlugoszewski with sculptor Ralph Dorazio, builder of her instrument designs (ca. 1962).
13. Composite of publicity photographs (date unknown; ca. 1960).
14. Page one of "Goat of the God," from *openings of the (eye)*, 1952–53.
15. Program for concert presented by the Living Theatre, 1952.
16. *Musical America* advertisement for the premiere of *Here and Now with Watchers*, November 1957.
17. Dlugoszewski's "Curtain of Timbre" program for the Five Spot Cafe concert, 1958.
18. Program for Composers' Showcase concert (shared with Netty Simons), 1959.

19. Complete score for *Music for Left Ear in a Small Room*, 1960.
20. Erick Hawkins and Lucia Dlugoszewski wedding portrait, 1 September 1962.
21. Wedding day family portrait, 1 September 1962.
22. First page of *Densities: Supernova/Corona/Clear Core*.
23. Advertisement for Erick Hawkins's dance classes (date unknown).
24. New York Philharmonic program for premiere performance of *Abyss and Caress*, 1975.
25. Composers assembled in Avery Fisher Hall, New York, on the occasion of conductor Pierre Boulez's retirement, 12 May 1977.
26. First page of notation for introductory percussion cadenza, *Tender Theatre Flight Nageire*, 1978.
27. Poster for Carnegie Recital Hall premiere of *Cicada Terrible Freedom*, 1982.
28. "To Lillian, Christmas 1982," graphic poem by Dlugoszewski.
29. Graphic poem for John Ransom Phillips, 22 December 1996.
30. Private diary writings ("duende scream"), 1987.
31. Private diary writings ("gauntlet of courage"), 1992.

ACKNOWLEDGMENTS

Thank you, Libby! It is no exaggeration to say that without the efforts of Elizabeth ("Libby") Smigel, dance curator and archivist in the Music Division at the Library of Congress, none of this would have been possible. Especially in the later stages of work on this book during the winter and spring of 2021, she and her staff overcame a seemingly endless onslaught of obstacles—pandemic shutdowns, Capitol Hill crises, and so on—to help me obtain what I needed, not the least of which were the photographs and other illustrations included here. I hope you are pleased with the results of your hard work! I also hope that this modest book inspires future scholars to delve deeper into your collection, to tell Dlugoszewski's story in even more nuanced detail.

I am also grateful to the following people for help—some personal, some institutional, some brief and anecdotal, some crucial and consequential: Benjamin Bates, Brett Boutwell, Lee Cannon-Brown, Richard Carrick, Renata Celichowska, Brigid Cohen, Rory Cowal, Leela Denver, Kaitlin Doyle, Joseph Finkel, Renee Flower, Sheryl Henze, Kelli Jurich, Mark Katz, Louis Kavouras, Julia Keefer, Al Margolis, Jim MacKenzie, Gloria McLean, Josiah McElheny, David Mahler, Bethany Morgan, Tracee Ng, Benjamin Piekut, Linda Quan, Anne Shreffler, Matthew Shubin, Mike Silverton, Don Stewart, James Thoma, Joel Thome, William Trigg, Ted Warburton, and Laura Pettibone Wright. Writers and diarists who influenced my thinking while working on this multiyear endeavor also seem important to mention. They include James Atlas, Robert Caro, Sophie Drinker, Leon Edel, Grace Hartigan, Jill Lepore, Gerda Lerner, Judith Malina, Suzanne Robinson, Wallace Stegner, Judith Tick, and Virginia Woolf. Strunk and White were also never far from my desk.

I am deeply indebted to the Ucross Foundation, which provided a four-week residency in northeastern Wyoming for uninterrupted work on the manuscript in the Big Red Barn during the summer of 2019. My research was also supported by several grants from the Committee on Research and the Arts Research Institute at the University of California, Santa Cruz, which enabled three trips to Washington, D.C.

I am thrilled to see this book appear in the California Studies in Twentieth-Century Music series hosted by University of California Press—the home of my first book some fifteen years ago. Editors Raina Polivka and Madison Wetzell ensured that the process from submission to production proceeded smoothly, despite the complicated logistical situation into which the manuscript was born. I am especially grateful for the advocacy of Richard Taruskin, the series curator, who motivated me to jump head-first into the writing of this book after hearing me give a presentation on Dlugoszewski at the Northern California chapter of the American Musicological Society regional conference in San Francisco in February 2019. Likewise, I am grateful for the generous and constructive readers' reports provided by Denise Von Glahn and Marian Wilson Kimber—scholarly role models of my own for whose support (and outrage) I am deeply thankful!

A few other very special people deserve special thanks: Dr. Diane Bridgeman, who, aside from being a gentle yet effective life coach, took time out of her own busy schedule to help me understand Dlugoszewski's psychological states of mind; John Ransom Phillips, for sharing both memories and precious original materials at his homes in Montclair, New Jersey, and Old Chatham, New York; and Katherine Duke, whose unwavering affection and advocacy for Dlugoszewski's legacy keeps the composer's spirit alive.

My mother Jane Garlinghouse and my sister Rebecca Beal have also supported this project from its tentative beginnings to its long breaks—breaks made necessary by a variety of medical sagas and natural disasters—to its final move toward completion in the midst of the global pandemic. (I promise my next book will be about Mel Brooks . . . or maybe Journey.)

Larry Polansky has had to live with this book's challenges, delays, frustrations, mysteries, and surprises for as long as I have. I am grateful for his patience, insight, encouragement, and careful reading of several drafts, but especially for his insistence that I simply shut a door in our very small house and allow myself to be a writer as often as I could—at least when we weren't fumbling through piano-mandolin arrangements of May Aufderheide rags. (I promise my next book will be about Hazel Felman . . . or maybe Froberger.)

Finally, this book is dedicated to Paul Tai, not only for suggesting I write it in the first place, but more significantly, for all he has done for noncommercial American music during his time as director of Artists and Repertory at New World Records. It seems a fitting tribute to someone whose behind-the-scenes vision shapes the body of what music we have available today—so much of which is in danger of being lost to the margins, shadows, and footnotes of history.

Margins, Shadows, and Footnotes

AN INTRODUCTION

To dangerously awaken the dangerous mind without fixing it![1]

LUCIA DLUGOSZEWSKI'S LIFE BEGAN IN DETROIT on 16 June 1925 and ended in New York City on 9 April 2000. She composed approximately one hundred pieces, invented around one hundred instruments, wrote poetry and prose, collaborated with filmmakers and the Living Theatre, and steered the musical direction of the Erick Hawkins Dance Company for nearly fifty years. Her compositions were praised by critics and championed by figures such as poet Frank O'Hara, writer Jamake Highwater, sculptor Isamu Noguchi, philosopher F. S. C. Northrop, and critics Alfred Frankenstein and Virgil Thomson, among others. The night she died, Dlugoszewski was missed at a dress rehearsal for a performance of her own choreographic piece based on the life of her friend, abstract expressionist painter Robert Motherwell.

After brief composition studies with John Cage and Edgard Varèse, Dlugoszewski followed her own creative path while confronting the musical issues of the time: expanded sonic resources; invented instruments and new ways of playing traditional instruments; alternative formal structures; interdisciplinary collaboration; the role of silence and "everyday sounds" in performance; and spiritual, psychological, and philosophical influences. Frequent concepts, influences, and key words running through Dlugoszewski's work may bewilder researchers: Logos and Eros, tenderness, sensual realism, Eastern philosophy, *suchness* and *thusness*, haiku, koans and the pursuit of the ungraspable, *radical empirical immediacy*, *quidditas*, *duende*, and *nageire*. "I believe in the poetic immediacy of sound," she explained.[2]

Beyond the simplicity of her youthful *Halloween Symphony* (a work for solo piano, despite its title; 1938) and *Song of Young Writers* (1941),

Dlugoszewski's works list reads like no other. Certain ideas appear frequently in her titles, including *everyday sounds, left ear, radical, cicada, naked, abyss, flight, terrible,* and *amor*, as seen in this sample list of compositions spanning most of her career:

>*Moving Space Theater Piece for Everyday Sounds* (1949)
>*Transparencies 1–50 for Everyday Sounds* (1951)
>*openings of the (eye)* (1951–52)
>*Archaic Timbre Piano Music* (1954)
>*Music for Left Ear in a Small Room* (1959–60)
>*Balance Naked Flung* (1966)
>*Densities: Nova Corona Clear Core* (1971)
>*Tender Theater Flight Nageire* (1971/78)
>*Fire Fragile Flight* (1973)
>*Strange Tenderness of Naked Leaping* (1977)
>*Amor Elusive Empty August* (1979)
>*Amor Now Tilting Night* (1979)
>*Startle Transparent Terrible Freedom* (1981)
>*Duende Newfallen* (1982–83)
>*Duende Quidditas* (1983)
>*Quidditas Sorrow Terrible Freedom* (1983)
>*Radical, Strange, Quidditas, Dew Tear, Duende* (1987)
>*Disparate Stairway Radical Other* (1995)
>*Depth Duende Scarecrow Other* (1996)
>*Exacerbated Subtlety Concert* (1997)

Dlugoszewski wrote over a dozen works for dances by choreographer Erick Hawkins, three experimental film scores, and three scores for productions by the Living Theatre. Many of the works were scored for her own percussion instruments or for "timbre piano," her distinctive inside-the-piano technique. Other pieces call for more classical chamber ensembles or orchestra, sometimes with theatrical elements, like the lighting and blowing out of matches. Only a few works include voice; not a single work includes tape or electronics of any kind.

Neither melodic nor motive-driven in a traditional sense, Dlugoszewski's compositional tendencies included the use of extended instrumental techniques, a focus on timbre, emphasis on abstract and philosophical/

metaphysical meaning, avoidance of fixed pitch through the use of sliding tones, and a preference for extreme dynamic ranges. She valued surprise and unpredictability—"the disparate element"—which she sometimes referred to as "giving the audience a flower at the right time."[3] Many compositions are listed in various sources as "work-in-progress"—Dlugoszewski reportedly had trouble finishing pieces, especially later in her life, as mood swings and psychological instability seemed to affect her with increasing frequency and intensity.

While striving to nurture her identity as a free-spirited artist, Dlugoszewski also struggled to balance her ongoing roles as daughter, muse, wife, and caregiver, roles that both inspired and oppressed her. (Dlugoszewski never had children, but felt the pressures of eldercare; after her mother's death in 1988 she wrote in her diary: "In search of myself again.") This is the story of a composer, but it is also the story of a woman who, in the words of Ruth Solie, shared "the restlessness of all women against patriarchy."[4] Dlugoszewski deserves an intervention of her own—both a recuperation of her life story through "fundamental fact-finding," as well as a critique of the gender issues that affected her compositional work and her career.[5]

· · · · ·

Women artists are currently being rescued, metaphorically, though not particularly rapidly, from the margins, shadows, and footnotes of history. Shadowy metaphors abound in mentions of forgotten females, as in musicologist Judith Tick's description of my 2015 book on composer Johanna Magdalena Beyer: "Beal ... allows us to appreciate the musical rewards in bringing someone in from the cold margins of conventional history."[6] Similarly, a 2017 description of an exhibit of the work of artist Sonja Sekula, who committed suicide at the age of forty-five in 1963, caused me to notice another woman lurking in another decentralized place: "This fascinating, welcome survey aims to rescue [Sekula] from the footnotes of the avant-garde."[7] A recent article on English composer Ethel Smyth similarly lamented the fact that she had "for too long ... been relegated to footnote status."[8] Linda Dahl, writing decades ago about the women left out of jazz histories, drew on the same metaphor: "Often they were buried in footnotes.... Under-recorded or, sadly, not recorded at all. Their slim oeuvre out of print. A blanket of silence."[9]

Margins and footnotes are where we put things that we allow to be overlooked, secondary to the main story. They are not unlike shadows, where things can hide, or be hidden. With this in mind, I could not overlook critic and composer Kyle Gann's peculiar praise, and then damning banishment, of Dlugoszewski: "Possibly the leading direct inheritor of Varèse's aesthetic, she lived a life of relative obscurity and died in 2000, having achieved little more than a shadowy reputation."[10] Gann's grim assessment of the (un)worthiness of Dlugoszewski's life not only caught my attention, it also perplexed me. (His dismissal of Dlugoszewski echoes Françoise Tillard's similar dismissal of Fanny Mendelssohn Hensel, who, according to Tillard, "did not really tackle life head on, did not complete her life's work, and never reached her full potential."[11]) Johanna Beyer received a similar assessment along with character descriptions such as antisocial, friend- and family-less, alcoholic, dark, unfriendly, lonely, and so on, none of which have been substantiated.[12] Likewise, Gann condemned Dlugoszewski, in a single sentence, to both obscurity—literally, darkness—*and* to the shadows. I imagine that such a description would have baffled this outgoing, prolific woman who loved passionately, and once wrote a graphic poem called "The Sun!" Extensive biographical and compositional evidence prove that she achieved much more than "a shadowy reputation." Once her "dangerous mind" had awoken, her creativity proved to be relentless.

In the early 1970s, during a critical junction in her career, Dlugoszewski made some of her most explicit statements about her views on the status of women in music, and how that status had affected her own work. Speaking to a reporter from her hometown of Detroit, Dlugoszewski asserted: "It isn't true that women can't compose great music. They can and do but they have been terribly put down in the past. Music is a very conservative field but there are some brilliant women composers coming along now who will, I think, change things."[13] In response to the question "Do women have stamina and single-mindedness?" Dlugoszewski reflected further: "I have never missed a performance or a deadline, even if it means working for 56 hours at a stretch.... I have missed having a family and I regret that, but it has been a necessary part of the sacrifice and struggle. I hope future generations of women composers will get more recognition and monetary rewards so they can enjoy both a career and a family."[14] The reporter Dlugoszewski spoke to on this occasion was all too happy to embrace a trope of neglect: "Until recently," the reporter wrote, "[Dlugoszewski] has worked in the kind of obscurity (and near starvation) which surrounds most serious composers, especially if they are women."[15]

During the winter of 1950–51, shortly after Dlugoszewski moved to New York City, writer Anaïs Nin described a public talk given there by Australian-born composer and *New-York Herald Tribune* critic Peggy Glanville-Hicks. Nin took note of Glanville-Hicks's explicit acknowledgment of the double standards women composers encountered while trying to build a professional reputation: "[Glanville-Hicks] mocks the composers and critics who interfere with the development of a woman composer. She is asked to recommend, to bless, to support lesser composers, to introduce them, help them on their way. But this help is not returned. It was the first time I heard a brilliant, effective woman demonstrate the obstacles which impaired her professional achievement because she was a woman."[16] Indeed, the social milieu Dlugoszewski entered into at the start of her career was not free of sexism, and women artists were taking note, at least in their own private journals, where they sometimes allowed their outrage to be aired. Just a year after Nin's writing about Glanville-Hicks, actress and Living Theatre director Judith Malina wrote in her own diary: "Paul [Goodman] says there are no women artists because a woman is too much concerned with her own body. I get angry."[17]

During the 1970s Dlugoszewski would write to a number of women composers, including Betsy Jolas and Miriam Gideon, expressing her admiration for their music and her appreciation of their presence in the world as role models for her own compositional career, though the bulk of her correspondence with other composers more frequently sought out prominent men like Virgil Thomson and Aaron Copland who had the potential to advance her career in ways that composers like Jolas and Gideon could not.[18]

. . . . .

In her introduction to an interview with Dlugoszewski published in 1993, Cole Gagne speculated about why Dlugoszewski's "long and distinguished career has received scant documentation from the press and the recording industry," suspecting that the composer's affiliation with the Erick Hawkins Dance Company had been "a double-edged sword," one that hindered her reception and "made her a difficult subject to research."[19] As it turns out, Dlugoszewski is no longer a difficult subject to research, thanks to a vast paper trail now available for study. With the help of those materials, I conceive of this book—admittedly focused more emphatically on her life than her work—as a first step toward reestablishing Dlugoszewski into the history of which she was a part. In this context, historian Gerda Lerner's words, from the introduction to her milestone 1979 book about discovering, resurrecting, newly interpreting, and "placing" women in history, ring true: "Women are made to fit into the *empty spaces* of traditional history."[20]

Margins, shadows, footnotes... empty spaces. (Dahl's "blanket of silence.") Virginia Woolf scholar Ellen Bayuk Rosenman echoed these metaphors, pointing out Woolf's challenges to claims of accidental absence instead of exclusion, while invoking a related image—the blank spaces "on library bookshelves where women's books should be." Rosenman writes:

> It is the "books that were not there" that tell the tale of women's literary history. Woolf implies here a politics of absence, continuing the spatial imagery of her title [*A Room of One's Own*] as well as the imagery of vision, by defining these empty spaces as having been created by gender inequities. Although there is nothing there, that "nothing" still has meaning, just as rests have meaning in a system of musical notation. This is another version of re-vision: to see *blank space* as its own kind of historical record.[21]

For some reason, which I hope to uncover in the process of describing Dlugoszewski's life and the times in which that life was lived, she has not been awarded what strikes me as an obvious seat at the table of not only the history of the New York School—the 1950s network of composers, musicians, dancers, artists, writers, actors, and directors—but also in the broader history of eccentric American composers whose creativity drives them to idiosyncratic music and ways of describing their aesthetics. Men like Harry Partch (1901–74) and Ornette Coleman (1930–2015)—to choose just two—have been celebrated for their autodidactic training and their refusal to follow an established path, as well as for their quirky and pugnacious characters (as in the case of Partch's legendary irascibility), or for their impenetrable theory (as in the case of Coleman's confusing *Harmolodics*). To be sure, Dlugoszewski was quirky, eccentric, and enthusiastic, and described her own music in such odd and opaque ways that she could give composer Anthony Braxton's *Tri-Axium Writings* a run for its money, but she was also productive, imaginative, and inventive. (She might have agreed with Revolutionary-era composer William Billings's proclamation, on the rules of composition, that "nature is the best dictator."[22]) Lucia Dlugoszewski was a rugged individualist in the truest American sense. Why does she (still) dwell in the shadows?[23]

· · · · ·

Soon after the 2015 publication of my book on Johanna Beyer, Paul Tai, artistic director of New World Records, wrote to me with an off-the-cuff yet serious suggestion: "Speaking of women composers, how about Lucia Dlugoszewski?"[24] To which I replied: "I don't know much about her." It wasn't the first time he had mentioned her to me, and the name started to stick in my mind. Only minimally curious at the start, I made my first trip to examine Dlugoszewski's papers at the Library of Congress in September 2015. At that time, I was only able to access three boxes of her materials, embedded within the Erick Hawkins Papers.[25] On my next visit, in December 2018, I was presented with several boxes of Dlugoszewski's New York letters to her parents written in 1950 and 1951, and an enormous, overstuffed scrapbook that documented her childhood in Detroit. In January 2019, the Library of Congress acquired over forty new boxes of her papers, materials that had been confiscated from her apartment by the State of New York when she died intestate and without heirs in 2000. This overwhelming amount of new primary sources became the focus of another trip to Washington in September 2019—one that yielded a significant amount of new information on Dlugoszewski's life and work. Other primary source materials—private letters, sketches of scores, unpublished essays, graphic poems and other art work—are scattered like Easter eggs around the country in other archival collections. By the time the COVID-19 global pandemic crisis exploded in early March 2020, I had more than enough material for an intense, shelter-in-place book project. (New primary source material surfaced at the Library of Congress during the final stages of preparing this book's manuscript, but could not be consulted in time for inclusion.)

In addition to this archival digging, I tried to gain a sense of Dlugoszewski's reputation among her contemporaries. I began by asking composers (and a few musicians and musicologists) what they knew about her. One composer appreciated her "because of her passionate temperament and what it produced musically." Another remarked that among musicians, "she had a wacky reputation." Another New York composer recalled: "I didn't personally know Lucia but I loved her work. . . . It empowered me to go ahead with my own feeble attempts at unusual instrumentation." A New York–based musician called her a "mysterious character"; another said she had "a 'downtown' temperament in an 'uptown' body." Another found her music disappointing, adding: "[My] impression was of a composer who didn't think very rigorously about her composing." Another composer admitted: "Sad to say, I know very little about her," while a musicologist who has written authoritative books and articles on American experimental music told me: "I have not heard of Dlugoszewski." Another expert on the same subject repeated this refrain: "I am one of those people who had never heard of Lucia Dlugoszewski." Another composer active since the 1970s apologized as well: "I'm sorry to say that I had not heard of Lucia Dlugoszewski."

A composer who lived on the West Coast during the 1970s recalled acquiring one of Dlugoszewski's few recordings at the time, an eight-minute brass ensemble piece called *Angels of the Inmost Heaven* (released on Folkways in 1975): "When I heard the recording," he wrote, "I just assumed she was well known and I was the only one who had never heard of her." Another composer who knew Dlugoszewski in the early 1950s remembered her as "kind of wild, and thinking the music [was] sometimes good, if somewhat all over the place." Another admitted: "In my ignorance, I regarded her pieces as being passé and uptown." Finally, a festival director who expressed skepticism about the quality of her music offered a challenge: "I do hope you prove me wrong."[26]

I intend to. I must admit though, that, like writer Delmore Schwartz's biographer James Atlas, who "fretted about Delmore's obscurity," I too have fretted over Dlugoszewski's lack of presence in histories of twentieth-century music, questioning both her worthiness *and* my ability to make a case for it in a piece of my own nonfiction storytelling.[27] But over time, I have become convinced of her right to be included in the history of the second half of the twentieth century. This is neither a tale of disappointed hopes nor the biography a tragic figure. Dlugoszewski was a skilled and inventive composer, a tortured creative whirlwind. Her life's work matters, and it deserves to be known. The following pages aim to tell the story of her life, and to document her creative work as accurately as possible: to shed light on Lucia.

A NOTE ON NAMES

The subject of this biography was born Lucille Ruth Dlugoszewski. At some point in her mid-twenties she started using the name Lucia (pronounced LOO-sha), and this is the name she used on her compositions, publications, and other creative works. At various times in her life she referred to herself in writing as "Lucy" (also "Lucie" and "Luci"), and people close to her called her this as well. In this book I refer to her as "Lucille" only in the first chapter, which documents her childhood in Detroit. In all subsequent chapters I refer to her by her family name, following the standard convention for composer biographies when the confusion of shared marital names is not a factor.

ONE

Lucille in Detroit (1925–48)

I think I wanted to be a composer even as a little girl because there are so many things that music can do, almost more than any other art. It can be faster and subtler, more sensual, more elusive. It can be larger and darker than we imagine, more mysterious, more violent. The dimension of its freedom is dizzying. Its sensitivity is unspeakable.[1]

FAMILY LIFE AND EARLY CHILDHOOD

Lucille Ruth Dlugoszewski was born in Detroit, Michigan, on 16 June 1925.[2] During the year of her birth, Calvin Coolidge was inaugurated to his first elected term, F. Scott Fitzgerald's "Roaring Twenties" era-defining novella *The Great Gatsby* was published, Igor Stravinsky conducted the New York Philharmonic during his first United States tour, and Louis Armstrong began fronting his own band. Less than a year after her birth, Detroit installed its first residential telephones.[3]

Lucille's father Chester (Czeslaw; nicknamed "Czesio") Dlugoszewski (1887–1975) arrived in the United States with an eighth-grade education in 1909. Before settling in Detroit he was employed as a sheet metal worker in Cleveland; in Depression-era Detroit Chester worked in the tool and die trade, eventually coming to work for Fisher Body, a branch of General Motors. Lucille's mother Jennie (nicknamed "Jolas") Goralewski (1903–1988) immigrated in 1913, having completed the equivalent of high school. Both parents were born and raised in the Polish town of Plock, on the Vistula River, some seventy miles northwest of Warsaw. Chester and Jennie married in Michigan on 1 March 1924; Jennie was naturalized in Detroit on 17 April 1931, and by 1940 Chester had been naturalized as well.

Lucille grew up fluent in Polish, and the Dlugoszewski household, which moved around frequently in Detroit during her young years, was one filled with Polish pride. A set of undated notes about her family background written down much later in Dlugoszewski's life include some details about family music making and her parents' courtship:

> [Jennie's sister] Helen played the violin and Jennie played the piano
> They played duets together for their parents + Jennie's husband, Chester fell in love with her when they played these duets
> Chester and Jennie used to go dancing every week at the Polish National Home in Detroit on Chene St. before they were married + danced to 3 o'clock in the morning
> when they were first married + Lucia was born they lived on MacDougall in Detroit[4]

In 1930, the Dlugoszewskis lived at 14637 Glenwood Avenue, in the northeastern part of the city near the well-to-do suburb of Grosse Pointe. Between approximately 1935 and 1940, they lived in a rented house at 5210 Moran Street, not far from the General Motors Hamtramck Assembly Plant. (The MacDougall Street mentioned [above] in Dlugoszewski's autobiographical notes also stood in the shadow of the GM Hamtramck Assembly Plant, just a few blocks from Moran Street.) In 1942, the year of Lucille's graduation from high school, Chester registered for the draft, and listed his address as 5327 Baldwin Avenue, about a mile away from their previous house on Moran Street, and this is the address Lucille used throughout her college years. By August 1948 the family had moved to 9894 Chenlot Avenue. Later in life she claimed to have grown up in Detroit's "slums."[5]

In an interview conducted around 1960, Dlugoszewski characterized her childhood in Detroit in unambiguous ways. She described the cultural background of her Polish-born parents, and described Poland—a place she never visited—as "a country vivid for rebellion, courage, exile." (She also referred to what she called the family's musical "chauvinism" with regard to their preference for Polish composer Frédéric Chopin.[6]) She described her father as being agnostic but raised culturally Catholic, with interests in mathematics, science, and dialectics. She described her mother as an amateur painter and as a person drawn to nature. Furthermore, she said, her mother displayed "simplicity, sensibility, respect for danger, lack of sentimental romanticism and idealism, [and a] delight in clear, radiant physicality." This trope remained consistent throughout her life: a feature article in the *Detroit News* published in 1972 explained that "Lucia credits her father, who was a toolmaker, with filling her head with liberal politics and intellectual pursuits; her mother, a painter and naturalist, nurtured her interest in the arts."[7] (In a separate, undated, typewritten "biography" Lucille described her father as an "ardent amateur in mathematics and political science" and her mother as a "painter.") She identified her hometown as "a factory city, therefore haunted, ugly, surreal, [and] slightly Charles Dickens." She recalled growing up surrounded by Midwestern dialects, French and Native American place names, and the unique terrain of the Great Lakes region: the "delicate blue uniqueness of [the] Northern sky and fresh water, exquisite bareness of deciduous trees..., much smell of snow."[8] The Michigan of Dlugoszewski's youth would remain a powerful source of metaphor and nostalgia throughout her life.

Her ambiguous reference to Dickens notwithstanding, Lucille's poetic depiction of her hometown neglected to mention the grim and gritty realities of the Detroit in which she grew up. Her "haunted, ugly, surreal" factory city was perhaps made so in part through the corruption of the Prohibition-era bootleg industry, strangled by organized crime's violent domination over liquor trafficking across the Detroit River between Windsor, Ontario, and Michigan speakeasies and "blind pigs"—illegal drinking locales, perhaps as many as twenty-five thousand of them in Detroit alone during Prohibition. As much as 85 percent of all the liquor smuggled into the United States from Canada is likely to have entered the United States in this way.[9]

The auto industry flourished alongside the organized distribution of hundreds of millions of dollars' worth of bootleg Canadian liquor.[10] As a result, Lucille and her family—especially her father, who worked in the auto industry—were eyewitnesses to the unprecedented and also violent union activities in Detroit, Pontiac, and elsewhere in the region, including the first "sit-down" strike at the General Motors Fisher Body Plant No. 1 in Flint on 30 December 1936, during the fight to establish the United Auto Workers. Racial tensions resulting from attempts to desegregate public housing were also on the rise during Lucille's childhood and teenage years. And as the United States entered the Second World War, Detroit's auto industry, suddenly known as "The Arsenal of Democracy," exclusively manufactured war materials like armored tanks, bomber planes, and other vehicles for use in the battles overseas.[11] In the immediate postwar era, while Lucille was in college at Detroit's Wayne State University, the metropolis saw large populations moving away from the inner city and out toward the automobile-friendly suburbs. Lucille's family, too, eventually moved to a wooded lakeside suburb outside the city.

The Detroit of Lucille's childhood was also one populated by Polish immigrants and second-generation Polish Americans, some three hundred fifty thousand of them by 1930, many of whom were drawn to the area because of the booming automobile industry. In particular, the Polish neighborhood of Hamtramck increased from just under four thousand in 1910 to a peak population of sixty thousand in 1928, and was by some accounts the most densely populated city in the United States at that time.[12] "Hamtramck was a very comfortable place for Poles," wrote local historian Dennis Badaczewski: "For immigrants especially it was a place where one could remain Polish—speaking the same language, following the same religion, living by the same customs, as in Poland."[13] Most Poles in Detroit during the Depression were Catholic churchgoers, many of whom belonged to the Polish National Catholic Church.[14] This hegemonic culture clashed with a new wave of immigrants from the South in the early 1940s, namely some estimated fifty thousand African Americans and two hundred thousand whites from West Virginia, Kentucky, and Tennessee, who came to work in Detroit's factories, bringing with them a new dynamic in racial conflict that caused the city to face "a rapid deterioration of race relations."[15]

In the shadow of these conflicts, Lucille's family seems to have adhered to certain Polish customs, including the typical Christmas Eve *Wigilia* ("vigil," in Polish) dinner, a traditional meal with holiday-specific foods, and festivities that began with the first appearance of the evening star.[16] Dlugoszewski invoked the spirit of *Wigilia* throughout her life, perhaps because it symbolized her Polish heritage and upbringing. The word itself would become obsessively recycled in Dlugoszewski's later writings, as did references to the appearance of the evening star. In several of those writings, she also analyzed the divergent influences her parents had on her psychological makeup, blaming her mother, on at least one occasion, for her own competitive nature:

> Jolas
> seduced me
> ravished me through aesthetics
> then lived through me
> so nothing I did was good enough
> and she made me think
> that she would stop loving me
> if I didn't get every prize
> every award
> and my one escape route
> where I was true
> was my creativity and the open door to that adventure
> also
> intellectual adventure

> which was
> always
> Czesio

Another writing made a similar comparison of her parents, with a more favorable depiction of her mother:

> Czesio courage
> courage thru intellect
> Face anything
> but this way *you know*
> *you understand*
> + that is worth
> the world + a whole life

> Jolas courage
> the gift of courage
> not through intellect
> but through love
> go sweet adventurer
> try the most dangerous challenge
> Have that ultimate fun of life
> of trying the limit of adventure
> don't fear, you have nothing to lose
> *because* I will always love you

In the late 1980s, for the benefit of a *New York Times* writer, Dlugoszewski described herself as "the only child and hope of a Polish immigrant family." "So I had to be a prodigy," she added.[17]

Lucille attended Detroit public schools and completed first grade at the Ferry School in Grosse Pointe Woods the day after her sixth birthday. Her elementary school report cards show that she was repeatedly given excellent marks in the subjects of literature, geography, and music. Lucille also wrote prolifically from an early age, and since her father worked away from home in Flint, Michigan, for an extended period while she was young, she had ample opportunities to practice her letter-writing skills. Her earliest extant letters, written to her father when she was just eight years old, revealed her enthusiasm for school, her love of learning, and her pride in her own academic successes.[18]

In other letters from this period she told her father about poems she was writing, and would relay conversations she had with people during the course of her days. She described receiving mail from the White House after she sent a letter to President Roosevelt (an executive branch spokesperson explained that the commander in chief did not have time to personally respond to every letter he received). In March 1934 she reported reading Harriet Beecher Stowe's 1852 novel *Uncle Tom's Cabin*; in April, she and her mother acquired a dog to complement their pet cat. (In a letter written in 1950, Dlugoszewski would remind her mother that as a child she "wanted to start an orphanage for cats and dogs."[19]) At least one letter to her father was written entirely in Polish. She would frequently sign off with some variation of "a thousand kisses goodbye" or "five kisses for Daddy." She even wrote to her parents when she was just away for the day on a school field trip. On one such occasion, she sent her mother a postcard from the historically preserved museum town Greenfield Village, just twelve miles west of Detroit near the town of Dearborn. Her language was formal and descriptive, as she wrote in inky cursive: "Dear Mother, We are having a very nice time. This picture is of an olden English cottage with many interesting things such as clocks and pottery. Best regards to Daddy, Lucille."[20]

During the summer of 1936, Lucille and her mother visited relatives in Owings Mills, a rural suburb just outside Baltimore, Maryland. Again she wrote numerous letters to her father, noting the antique features of the 150-year-old farmhouse where they were staying. She recounted feeding the pigs and chickens, cutting grass with a scythe, stripping dried corn from cobs with a barn machine, harvesting vegetables from the garden, and collecting dried wood from the forest. She and her mother took day trips to the Chesapeake Bay area and visited Revolutionary War–era historical sites.[21] A week later, she wrote of visiting Washington, D.C., and Mount Vernon, signing off as "your sweetheart" and begging her father to answer her letter.[22] Her father might have been busy at work; as the nation started digging out from the Depression, Detroit initiated its road to recovery, as "a car-hungry nation began again to buy automobiles."[23]

By the time Lucille was about ten years old, her father owned a number of pedagogical drafting books on mechanical drawing, perspective sketching, methods of pictorial representation, and sheet metal drafting, books published by the Detroit Board of Education in the 1930s. As a tool and die worker, Chester seems to have been studying drafting as a way up the workforce ladder. A book in his possession explained that the course for which this book was used had the purpose of developing "the student's ability to visualize, interpret working drawings, and to draw objects freehand and mechanically in picture form."[24] He used an assortment of straight and curved drafting tools, which Lucia kept among her own possessions until the end of her life. A large collection of surviving drafting exercises shows that in 1935, Chester was taking classes in the Mechanical Drawing department at Cass Technical High, one of Detroit's public schools. Chester diligently sketched bench hooks, brackets, tool posts, T-slot blocks, universal joints, bracket bearings, yokes, press screw blocks, belt shifter brackets, step cylinders, and vise jaws. His proficiency in mechanical drawing must have been a fascinating source of visual inspiration for young Lucille. Much of her correspondence throughout her life included sketches and drawings, and many of her dozens of graphic poems displayed drafting-like designs filled with lines and arrows, shaded and overlapping geometric shapes with a sense of three-dimensionality—the combination of which look strikingly similar to many of Chester's homework sketches.[25] She would make this connection herself, later, writing to her mother in early 1951: "I'm starting copying out the sonata on onion skin with India ink and a stub [fountain] pen and I feel like a architectural draftsman—boy daddy should tell his fellow workers what a precision job his daughter has," she joked.[26] Just a few months earlier, she had determined: "Czesio is the most artistic die maker in all of Fisher Body."[27]

Much of Lucille's early life in Detroit can be reconstructed with the help of a thick, leather-bound scrapbook (now housed at the Library of Congress), which features her name embossed in gothic gold script on the cover. This scrapbook includes programs from piano recitals, photographs, newspaper clippings, published poetry by Lucille in both English and Polish, school records including report cards from elementary school through high school, correspondence sent to and from Lucille, and many other documents that demonstrate how full of music, literature, and other activities her life was from a young age. Poems and letters to her parents reveal a devoted daughter who was emboldened to cultivate her ambitious nature. Clearly raised with a healthy dose of self-confidence, Lucille faced few barriers in exploring different avenues of creativity: "go sweet adventurer / try the most dangerous challenge," she would later write in a notebook to herself, echoing her mother's encouragement.

EARLY MUSICAL EXPERIENCES AND POETRY

As Adrienne Fried Block wrote in her 1998 biography of Amy Beach: "There is a mythic aura about a child who instinctively knows how to play the piano and compose."[28] Lucille began both activities early, and later claimed that she decided to be a composer when she was six years old.[29] "I was never inhibited by the sexist dictums that girls don't do certain things," she told a reporter in the early 1970s, adding: "I always wanted to be a composer, and no one said 'don't.'"[30] As a young girl she is likely to have been listening to the music of her home life and her community, possibly the music of the church and the dance halls, but also Depression- and wartime-era radio: by 1933 wireless radio was part of everyday American life, and on 30 January 1933—the same day Adolf Hitler was named chancellor of Germany—*The Lone Ranger* debuted on the Detroit station WXYZ and could soon be heard nationwide.[31]

Lucille took her earliest piano lessons with her mother, but soon moved on to local music schools. By the time she was ten years old she seems to have had two piano teachers: Adelgatha Morrison at the Detroit Conservatory of Music, and Carl Beutel at the Carl Beutel Piano School.[32] Lucille's piano training was conventional—a mix of Burgmüller, Czerny, and Beethoven—alongside courses in theory and composition. She memorized music easily, and had a particular fondness for Bach.[33] She soon entered a number of local music competitions and festivals; during the month of her fifteenth birthday, she won a gold medal during the Detroit Musicians League Honor Student Recital for her performance of Chopin's *Grand Valse Brilliante* (op. 18).

Piano practice dominated her early teenage years, as her repertoire expanded to include not only music by Bach, Beethoven, and Chopin, but also Grieg, Haydn, Liszt, MacDowell, Mozart, and Rameau. ("Long hours of daily [piano] practice cut her off from the normal world of childhood," a newspaper profile of the composer would claim, "but the Polish cultural community of her parents was a rich substitute.")[34] A number of "Adjudicator's Comment Sheets" from competitions and other assessment processes describe Lucille's early musicianship. One such evaluation, undated but signed by another of her piano teachers, Edward Bredshall, reported on her memorized performance of Mendelssohn's *Rondo Capriccioso*: "Occasional nervousness did not mar the general effort of contestant's playing which is well controlled and studied. Shows good talent. Excellent assurance. Natural musical feeling. Good control of tempi. Performer seems to stiffen muscularly in climatic passages. Finger technic [*sic*] could be further developed." She performed Mendelssohn's formidable work again on 8 May 1941 as the only soloist in Northeastern High School's spring music festival concert. During her high school years Lucille would continue to earn certificates of honor with ratings of "superior" from the National Guild of Piano Teachers' National Honor Roll.

Composing seems to have gone hand in hand with piano playing for the young musician. When she was just eleven years old, the *Detroit News* featured a photograph of Lucille at the piano, announcing that she had performed her own original solo piano piece, called *Halloween Symphony*, at a Young Writers event sponsored by the newspaper; a few months later, the paper featured another photo of Lucille at the piano, this time with ribbons and curls in her hair.[35] Around this time, Lucille recorded her *Halloween Symphony* on Presto Recording Phonograph for the Grinnell Brothers Radio-Television Show.[36] At the Civic Detroit Children's Theatre one December, Lucille performed another original composition titled *The Bell's Story of Christmas*. During her childhood and early teenage years Lucille wrote a number of other pieces, now lost: *Bell Buoy* [sic] No. 13, *Evolutionary Joe*, and *Chromium Nitrate*, to name just a few.

An undated, unsigned newspaper article (ca. 1939) included in Lucille's scrapbook, titled "Composing Brought About by Mother's Challenge," documents her early compositional beginnings on the occasion of the fourteen-year-old's "debut before a concert audience," performing *Halloween Symphony* at the annual convention of the Musicians' League:

> A challenge by her mother started Lucille composing her first piece at eleven. A month later, she played at the Michigan Composers Contest. Lucille states, "When I compose a tune, I want my audience to get my thoughts and feelings from the music rather than draw their own conclusions." Lucille likes the originality of Beethoven, Chopin's smooth simplicity, and Wagner's style of portraying characters. She devotes all her time to music, and never leaves a tune unfinished once she begins work on it. Harmony and the right chords are the pattern for her work. When something is difficult she tries to excel in it to conquer it.

A further motivation to compose came from a woman—"Aunt Kaye"—who worked with the Young Writers' Club for the *Detroit News*. In September 1939, writing on the newspaper's letterhead, Aunt Kaye invited Lucille to compose a song for the Young Writers' Club.[37] By December, Lucille had finished the piece, "Song of Young Writers," a twenty-four-measure song for voice and piano; it was scored in C major and set in cut time, "Tempo de Marcia." The tonal harmony ventured only as far as a secondary-dominant chord. Much like its young composer, the text, which she wrote, was emphatic and full of optimism, with a fermata over the penultimate word, "try":

> Let's get armed with pens and paper and march onto victory;
> Keep on climbing working trying till success will ours be;
> Hold our heads up high young writers, Make Dreams the Real and True;
> Grow to be the great and lasting, Swell American Pride A-new;

We're the ev'ry hope of Future; We will be past's Lasting men;
Laughing, Happy, Always eager, Ready to Try again.[38]

Aunt Kaye made copies of the song for distribution to audience members during the entertainment portion of a December 16 meeting of the Young Writers' Club, and invited Lucille to come and play the piano part herself.[39] Just over a year later, Aunt Kaye again asked Lucille to perform one of her "little stories with musical accompaniment" at the Young Writers' Entertainment in the studio auditorium of the *Detroit News*, on 18 January 1941.[40]

Lucille claimed she began writing poetry at the age of six. "I usually write poetry about the night because you can pretend better and it isn't so realistic as the day," she remarked in a newspaper interview conducted while she was in tenth grade, adding: "Poetry is based on the imagination."[41] Lucille's fascination with nighttime and the creative potential of working at night would remain consistent throughout her life, leading her to go for days without sleeping, instead composing or writing poems about the night sky and other nocturnal subjects. In a letter written to a friend in the mid-1980s, Dlugoszewski would recall: "When I was a little girl I would do this. I would secretly creep out of bed in the middle of the night and look out the window at the beautiful quiet night and strange wordless poetry would well up from my tragic child's heart." Nearing the age of sixty, she added: "I guess I haven't changed very much."[42]

During junior high and high school, Lucille wrote and published dozens of poems, on topics ranging from mundane domestic work to religious and civic holidays, from patriotic expressions ("New Year's Greetings to America") to celebrations of her parents.[43] Some offered careful observances from everyday life, like her descriptive "Ode to Housework," with its subtitle "The Electric Iron," published in a newspaper when she was fourteen years old. Others poked fun at the oddities of her school, as in "Where Are Those Elevators?," which described a prank her school's seniors played on freshmen. Lucille's more serious poems contemplated history, patriotism, and nationality, and several were published in Polish. One poem, titled "Thoughts of Home (As Told by a Polish Refugee)," might have been inspired by her parents' own descriptions of Poland, and made mention of the Vistula River, which passed through their hometown. One poem published in Polish was simply titled "Szkola" (School). Other poems offered reflections of her urban surroundings ("City's Child"), gratitude for the richness of her environment ("Make It Another Thankful"), descriptions of the changing of the seasons ("The

Pumpkin and the Cornstalk"), and homages to friends ("Carillon Music, ['to Nancy Brown']"). Lucille's poems reveal a child with an observant eye and a sense of humor. Her intellectual engagement with current events would remain a characteristic of her personality as she grew into adulthood.

NORTHEASTERN HIGH SCHOOL

After completing the ninth grade at Greusel Intermediate School in January 1939 (and collecting many scholastic honors along the way), Lucille entered Detroit's Northeastern High School, where she would graduate on 28 January 1942 in a class of 172 students. As in elementary and middle school, Lucille was an outstanding student. High school report cards show that she excelled in diverse subjects: advanced algebra, art, band, biology, chemistry, choir, civics, debating, economics, English, geometry, harmony, history, Latin, news, physics, swimming, typing, and trigonometry. From 1939 until 1941 her high school named her as a Jane Addams student for "High Distinction in Scholarship" during their annual honors days. The *Detroit News* listed her as a straight-A student, and she was consistently praised for her perfect attendance.

Though naturally drawn to music and poetry, Lucille also participated in a variety of sports and extracurricular activities. As a member of the Jane Addams Sardines (a squad of the high school swim team), Lucille won second prize in a "swimming marathon," having swum 327 lengths of the pool; she also completed Red Cross life-saving training. She played glockenspiel in her high school's marching band and served in the "Officer's Club." According to her 1942 yearbook, she also wrote a play with classmate Ted Kokubo, which was described in the yearbook as a "super colossal, stupendous, gigantic operatic performance." (Nothing more is known about this piece, other than that she was listed as "playwright" and Kokubo was listed as "financial backer" in their Class of 1942 yearbook.) Her high school music teachers included L. Russell Johnson, William Fishwick, and Leland H. Olmstead.

In the fall of 1940 Lucille served on Northeastern's student council, and also worked on the editorial staff for the school's newspaper, *The Review*. (A gossip column in that paper called "Petticoat Prattle" described Lucille as "a well-dressed lassie" with "long curls and accordion pleats.") With eleven other members of the paper's editorial "staff," she traveled to Cleveland in late November 1940 for the National Scholastic Press Association Convention.

Lucille wrote letters to her parents describing her experiences during the trip, starting with a card from the short train ride from Detroit. On the second night of the convention, foreign correspondent and Pulitzer Prize–winning journalist R. H. Knickerbocker gave a keynote address titled "At the Ringside of History." Lucille took detailed notes during his speech, which focused on the role of France and England in the young European war. After a vivid description of the view out her Hotel Cleveland window into the city's downtown nightscape, she offered her parents an impression of Knickerbocker's speech:

> He told us an uncensored story of the battle of London and it was his belief that England is our first line of defense and we should make every effort to insure her victory. Don't you think so Daddy? He said that Paris and France fell 90% because of lack of morale and 10% because of German fighting superiority. He was living in Paris when France surrendered. The people didn't even know what was happening because the press was censored so by government authorities. He said that Winston Churchill is the man that is holding the English morale.[44]

Returning to her room from a ball the next night at 1:45 a.m., she wrote of less political matters, and pronounced herself "a lady," because, as she proudly announced, she "drank coffee instead of milk."

Under different circumstances, Lucille might have turned toward a career in journalism. Throughout high school, she pursued her interest in writing, and in April 1941 she won an award for an essay titled "What American Democracy Means to Me." The Civitan Club of Detroit held its Annual Citizenship Essay Contest Banquet at the Whittier Hotel on 30 April 1941. A few days later, the *Detroit Free Press* ran a short article titled "Civitan Club Awards School Cup," with a photograph of young Lucille accepting an enormous silver trophy: "The Northeastern student champion among 4,000 essay students in 19 Detroit high schools received a desk lamp, and a chance at district and national honors."[45] An excerpt of Lucille's essay was published in *The Review*.[46] It offered a utopian view of her Detroit neighborhood, while ridiculing political ideologies that demonized foreigners and immigrants:

> There's a street in our city—a fine street where each lawn is as neat as every other and each crosswalk as clean as every other. Yes, Baldwin Avenue is a fine street. Yet, that doesn't make it so. It's times when the man next door fixes his neighbor's lawn mower or the lady across the street gives away slips of her prize roses.

I know the street well for my house borders their homes and in my garden grows one of those prize roses. I know, too, some startling facts about Baldwin Avenue, things that would prove a thousand times that oft quoted phrase referred to America—a melting pot! I know a lady on the corner who is German and my next door neighbor is Canadian. The woman two doors away had come from Italy only a few years back and her neighbor speaks with a soft Slavic accent.

We all hear of lands where people are taught that the best harvest comes by plowing up the bad in others. The voices of their superior officers repeat day after day, "It is the survival of the fittest and we are the superior race! Hate him who lives across the border—hate him! He is different from you. He is beneath you. He is your enemy."

I hear of those lands every day on the news broadcast. Yet when the same people enter our shores carrying their little bundles of worldly goods, they eventually leave those little bundles on the big pile of common good. I used to wonder why, but today as I walked up our street I found the answer.

We are allowed to appreciate ourselves as well as criticize ourselves. We are allowed to help each other. But no—that is no boon given us ... we are not allowed. These are our unalienable rights, for ours is the philosophy of democracy.

During her senior year, Lucille took over the editorship of *The Review*, sharing the post with fellow classmate Mary Staltman. Alongside editorials and current events pieces, she also wrote a gossip column called "All about Us." Lucille's writer's voice, even in adolescence, brimmed with cheerful curiosity. Like "What American Democracy Means to Me," an article titled "Our Youth" showcased Lucille's American spirit, one that questioned given truths and empty patriotism, while calling on her generation to political activism despite the caution learned from growing up during the Great Depression:

We are youth! Yes we are a different youth, schooled in the shadow of the first great war, taught to distrust, to analyze—cautious and afraid. Though we still stand on firm rock, all around us is doubtful ground. With each new step we may sink into the mire. Those who warned and taught us to distrust have turned to flag-waving and band-playing. We are afraid to believe anything anymore. There's the urge to turn and run—to run away.

Yet will we remember Plymouth Rock, the spirit of '76, the hopes of 1865, the trail of the covered wagon? Will we remember the courage that preserves us as a nation? We are the youth of America and we cannot forget. We cannot forget to analyze, to explore, to search—to accept only that which benefits the majority. We cannot run away!

Lucille's ambition did not go unnoticed by her peers. Just a few weeks before graduation, *The Review* ran an article titled "This Month's Luminaries Radiate and Scintillate," which spotlighted her "lengthy list of accomplishments"—including writing poetry, playing the piano, and working on her algebra—while calling "Lucy-belle" "brilliant," "humorous and witty," and "serious when she so chooses." Claiming that she enjoyed Schubert, mystery stories, white shirts, dogs, and "walks alone at midnight," the article also announced that "Lucy's prince charming must be a big game hunter or an ambassador; a reasonable facsimile of Sherlock Holmes will do." Her high school peers were impressed that she intended to study medicine at Wayne State University, though, they wrote, "music will be her sideline."[47] Her Class of 1942 yearbook also described the graduating senior in complimentary terms:

> Now comes a tale of one so extraordinary in everything participated in that its doer was automatically called "Brain Trust" and "Genius." Lucille Dlugoszewski was a member of the Student Council, the winner of the Civitan Essay Contest, a varsity swimmer, a member of the choir and the band, a varsity debater, editor-in-chief of *The Review* and co-editor of the Senior Issue; and she had the honor of giving the traditional Jane Addams speech. Lucille was referred to as a pianist and composer. The scholarship to Wayne for four years was awarded her.
>
> A possessor of the desirable qualities to make the greatest doctor-to-be faced the world when Lucille Dlugoszewski closed the door on her last day in high school.[48]

Friends and admirers covered the pages of her yearbook with encouraging and revealing messages. ("To the piano player who can't even play chopsticks," one boy wrote; "To Lucille, specialist in heartache," wrote another.) Lucille graduated from high school in January 1942, just weeks after the bombing of Pearl Harbor.

WAYNE STATE UNIVERSITY

Lucille's first year of college took place in the context of the new war. Practice blackouts required people to stay indoors while "the city's air raid wardens, equipped with gas masks and wearing steel helmets, patrolled the darkened streets."[49] The month she entered college, the auto industry's production moved toward the manufacturing of war materials, producing the last automobile made on a Detroit assembly line for some three years.[50] Also in February 1942, racial clashes at Detroit's Sojourner Truth housing project were triggered by the relocation of Black residents into new homes in largely Polish and all-white neighborhoods in northern Detroit.[51] Political, economic, and social struggles hovered on the edges of Lucille's university experience.

Lucille matriculated at the College of Liberal Arts at Wayne State University in February 1942 as the only student from her high school to receive a full scholarship from the Detroit Board of Education, with the possibility of a three-year renewal if her scholastic performance remained high.[52] The Detroit Board of Education continued to renew her college scholarship through at least the fall semester of 1943.[53] She followed a diverse curriculum and declared a major in chemistry in September of 1944; she transferred to pre-med in February of 1945.[54] Later she recalled that she adopted William Carlos Williams and Anton Chekov as her models: creative men who made their living as doctors while privately pursuing their art.[55] Lucille's Wayne State University transcripts show that she attended eight regular semesters plus several summer sessions. By March of 1946 she had reached the maximum number of allowable credit hours, and requested to be transferred to "non-matriculated status." In that status she continued taking classes through at least February of 1947. There is no record of a degree having been awarded, though she later claimed she had earned a Bachelor of Science degree in chemistry.

Beyond a variety of entry-level courses like introductions to psychology, philosophy, and Western civilization, her curriculum included: languages (French, German); literature (Shakespeare, Nietzsche, Goethe, Thomas Mann, Modern Poetry); arts (drama, visual arts, "Great Old Masters," "Foundations of Modern European Art"); physical education (folk dancing, tap dancing, swimming, field hockey, badminton); philosophy and history (aesthetics, American government, Plato and Aristotle); and a variety of math and science courses (analytic geometry, calculus, organic chemistry, general zoology, and "comparative vertebrate zoology," which she repeated several times). Lucille's choice of curriculum reflected her parents' influences—science from her father, arts from her mother—though, for a declared chemistry/pre-medicine major, she seems to have favored languages and literature over subjects in science. She later recalled that during this time she was also "deeply influenced" by Chester Kuhn's poetry seminar at Detroit City College.[56] Many years later, she would write of her college years as her "high heel existence," recalling "the fine days when I awoke in my adolescence."[57] Year after year, she received honors for "outstanding scholastic achievement."

During her later college years Lucille maintained a competitive level of writing, performing, and composing. Her prose writing won a variety of awards, including a prize for a stream-of-consciousness short story called "All on a Summer's Day," and another for a story called "Gratiot Avenue," referring to a main artery cutting through downtown Detroit close to MacDougall Street where her parents lived when she was born.[58] Her poetry was recognized as well: in the mid-1940s, a Board of Judges for the National Poetry Association chose Lucille's poem "Uncalled" to be published in *The Second Annual Anthology of College Poetry*, a nationwide compilation of selections chosen from thousands of submitted poems.[59]

During her college years, Lucille's musical activities continued alongside her prize-winning writing, and she occasionally won awards in local piano competitions as well. She performed classical repertoire—Bach, Beethoven, Chopin, Debussy, Handel, Ibert, MacDowell, Mendelssohn, Ravel, Scarlatti—at the Carl Beutel Piano School in solo and group recitals, and also appeared as a soloist for the Detroit Musicians League, the Detroit Musicians' Association, and at the Polonia Society, where she gave an all-Chopin/Paderewski program in conjunction with a Polish art show at the International Center in Detroit. (On this occasion she was described in a newspaper as a "seventeen-year-old composer and poet from Detroit, who is a pre-medical student at Wayne University.") For what might have been her first professional engagement as a composer, Lucille wrote incidental music for The Vespers Players' production of W. H. Auden's *For the Time Being: A Christmas Oratorio*, which was performed for three nights at the Greek Theater in Cranbrook (Bloomfield Hills, Michigan) in 1946. A newspaper article announcing the performance featured a photograph of a glamorous Lucille posing at the piano, with a caption that identified her simply as: "Composer."[60]

MOVING ON: MEDICINE OR MUSIC?

Later in life Dlugoszewski would repeatedly explain that her move toward music as a profession was a decision necessitated by being rejected from medical school. But scholars and critics have suggested less of a passive move: "Although she did well in school, *she found the science courses too anti-art*.... As soon as she graduated, *she abandoned the idea of medicine* and came to New York to study music," wrote a scholar who interviewed her in 1977.[61] Similarly,

Dlugoszewski's friend Jamake Highwater framed her move toward music as a deliberate action, one in which she "*decid[ed]* in favor of the humanities and le[ft] medicine behind her."[62] Another interviewer in the early 1990s made a similar assumption: "Frustrated by the sexism and ageism that blocked her attempts to enter medical school, [Dlugoszewski] *abandoned* her idea of becoming a doctor and instead accepted an opportunity to move to New York and study with Grete Sultan in 1952."[63] In the same interview, Dlugoszewski herself reinforced this version of the story:

> The first blow came when I applied for medical school. I was only 15, and I think I looked 10. My grades were great, but at that time, the male-chauvinist business was so great in pre-med. And a girl—and with a Polish name on top of that? Forget it. But the joke is that I had this crazy idea that I would earn my living as a doctor, the way Chekov did or the way William Carlos Williams did, and then do the music! I mean, can you imagine that? It would have been a battle just to become a doctor then. And then the music too! The blow of being rejected that first time around at medical school was a very big trauma. I just couldn't understand it, and my parents couldn't understand it.[64]

"I was hitting the two most male chauvinist outposts, music and medicine," she said to yet another interviewer.[65]

In reality, Lucille might have been sidetracked by an unexpected opportunity, one that came to her through a series of connections made by one of her three Detroit piano teachers, Edward Bredshall.[66] A classical pianist and former Nadia Boulanger student with ties to the League of Composers and the Pan American Association of Composers in New York during the 1930s, Bredshall befriended a German-Jewish émigré pianist named Katja Andy (born Käte Aschaffenburg; 1907–2013), who settled in Detroit in 1938.[67] Through Bredshall, Lucille met Andy, and through Andy, she met pianist Grete Sultan (1906–2005), also a German-Jewish émigré. (Both Andy and Sultan had been students of pianist Edwin Fischer's in Germany prior to the war.) Since Sultan specialized in both Bach and contemporary music, she seemed like the ideal next teacher for Lucille as she began to seek a path for moving beyond her medical school plans, and eventually out of Detroit.

The Berkshire Foundation of New York City seems to have facilitated Lucille's move to New York to study piano with Sultan. In the summer of 1948, the Foundation's Office of Finance sent Lucille a letter:

> I am happy to inform you that the Berkshire Foundation has chosen to honor you with one more year of education. This should be expected under

the guidance of Grete Sultan, Varèse, Saltzer [sic], John Cage, and Julius Hereford.

And, because of your special talents, the Foundation has decided unanimously to award you one additional year after the above fellowship is completed to allow you full independent maturity as a composer without the warping effect of economic considerations. Whatever instruction will be necessary to you in this period will be chosen and approved a year from now. Both fellowships, of course, include complete living expenses.[68]

Lucille's New York connections to composers John Cage and Edgard Varèse, theorist Felix Salzer, and music historian Julius Hereford were most likely established through her association with Katja Andy, Edward Bredshall, and Grete Sultan. It is unclear how early Lucille first came into contact with the Berkshire Foundation, what the "one more year of education" referred to, or exactly when she left Detroit for New York City. By the summer of 1949 Lucille was writing home from the East Village address of 211 East 17th Street, in a neighborhood situated between Union Square, Gramercy Park, and Stuyvesant Square Park.[69] And by January 1950 she was writing daily letters to her parents about her prolific musical and social activities, sparing no detail about her budding career. Though she returned to Detroit frequently throughout the rest of her life, New York City would remain Lucia Dlugoszewski's permanent home for the next fifty years.

TWO

Letters from New York (1949–51)

You know Lucia, the great composer![1]

BETWEEN FEBRUARY 1950 AND JUNE 1951, Lucia Dlugoszewski wrote her parents in Detroit over 250 letters describing her experiences in New York City in enthusiastic detail. While the Berkshire Foundation continued to support her music studies, her parents regularly sent her money orders and postal stamps—as well as *paczki*, jelly-filled Polish donuts her mother baked for Fat Tuesday. Often writing to each parent separately on the same day, her letters display spontaneous and emphatic humor ("ha ha ha," she liked to write), vanity, and increasing boastfulness about her successes. She tended to open her letters with a casual and elliptical "Well . . ." and sign off with "millions of *Buzi* [kisses] to you," or some other expression of endearment. She frequently included words or phrases in Polish, and referred to herself in the third person (Lucy, Luci, or Lucie), or as "*dzidziuś*" or "*dzidyinsyka*," Polish terms for "baby girl." After the Brooklyn Music School hired her as a teacher in the fall of 1950, she proudly referred to herself as "the professor." Clearly "wanting to make it big as a composer," she was hardly "the typical sheltered little girl from the Midwest," as a reporter later claimed.[2]

The New York City Dlugoszewski embraced as her new home around 1949 vibrated with interaction between the performing arts and the visual and literary arts, especially in the Greenwich Village community where she soon found herself living.[3] Friendships and rivalries between various "New York School" groups—painters, writers, actors, dancers, and composers—dominated activities at certain cultural hubs, including the 8th Street Club, a site for panels, lectures, and spirited aesthetic exchange; the Cedar Tavern, a favorite drinking establishment among the abstract expressionists and their allies; the Living Theatre, a revolutionary ensemble created in 1951 that sometimes programmed new music events; and the White Horse Tavern, a Hudson

Street bar frequented by writers like James Baldwin and Dylan Thomas. European immigrants, including artists Josef Albers, Marcel Duchamp, and Hans Hofmann, and composers like Edgard Varèse commanded old-world respect, while young innovators like composer John Cage, choreographer Merce Cunningham, poet Frank O'Hara, artist Robert Rauschenberg, and dozens of other avant-gardists propelled American experimental arts into uncharted territory. This dynamic artistic community electrified the young Dlugoszewski, whose extroverted personality steered her toward collaborative and interdisciplinary approaches to creativity.

In her letters, Dlugoszewski delighted in both the lofty and the quotidian, and spared few details about her daily encounters with both city life and the contemporary art community surrounding her. She discussed her compositional activities, but also the day-to-day minutiae of her life, like going to the movies, or taking care of the plants she kept in her apartment's window boxes: jade, begonia, elephant ears, and geranium. She shopped for clothes at Wanamaker's department store (to avoid "the sale crazed ladies at Macy's").[4] And she frequently described her wardrobe—dresses, coats, hats, and jewelry. Her mother, Jennie, sewed much of her clothing at the time, and their correspondence discussed recent trends in fashion, with Dlugoszewski often sketching drawings of new styles or describing patterns she had seen in magazines. In early 1950 she wrote of a drought that was plaguing the city, mocking New Yorkers who "prayed for rain" in church. She kept up with breaking news, paying close attention to the activities of labor unions that affected her father's work, like the historic John L. Lewis–led coal strike of 1950, which allowed steel and autoworkers to establish a five-day workweek.[5] This collection of letters sheds light on Dlugoszewski's youthful personality, attitudes, and relationships as she embarked on adulthood and the beginning of her professional life in a city poised to alter the world's perception of contemporary culture.

THE STUDENT

Dlugoszewski's life in early 1950 was filled with practicing the piano at Steinway Hall, taking music theory, ear training, and score reading classes at Mannes School of Music, studying composition privately with John Cage, composing and preparing for performances of her own music, and attending as many concerts as she could: by February she reported being "deep in the concert season."⁶ These performances had a profound effect on Dlugoszewski's development, as she claimed that she was "going to constant concerts these days which is the best thing you can do for composing." Echoing generations of young artists who moved to New York City in pursuit of creative inspiration, she added an unequivocal affirmation of her experiences: "This is the best kind of life for me—I love it."⁷

Dlugoszewski's concert-going companions included some of the mentors assigned to her by the Berkshire Foundation, including Mannes professor Felix Salzer, who took her to a performance at Carnegie Recital Hall in early February.⁸ Her piano teacher Grete Sultan—whom fellow piano student Christian Wolff later described as "a quiet, modest person, but firm and with strong integrity ... without any strain or fuss, a model of discipline and devotion"—quickly became a friend and constant companion.⁹ Dlugoszewski's other mentors took her to many other concerts throughout her first year in New York: Julius Hereford and Edgard Varèse escorted her to a piano recital given by Armenian pianist Maro Ajemian; Hereford and John Cage took her to a reading by poet William Carlos Williams; Hereford and composer William Schuman (then president of Juilliard) accompanied her to a performance of the New York Philharmonic conducted by Dmitri Mitropoulos.¹⁰ She attended classical concerts at Juilliard (Haydn, Schubert, Debussy, Bartók) as well as more avant-garde ones, like the 1950 WNYC American Music Festival Composers Alliance Concert (Cage, Wallingford Riegger, Varèse). In February she attended a concert of Bartók's orchestral music conducted by Leonard Bernstein; she also attended an orchestral performance of music by Virgil Thomson. At a Town Hall concert of Romanian composer George Enesco's music, she met the composer himself: "A wonderful man," she decided.¹¹ John Cage took her to a poetry reading given by Dylan Thomas; a few months later he surprised her with tickets for two to a new play starring the popular Broadway actors Alfred Lunt and Lynn Fontanne.¹²

John Cage was a constant presence in Dlugoszewski's daily life during this period, and their brief but intense friendship and subsequent rift seems to have been the source of a lifelong obsession for her. Born in Los Angeles in 1912, by the late 1930s Cage had established himself as a pioneer in percussion ensemble music; in 1940, he invented the "prepared piano," an innovation that reimagined the sonic possibilities of that centuries-old instrument. During the 1940s Cage also experimented with radios and phonograph records as sound sources, and began collaborating with dancer-choreographer Merce Cunningham. Around the time when Cage and Dlugoszewski would have met in New York City, he was starting to develop the unprecedented compositional technique that would come to be known as "chance operations," based on the ancient Chinese oracle *I Ching*. Dlugoszewski attended many performances of Cage's music, including his *Sonatas and Interludes* (1946–48) for prepared piano, played by Maro Ajemian at Carnegie Hall in early March 1950.[13]

Dlugoszewski occasionally performed her own new work at Cage's studio during 1950, and took pride in telling her parents how well her performances were received by his invited guests—"the composers said I have a wonderful ear for creating beautiful sounds," she reported.[14] On other occasions she described Cage's pleasure in "the composer Lucia['s]" compositional progress, and his assessment of her "great and sensitive musicality."[15] Cage urged her to learn more about orchestration for strings and woodwinds: "Maybe I'll be like Papa Haydn and know all the instruments," she mused.[16] Inspired by the knowledge, encouragement, and enthusiasm Cage imparted on his student, Dlugoszewski admitted to her mother: "I just never want the lesson to be over for the day."[17]

On one occasion, Cage invited Dlugoszewski to play one of her new piano pieces in a class he was teaching at Columbia University.[18] On another, Cage invited her to a "New Music luncheon," where she gave a "little speech" about her "method of composing" and her "philosophy for composition." Reporting that her presentation was a great success, she also praised Cage's cooking for the event: "All sorts of exotic delicacies—chicken livers and mushrooms and almonds in some cream on toast—and that sort of thing."[19] As a pioneering figure of the New York avant-garde around whom artists of all types orbited Cage would have had to limit the time and attention he gave to any one student, yet he took the young woman from Detroit under his wing, and into his inner circle.

Like Cage, composer Edgard Varèse (1883–1965) mentored Dlugoszewski during her early days in New York, inviting her to many performances and events, and visiting her on social occasions. The French-born composer had come to the United States in 1915, and by the 1920s he had established himself as a leader in the ultramodernist scene, cofounding important organizations for contemporary music including the International Composers Guild (1921) and the Pan American Association of Composers (1926), an organization with which Dlugoszewski's Detroit piano teacher Edward Bredshall had been associated. Like Cage, Varèse had been a pioneer in percussion ensemble music. Following the stylistic innovations of Igor Stravinsky,

Varèse's orchestral compositions tended to place string instruments in the background of his orchestral textures, instead foregrounding winds, brass, and large percussion sections. His focus on timbre and texture over melody and harmony influenced Dlugoszewski's own compositional style, an influence that would become especially apparent with her ensemble works composed during the 1970s. Varèse's vast interest in sound broadened her own horizons: In February 1950 he took her to a concert of early music where she encountered Renaissance instruments like the viola da gamba for the first time.[20] According to her own autobiographical sketches and accounts given in interviews, Dlugoszewski studied composition with Varèse for some short amount of time during her early days in New York, though her letters to her parents exclusively report on her studies with Cage.

In April 1950, composer Ruth Crawford Seeger (1901–1953) returned to New York from Washington, D.C., to attend a performance of her String Quartet (1931), which had been programmed a year in advance by the International Society for Contemporary Music.[21] Dlugoszewski attended the concert at Columbia University's McMillan Theater, describing the composer to her parents as "the lady" who was "Varese's greatest pupil (since me—ha ha)."[22] (Crawford had not studied with Varèse, as Dlugoszewski erroneously claimed, and had been absent from the New York contemporary music scene for many years.) "Of course we are all going to hear it," Dlugoszewski added in a letter to her father.[23] Later in life Dlugoszewski would frequently refer to Crawford and her String Quartet in reverent tones, remarking on her use of dynamics as the main musical parameter in the "startlingly exquisite" quartet's mysterious third movement. Dlugoszewski concluded that Ruth Crawford was "not only one of the greatest American composers but also, one of the world's great composers."[24] While teaching a composition class for dancers at Hunter College in the late 1960s, Dlugoszewski would again use Crawford's quartet as an example of the compositional versatility of dynamics.

Dlugoszewski's new friends continued to take good care of their young charge: on Easter Sunday Grete Sultan gave her an edition of E. E. Cummings poems, while Cage and Varèse together bought her a metronome.[25] A few days after Easter Dlugoszewski visited the Botanical Gardens in the Bronx with Sultan and Cage.[26] She frequently went on picnics in Central Park with a group she now referred to as "the artists," including Cage and others in his circle of friends.[27] Dlugoszewski and Sultan, who had quickly become friends beyond Dlugoszewski's piano lessons, made plans for entertaining Katja Andy during her upcoming New York visit.[28]

The young composer-performer also quickly embraced an attitude of the *artiste*, insisting on her needs as a creative person. In anticipation of a visit at home with her parents for several weeks in March 1950, she adopted a strict tone while informing her mother of her need to practice undisturbed for about six hours a day. Oddly assuming male pronouns, she insisted: "I'm sorry that's the rules for a musician but he always must practice for his health so I think about it now and if we agree on this all will go smoothly on my vacation."[29]

According to her own accounts, Dlugoszewski's compositional work during this period included a suite for viola and alto voice, a work for strings and woodwinds, and a series of sonatas.[30] A performance of one of these sonatas was reportedly "very well appreciated" by an audience that included Lou Harrison, Wallingford Riegger, and Virgil Thomson: "You know Lucia, the great composer!" she exclaimed.[31] Though the works she composed during this period are not known to us today, her letters allow some insight into some of the musical issues she was thinking about, including rhythmic structures, and what she referred to as "new kinds of melodies." Getting used to these new sounds required a new way of hearing, which she saw as a new paradigm: "It's just like it was for the people in Galileo's time who always thought the world flat and then he told them that the world was round."[32] Others seem to have played some of these early piano works as well. In the summer of 1950, Cage gave a concert at the University of Louisiana that included one of her sonatas.[33] On another occasion, Dlugoszewski bragged to her father that Grete Sultan planned to play her most recent sonata in an "informal recital" at the Frick Museum.[34]

During May 1950, Dlugoszewski's cultural education continued, including a performance of Varèse's *Density 21.5* for solo flute (1936) at the New School Auditorium, a visit with Cage to the Metropolitan Museum of Art exhibit titled "Art Treasures from the Vienna Collections," an evening with Cage, Sultan, and Varèse at "The Columbia Alice Ditson Foundation for modern composers," and a dance recital by Merce Cunningham accompanied by Cage.[35] On a rainy Thursday evening in May she relayed an anecdote about another concert she had just attended, one featuring music by Aaron Copland:

> Mr. Cage told Mr. Copland that his work was mediocre and Mr. Copland told him: "Well, John, you're younger than I am so you're not so money hungry and have time to write good music." Mr. [Henry] Cowell was there, too, and he laughed and so did Mr. [William] Schuman—Then Mr. Cage pointed

to me and said "well here's one even younger and more idealistic than I am so you old fellows better watch your step." And then I said that they didn't have to worry because they had seniority and then they all laughed some more.[36]

"You see," she wrote her parents, "these musicians like to crack the joke just like anybody else—just like the die makers playing hide and seek when they come out of Fisher Body," she wrote, making reference to her father's workplace.

As the spring turned toward summer, Dlugoszewski began thinking about her future, and about whether she should try to stay in New York permanently. Seduced by her newfound independence and the bohemian lifestyle of the artists she was getting to know, she became less and less inclined to return to her midwestern hometown. Writing at the end of May, she implored her mother to accept her decision to stay in New York where she could enjoy many more professional opportunities, rather than "go to seed" in Detroit like her former teacher, Dr. Carl Beutel. Citing her upbringing as less than ideal for an aspiring artist, Dlugoszewski chastised her mother: "You mustn't be too impatient with my development because you know I had to do it more or less the hard way because none of us had the kind of cultural background that could choose from the beginning the proper teachers, etc."[37] While lamenting the disadvantages of her Detroit-based education, she also sought out opportunities in New York that would connect her to her Polish heritage. During the summer of 1950 she contemplated taking a night class on Polish culture at Columbia; later that summer she would tell her father: "Once in a while I listen to the lectures in Columbia University on Polish Culture."[38]

On the sixteenth of June 1950 Dlugoszewski turned twenty-five years old, and her New York friends treated her to a surprise party in her own apartment. She wrote a long description of the party to her mother, explaining how her friend Mary Norton orchestrated a ruse in order to decorate Dlugoszewski's room with flowers, balloons, and gifts while she was out practicing:

> When I came home at 7:00 p.m. everybody yelled surprize.... The bed was pushed against the window to give room for extra chairs and the coffee table was set and there was Mary, Miss Sultan, Mr. Cage, [the Berkshire Foundation's] Mr. Lovisco, Mr. [José] De Creeft and Mr. Varèse. Mr. Lovisco brought a bottle of Lacrima Christi [Italian wine], Mr. Cage brought me a cake he baked, Miss Sultan brought me the *Russian Reader*, Mr. De Creeft brought me a little original sculpture, and Mary brought me the complete *Cantos* of Ezra Pound. And after we drank the wine and blew out the candles I opened

the wonderful package from [Detroit] and was overwhelmed.... And after all this Mr. Varèse took us all to see Charlie Chaplin in *City Lights*.[39]

A few days after her birthday, she again expressed frustration about what she seemed to perceive as her parents' clinginess. Asserting herself as "an artist and a *powsinoga* [gadabout]," she pleaded: "You did all that is necessary for me and were more than wonderful parents to me and now is that time to relax and forget a little bit about that troublesome *dzidyinsyka* for awhile—okay?"[40] She also relayed her summer plans, which involved staying in New York and continuing to work closely with Cage and Sultan, with the financial support of another Berkshire Foundation scholarship.[41] She also sought out possible teaching positions for the coming year. Her options included the Mannes School ("a horror" because of its low pay), the "experimental" Greenwich Music School ("where the composer Lou Harrison teaches"), and the Brooklyn Music School, which paid six dollars per hour—one dollar more per hour than the Greenwich Music School.[42] She outlined other ambitious plans that would only be possible if she stayed in New York, including her assumption that she could "probably get a commission eventually to write ballet music for Martha Graham or others," since, she explained, "that makes a composer famous quicker than anything."[43] (Later that year, she would write that Cage had been encouraging her to write music for dance, which, she speculated, "might be a very good opportunity for doing something practical with my composing but we'll see what happens before I say any more about it."[44])

"Lucia is soon to become a very mature composer to carry on the name of Dlugoszewski," she reported to her father in the beginning of July.[45] The soon-to-be-very-mature composer spent the summer of 1950 practicing, composing, taking composition lessons, writing poetry in the park on warm afternoons, and taking in an Edvard Munch exhibit at the Museum of Modern Art. She socialized as well, relaxing in Central Park with "the artists" on picnics. She justified her bucolic leisure time as a path to inspiration:

> Sometimes you become more inspired to compose when you are just relaxed and enjoying yourself than when you are always working and so this July 4th holiday Luci is going to take a holiday and then will see the results. As to the members of the picnic they all sent you their best regards to get well.[46] There was Mr. Cage and Mr. Varèse and Miss Sultan and Mr. Lou Harrison and Mr. Ben Weber and even Mr. Arrau and his wife and we really had a grand time. Miss Sultan, Mr. Cage, and Mrs. Arrau prepared the food and we didn't get home till midnight.[47]

As early as the summer of 1949, when she and Sultan attended his NBC Telephone Hour appearance, Dlugoszewski had counted the pianist Claudio Arrau (1903–91) among her acquaintances, and now in the summer of 1950, she found herself enjoying "sun and fresh air and quiet and gardens" over a weekend with Sultan at Arrau's country estate in Douglas Manor, Bayside-Douglaston, by Long Island Sound.[48] Arrau lent Dlugoszewski and Sultan a tape recorder so they could record and study their own piano playing.[49]

As the active conflict in Korea escalated, Dlugoszewski reported "feeling quite happy in spite of the war news." She added: "You know when a person is creating something in art it always keeps him strong and not melancholy no matter what may be happening."[50] As the Korean War heated up, so did New York's temperatures, and Dlugoszewski tried to work in the mornings, the coolest part of that hot summer. A letter to her mother mixed the mundane with politics and culture. Claiming she "went crazy with the heat" and conducted a number of "irrational acts," she reported buying nylon lace gloves and lingerie at Wanamaker's department store: "You know even [an] artist must act like a crazy woman some time." She added that she had been listening on the radio to commentator Frank Edwards, who was sponsored by the American Federation of Labor, and that she was reading Albert Einstein's new book *Out of My Later Years* (first published in 1950), "in which he devotes one whole chapter in tribute to Misses [sic] Curie."[51] She continued on this political bent in a letter to her father the following day, noting: "Congress is trying to evade the Social Security Bill."[52] Commenting on the rainy weather that followed the heat, she added: "This city is getting to be just like the Bible—7 weeks drought and 7 weeks rain. I don't know if the churches or the scientists are to blame."

During the summer she also made preparations for upcoming performances—for the "New Music Federation of American Composers" and/or "the Publishers of New Music for American Composers committee." The positive reception garnered by her performances prompted her to pursue a publisher for her growing body of work. She described meeting a publisher who allegedly told her that she was "the most talented young writer he's ever met," though she was also advised to establish a more developed portfolio of her work.[53] In fact, Dlugoszewski would have to wait another twenty-seven years before seeing a single piece of her own published.

On 26 July 1950, Dlugoszewski and a Michigan-born sculptor named Ralph Dorazio (1922–2004) applied for a marriage license in New York City—an event that went unmentioned in her letters home.[54] In fact, Dlugoszewski made not a single reference to Dorazio in any of her (currently available) letters of 1950 or 1951, and there is no evidence that they in fact married, though many people close to her later in life believed that they had.[55] A child of Italian-born immigrants a few years Dlugoszewski's senior, Dorazio graduated from Detroit's Eastern High School in January 1939; Dorazio and Dlugoszewski seem to have known each other in Michigan, and had moved to New York together, along with Dlugoszewski's friend Mary Norton.[56] (Dorazio and Norton married in 1961.) Working for a time as a studio manager for architect Frederick Kiesler, Dorazio rented a large studio on 23rd Street where he would occasionally host events, including some of Dlugoszewski's own early performances of her music exploring "everyday sounds." Dorazio's lack of presence in Dlugoszewski's otherwise detailed correspondence with her parents during the summer of 1950 remains one of the mysteries of her biography.[57]

Dlugoszewski traveled home to Michigan on 14 August, where she stayed for several weeks. Prior to her visit, she again outlined her daily needs while at home, including five to six hours of uninterrupted time for practicing and composing: "I don't think that's so much time to ask for me and if you and Czesio try very hard to make this possible for me I'll be much more happy," she added, "and will feel better too because I have to always be a musician."[58] When she returned to New York, Cage and Sultan picked her up at the train station and helped her get home with her luggage. She returned to the city with new clothes, vitamins, and homemade strawberry jam.[59]

THE PROFESSOR

Following up on the job possibilities she had outlined at the beginning of the summer, Dlugoszewski soon visited the Greenwich Music School, the Brooklyn Music School, and the Henry Street Settlement House "to discuss her jobs and pick the one she wants."[60] (During this period of job hunting, Cage and Sultan helped her try to buy a piano from a wholesale piano warehouse.) She announced her decision about the jobs soon after, opting for a position at the Brooklyn School because it offered a better schedule—two six-hour days per week at a rate of six dollars an hour—and was only a three-minute subway ride away from where she was living, "not way deep in Brooklyn where I used to live."[61] She was choosy about her schedule and instinctively protected her time for composing; the Greenwich Music School would have required her to teach every day.

September 1950 was a busy time for Dlugoszewski, as she prepared to move at the end of the month to a new apartment at 292 East 3rd Street with Mary Norton. Dlugoszewski started teaching at the Brooklyn Music School on Thursday, 21 September; she and Norton moved on the last day of that month. Even before she had started her new job, she began referring to herself as "Professor Dlugoszewski."[62] Finding common cultural ground with her new colleagues, she reported that there was another female teacher at the school from the Warsaw Conservatoire, and that a "Professor Pasternak" addressed Dlugoszewski in Polish. On 20 September, the day before beginning her job, she wrote her mother: "And now I must go to Mr. Cage with my new composition—I will teach a composition student tomorrow myself—*Lucia professor* now." Enchanted by her new professional title and empowered by a sense of maturity, she chastised her father on her first day of work: "Today I begin as Professor Lucia so please consider me an adult now and don't offend [the] artist by asking in such incredulous tones what I do the rest of the time because I am very busy practicing and composing and that should be something of importance to you."[63] "Professor Lucia talking!" she exclaimed at the start of a letter to her father a few weeks later: "It's so much fun being professor—I never would have imagined." She went on to brag about her "logical and analytical" thinking that allowed her to "explain everything so clearly to the students." She fantasized about creating a seminar through the Berkshire Foundation for which she would "lecture on modern music."[64] A few months later she would describe her own teaching as "the work of bringing sweetness and light and art to the masses."[65]

Dlugoszewski's mother wanted to come to New York to help with her move to the new apartment, but Dlugoszewski implored her not to: "Remember the *child* is 25 years of age and it's time she attended to her own affairs. . . . Please leave me alone to solve my own adult problems and be somewhat independent." Insisting that she was not starving, as her mother presumably thought, Dlugoszewski explained her finances: "I get paid today $68 pay for my professorship and with the fifty dollars you sent I paid Grete back my thirty dollars for the rent and with the rest I'll have some cleaning done. And put it in the bank so you needn't worry about me budgeting—I *don't* tip anymore."[66] (Later that autumn, she wrote her mother: "Don't worry about me financially. After all I'm [a] professor!"[67]) Though Dlugoszewski insisted on her independence as a breadwinning adult, her mother continued to send her dresses, aprons, embroidered pillowcases, and postage stamps, as well as homemade cookies. Struggling to distance herself from her parents' constant attention, she asserted her autonomy again and again: "You know doctors say the overprotected child is the greatest misfortunate as an adult," she scolded.[68]

Despite the demands of her new job and the logistics of settling in to her new apartment, Dlugoszewski maintained a busy social agenda. Escorted by sculptors Alfred Van Loen and José de Creeft, whom she probably met through Ralph Dorazio, she attended a party "where all the society of New York was gathered." She wrote to her mother: "Lucia just improvised for them on the piano and everyone was so impressed and actually I didn't do very much and I felt just like Beethoven in society—very contemptuous. Ha ha."[69] The added laugh suggests perhaps she felt not contempt so much as amazement at finding herself at the center of such a heady cosmopolitan scene. A few nights later, she went to the Metropolitan Opera with Cage, Van Loen, and composer-critic Peggy Glanville-Hicks. In October she attended a Friends of Modern Music concert with Cage, a memorial concert for Béla Bartók with Varèse, and a party in honor of de Creeft at Van Loen's studio: "You forgive the artist," she asserted in a separate letter to her father that same day, while apologizing for not writing more.[70] That month she also enjoyed a "very enthusiastically appreciated" performance of her new sonata for two violins—"so beautiful angels could have written it," she asserted. Acknowledging her arrogance as a "full composer" inclined to "brag about her own work," she blamed this attitude on teaching, which, she claimed, "gives me so much self-assurance because I'm always being called professor and you know the head begins to swell."[71]

In November, Dlugoszewski described an encounter—also initiated by Cage—with Arnold Schoenberg: "I heard Mr. Schoenberg's orchestral variations and he was in the audience and after the concert we went to Mr. Cage's studio and I played my newest sonata and Mr. Schoenberg said mine is the new courageous music that he is too old to write anymore and I was so flattered."[72] A few nights later she attended a celebration for Aaron Copland's fiftieth birthday at the Museum of Modern Art; she might have celebrated too enthusiastically, as she was too exhausted the following morning to write her mother anything more than a short note.[73] A few days later she told her father that she was writing yet another new sonata; soon after that she wrote to her mother: "I didn't write yesterday because after teaching I had to go to a recital of works by Mr. Varèse and then I got such an inspiration to write something myself that the time slipped by."[74] A day later she attended a concert of Dane Rudhyar's music. She was amused, perhaps sardonically, by the fact that he was finally gaining professional recognition at age fifty-five.[75]

Dlugoszewski and Norton hosted a Thanksgiving dinner party, featuring pan-broiled chicken with cranberry sauce. She reported to her mother: "Mr. Cage is going to bake in his oven pumpkin pie and Mr. Lovisco is going to bring the wine and Miss Sultan will come."[76] The rest of the holiday season was spent preparing manuscripts to bring to a publisher, attending a concert of Cage's "6 Sonatas for the piano" played by Maro Ajemian (probably excerpts from Cage's *Sonatas and Interludes for Prepared Piano*, dedicated to the pianist), and hearing twenty-five-year-old David Tudor play the American premiere of Pierre Boulez's Second Piano Sonata at a League of Composers concert in Carnegie Hall. Full of excitement for this new music and the possibilities her own musical future might hold, she went home to Detroit for Wigilia and the Christmas holiday.

MEETING ERICK HAWKINS

After returning to New York in early January 1951, Dlugoszewski resumed her correspondence with her parents, describing copying out a sonata, practicing for an upcoming performance of her own music at Sultan's studio, writing a new suite for oboe and percussion that she described as "very mysterious," and reading "a new book on the physics of sound from the engineering standpoint."[77] On 10 January she sent her mother a program from a Martha Graham concert "that we all went to." Around this time Dlugoszewski and Sultan began shopping more intently for a piano; Dlugoszewski's mother sent her a check for $200 for the purchase.[78]

Close on the heels of the Martha Graham performance, Dlugoszewski wrote a letter to each of her parents separately, in which she first mentioned her new acquaintance with dancer-choreographer Erick Hawkins. To her father, she wrote: "Well, Luci is very busy these days teaching and practicing and composing and trying to create a ballet with Erick Hawkins and Martha Graham. And any one of these projects may bring something very good with them but it's hard to say which one just now. You know a musician is just like a stock market operator. He has to gamble a little bit and then sell short a little bit and then see what happens."[79] To her mother she wrote: "Well, I'm on the subway to go to the studio of Erick Hawkins and Martha Graham to try to create a ballet with them with music—you know Mr. [William] Schuman did one with Martha this summer and it's going to be presented in Carnegie Hall this week."[80] Poetry written by Dlugoszewski to Hawkins implies that the two had already become lovers by early January 1951; though she did not make this explicit to her parents, his name appeared with increasing frequency in her letters home.

Born in Trinidad, Colorado, a small town just fifteen miles north of the New Mexico border, Frederick [Fred; Erick] G. Hawkins (1909–94) was the fourth of five children, and the only boy in the family. His parents, Eugene Gilbert Hawkins, born in Missouri, and Myrtle Minnie Cunning, born in Nebraska, moved the family to Kansas City, Missouri, where Hawkins attended high school, graduating sixth in a class of 459 students in 1925, the year of Dlugoszewski's birth. After high school, he worked for one year in the advertising department of the Palace Clothing Company in Kansas City. His father, a machinist and inventor, had financial difficulties due to a "defunct business." In April 1926, Hawkins applied to Harvard University, even though, as he wrote in his college application essay, his friends had advised him to attend a western school due to their "more progressive spirit." Still, Hawkins set his sights eastward: "Western universities may exert a desirable influence over a boy in this respect, but in my estimation, this western spirit is over balanced by the very atmosphere and the traditions of a great and famous university like Harvard." Citing the institution's "unsurpassed" professors and equipment, he concluded: "At my present stage of life my most compelling ambition is to be a student at Harvard."[81]

Hawkins entered Harvard as a member of the Class of 1930; due to a number of leaves of absence necessitated by his family's dire financial situation—Hawkins took time off to earn money working as a tutor—he did not earn his degree until 1932. Though his college application had listed history, literature, and music as his chief fields of interest, he gravitated toward Latin, and then Greek, eventually earning a degree in Classics. Hawkins's interest in ancient Greek culture and mythology, combined with his early childhood exposure to Native American traditions of the Southwest, would come to have significant influence over his own creative work throughout his career.

Moving away from academics, Hawkins became fascinated with the style of German dancer Harald Kreutzberg, with whom he studied briefly in Austria before entering the American School of Ballet in 1934. A few years later, one of the founders of that school, Lincoln Kirstein, invited Hawkins to join his newly instituted Ballet Caravan, for which Hawkins created his first choreography, *Showpiece*. Hawkins's work impressed Martha Graham when the Ballet Caravan performed *Showpiece* at the Bennington [Vermont] College Summer Festival in 1937. After studying briefly with Graham, and entering a romantic relationship with her at the same time, Hawkins became the first male dancer in her company, dancing a number of lead roles during the 1940s, including "Husbandman" to Graham's "Wife" in the premiere of *Appalachian Spring* in 1944.[82] Four years later, the couple married in Santa Fe, New Mexico. Hawkins's growing ambition as a choreographer in his own right created tension in both their professional and private relationships, and during the summer of 1950, while on tour in Europe, the couple separated. (They would not divorce until 1959.) When Dlugoszewski met Hawkins, probably in late 1950, he was just starting to redefine his career as a choreographer and as a soloist of his own work, looking for something more inherently American: "Balanchine was a wonderful man, but his eye was still on St. Petersburg," Hawkins would write late in his life.[83]

Though Hawkins was still married to Martha Graham in early 1951, increasingly, he turned his collaborative attention toward Dlugoszewski, whom he met through Grete Sultan when he asked her to recommend a pianist as a possible dance accompanist.[84] Hawkins recalled: "I didn't find somebody who would play the Spanish guitar for me, but I found Lucia Dlugoszewski. After I got to know her, I could see she had a talent and a very great aesthetic sensibility, and so I asked her to write a piece for me. It is quite the equivalent of anything I was able to produce in the dancing."[85] Like many of the private workspaces Dlugoszewski's friends occupied around New York City, Hawkins's dance studio became a venue in which she performed. In early February 1951 she gave recitals of some of her new sonatas at both Cage's and Hawkins's studios. (Clearly enjoying the attention these situations brought her, she told her mother of a concert at which "Mr. Cage kept introducing me as 'My dear friend, the composer, Miss Dlugoszewski.'")[86] Describing her work to her father in mid-February, she reported: "Lucia is now working on the Orpheus score and she has to read Greek mythology for it and use all kinds of orchestrations so that keeps her quite occupied and of course the teaching is lots of fun because you try to give that joy that you feel for music to other people."[87] "The Orpheus score" referred to a piece Hawkins commissioned from Dlugoszewski—the first in a lifetime of collaborations—which resulted in a piece called *openings of the (eye)*.[88] Not much time passed before Dlugoszewski sent her mother a photograph of Hawkins: "You know I'm writing music for his dances so I thought you might like to see what he looks like," barely concealing her delight at his physical appeal.[89] Two weeks later, she mentioned taking a cold but beautiful ride on the Staten Island Ferry with Sultan and Hawkins, admitting: "Of course the idea for the excursion was mine."[90]

As winter turned to spring, Dlugoszewski defended her decision to spend her time composing instead of writing lengthy letters to her mother. What had been the cheery responsibility of a dutiful daughter now became a burden that interfered with her desire to fully engage with her new identity: "I hope you excuse the haphazard mail but when you are trying to be a great composer it takes a lot of time" (18 March); "I'm very busy writing some new music and it makes letter writing a little hectic but I hope you'll understand" (21 March); "Sorry I didn't write but I'm writing music now that's sure to be performed if I only get it done so I'm pretty busy" (5 April); "Please excuse this sketchy writing but I know you want your daughter to get famous and that keeps you busy you know" (16 April). She was also quite likely distracted by the thrill of her new affair with Hawkins. Nonetheless, she found time for concerts—music by Caturla, Cowell, Harrison, Hovhaness, Ruggles, and Wigglesworth at the Manhattan School of Music, for one—as well as musical experimentation, and leisure time with her friends: "You know Lucia created a prepared piano more beautiful than Mr. Cage ever imagined but then your daughter is very gifted—ha ha—And just be patient about the fame. It may come sooner than you think. I just don't want to say anything until there is no doubt. So just be happy Jolas because Luci is doing very well. Tomorrow for relaxation I'm going to a Polish movie with Mr. Cage, Miss Sultan, and Mr. Hawkins and I will educate them in Polish culture."[91] Dlugoszewski's "prepared piano," which would soon come to be known as the "timbre piano," contributed a variety of sonic possibilities to the score she was writing for Hawkins, which now had replaced an originally planned cello part with percussion: "I'm quite enchanted with my new creation," she admitted.[92]

As her school year came to a close, Dlugoszewski had to sacrifice some of her composition time for grading theory papers and other academic obligations. The Brooklyn school paid well and her finances were stable, she reported to her father, adding "for July and August the Foundation would like me to teach some private students and I can arrange the schedule to suit myself so I can arrange my summer vacation according to that."[93] Dlugoszewski also made plans for her summer practicing, explaining to her mother: "Mr. Hawkins has offered me his studio for my private students this summer since he will be away for certain days teaching himself so if I don't get my piano in time I'll do that."[94] Just a few days prior, she described a rare occasion on which Cage, Cunningham, Dlugoszewski, and Hawkins are known to have been in the same room: "Well, I was very good on Sunday with my sonatas—Mr. Cunningham and Mr. Hawkins and Mr. Cage were all there and they all enjoyed it very much."[95]

The Dlugoszewski-Hawkins alliance, lasting from 1951 until Hawkins's death in 1994, would come to be one of the longest-standing collaborations between a composer and a choreographer in the history of modern dance, outdone perhaps only by the collaborative work created by Cage and Cunningham between 1942 and 1992. Hawkins would later proclaim that Dlugoszewski was without equal in having created a new standard of music for contemporary dance: "There is no composer who has been more inventive, more poetic, more theatrically imaginative, and technically successful in creating a true music for dance," he wrote of his creative partner—and by then, wife.[96] Evolving beyond the relationships of her early days in New York, Dlugoszewski embarked on a lifelong journey with Hawkins. This journey began with their first performance together: the above-mentioned, cryptically titled *openings of the (eye)*, a five-movement, solo dance piece scored for flute, "timbre piano," and percussion, which premiered in New York City in January 1952. Moving swiftly from student to teacher to professional collaborator, Dlugoszewski embraced her new role as composer.

THREE

New York Beginnings

A BROADER VIEW (1950–53)

> because you and i know what everyone else does not know that the natural state of man's mind is delight.[1]

DLUGOSZEWSKI'S NEW YORK LETTERS to her parents paint a rosy picture of being enfolded in a vibrant circle of friends as she worked to establish herself as a legitimate composer in the middle of a blossoming avant-garde scene that would come to be known as "The New York School." Her pride and enthusiasm might have been exaggerated for the sake of her parents, but she never expressed any apprehension about her ability to participate in this creative and erudite crowd: hesitation and self-doubt do not seem to be qualities she possessed, at least not during this period of her life. Journal and notebook writings from decades later reveal that she eventually lost her youthful bravado and gained instead a sense of rage and despair, fueled by conflicts with Hawkins, exhausting insomnia, and a relentless, self-imposed work schedule.

If we take her early letters at face value, she was a full-fledged member of the New York School, at least for a short time. However, descriptions she gave of this period in her life many decades later contradict her own eyewitness accounts of her relationships during her early years in New York, and call into question both the accuracy of her memory and her intentions in distorting aspects of her own experience. Revising her own history from a distance of decades, Dlugoszewski created a mythical origin story about herself, making no mention of the multiyear support provided by the Berkshire Foundation, while downplaying the companionship and encouragement she received from "the artists," in particular, the friendship and mentoring she enjoyed with John Cage.

When discussing this part of her life later on, Dlugoszewski claimed that she took theory and analysis lessons with Felix Salzer before meeting other composers in New York.[2] Salzer (1904–86), a Viennese-born theorist and musicologist who had studied with Heinrich Schenker prior to immigrating to the United States in 1939, taught Schenkerian analysis and other topics at the Mannes School of Music. By working with Salzer, Dlugoszewski maintained that she was "looking for validation that she could become a composer.[3] Salzer thought she was a "logical" person, as she remembered later, but he found her compositions themselves "not logical." This recollection is validated by a letter to her mother, in which she reported: "You know I wrote my new opus and it's with poetry too and Mr. Salzer wanted to see it and guess what he said—'you must be a genius because I can't understand [it] at all and yet it looks very profound.'"[4]

Dlugoszewski later claimed that Salzer recommended that she seek out five composers in New York: John Cage, Gian Carlo Menotti, Vincent Persichetti, Edgard Varèse, and Ben Weber.[5] This assertion is odd, and almost certainly inaccurate, since the 1948 letter from the Berkshire Foundation (quoted in chapter 1) named Salzer, Cage, and Varèse (among others) as preassigned mentors. In a later version of the same story, Dlugoszewski took an original composition of her own to each of the five: "I had this feeling that every composer was a master and could tell me the whole truth," she recounted. In every case, she insisted, they "made fun" of the other four. Though the letters to her parents suggest that she studied with Cage in 1950 and 1951, she later claimed in interviews that he merely wanted "clones," and that she was unwilling to accept that kind of heavy-handed mentoring. On the other hand, she recalled, Varèse did not want her to imitate him. Out of the five composers Salzer had recommended, she felt most aesthetically aligned with Varèse, and took "informal" but "intense" lessons with him for some time: "[Varèse] showed me courage, independence of thought . . . all the good things. . . . He taught me the power of philosophic thought in terms of sound. . . . He taught me that the greatest excitement for an artist is facing the unknown. . . . Varèse gave me the world."[6] Just a few months before his death in November 1965, Dlugoszewski wrote to her former mentor, praising him for his "glorious ears," his "shattering imagination," and his "towering spirit." Embracing him as a father figure, she wrote: "Without you there would be no music for me."[7]

Dlugoszewski might have begun studying with Varèse in or after 1951, during a time when letters to her parents are not available. (No tangible evidence of their lessons has been located.) She recalled Varèse talking to her about his own work, but also introducing her to classics of modernism, including Ruth Crawford Seeger's String Quartet 1931 (which she had seen performed in April 1950), Boulez's Second Piano Sonata (which she had seen David Tudor perform in December 1950), Ives's spatial experiments, the music of Erik Satie, and Webern's Symphony Op. 21, which she would have had an opportunity to hear in its American premiere in New York in January 1950 (indeed she might even have attended this concert with Cage, the legendary occasion on which he first met Morton Feldman).[8] Dlugoszewski had not heard any of Varèse's music while growing up—"nobody was playing Varèse in Detroit, Michigan!"—and she later recalled that hearing his chamber piece *Octandre* (1923) for the first time "made [her] hair stand on end."[9] Decades later she would claim that having Varèse as a composition teacher allowed her to escape "the rigid dead-end dogmas of both serialism and aleatory disciplines," and throughout her life she stayed true to his advice, perhaps the most consequential she ever took to heart: "Go to the direct exploration of sound," Varèse instructed.[10]

Though she later placed Varèse at the center of her development as a young composer, it is clear that her early encounters with Cage also made a lasting impression—one that she felt impelled to rebel against for the rest of her life. Reflecting on the role Cage had played in influencing her ideas as a composer, Dlugoszewski told an interviewer of an important encounter with him during her early days in New York (while claiming that she was a "teenager" when she arrived—she was at least twenty-three at the time):

> He said: "You know, what I think is beautiful may not be what you think is beautiful." And that scared me a lot, because he was right. And then, him being a devastating intellect and a very logical man, he said: "Therefore, there's no point in doing anything beautiful." And I thought: "God, I think he's right there, too!" But it scared me.... I still agree that what I think is beautiful may not be what you think is beautiful. But what I want to get across in my motive is: If the sounds are strange they're still strange in terms of aliveness and beauty, by my standards. They are not to provoke you into discomfort.[11]

In other situations Dlugoszewski characterized Cage as downright hostile, even claiming that he tried to harm her career: "Concerts Cage controlled were shut to me," she said, adding that Cage "was so offended that I didn't choose him as my teacher that he did everything he could to not let me be heard as a composer."[12] These statements deny the dozen or more occasions in 1950 and 1951 on which Cage invited Dlugoszewski to perform her own music, or otherwise praised or encouraged her. In part, Dlugoszewski blamed what she recalled as a hostile atmosphere on Cage's younger colleague Morton Feldman (1926–87), who, according to Dlugoszewski, "was very responsible for barring me from concerts because he was so close to Cage."[13] But far from being "offended," at least throughout 1950 and the first half of 1951, Cage seems to have been fond of Dlugoszewski, to the extent that their social and musical activity included holidays and birthdays spent together; offerings of home-cooked meals and other gifts; visits to concerts, museums, poetry readings, parks, and the theater; and an ongoing exchange of musical ideas. It is also notable that in October 1950, Cage encouraged Dlugoszewski to compose for dance, at least according to what she reported to her parents at the time.[14]

Why did Dlugoszewski misremember the reality of her early years in New York, and distance herself so vehemently from Cage? By entering into a personal and professional relationship with Erick Hawkins in early 1951, Dlugoszewski implicitly took sides in the rivalry between Hawkins and Merce Cunningham (1918–2009), Hawkins's most immediate and consequential rival. Hawkins had become the first male dancer in the Martha Graham Dance Company in 1939; Cunningham would become the second, also joining in 1939, and both danced in the premieres of *El Penitente* (1940) and *Appalachian Spring* (1944), among other milestone works of Graham's. This connection led to inevitable comparisons of Hawkins's and Cunningham's work—their choreography, their collaborators, their companies, their design styles, and their choices of music.

Martha Graham biographer Mark Franko has written of the rivalry between the two former Graham dancers: "Once Hawkins became an independent choreographer with his own company he continued to compete with Cunningham for recognition as a leading avant-garde choreographer."[15] Or, in the more blunt words of composer Eleanor Hovda (1940–2009), who worked as a rehearsal accompanist for both Cunningham and Hawkins at various points in her career: "They hated each other's guts."[16] Writer Jamake Highwater, who became a friend of Dlugoszewski's during the 1970s, contemplated the difference between Hawkins's approach and Cunningham's in a more developed way:

To find an animal body within himself Hawkins had to abandon the narrative dancing he performed in the early days with the Martha Graham company. That kind of dancing was so intent upon the human psyche that it very nearly ignored the human body. Merce Cunningham also left Graham to get away from psychology. Both Hawkins and Cunningham went in search of a new principle of movement by going back to basics. Cunningham is stupendously rational; and so he became convinced that classicism was the fundamental stuff from which everything evolves. Hawkins is impelled by something more primary. He wanted a physical, not a logical, reason for dancing. And he knew that he could find it in the body which exists within our bodies—the spiritual body.[17]

Though on the surface the choreographer-composer pairs had similar goals—advancing American modern dance and promoting its use of live, experimental music—at some point they stopped interacting in the same social circles, and their artistic orientations diverged. Perhaps Cage and Cunningham's embrace of chance operations as their guiding compositional principle provided a breaking point. Cage began working on his first major chance composition, *Music of Changes*, in February 1951, right around the time Dlugoszewski was starting to collaborate—and fall in love—with Erick Hawkins.[18]

OPENINGS OF THE (EYE)

As early as January 1951, Dlugoszewski started writing poetry that suggests that a romantic and physical relationship with Hawkins had already begun. Many poems from this early period of their courtship display traits typical of her poetry and writing in general: nature and nocturnal imagery, visceral physical references, fantastical sensuality, and surreal eroticism (with a nod to E. E. Cummings). She would continue to write erotic love poetry to Hawkins throughout their relationship. The earliest known of these poems exists as a typescript dated 17 January 1951:

AND A

(Poem to the April of a Protestant Lover)

from the skin splintered moon
(distilled over distance) comes
smooth to the (i)
    and
i becomes black to the moon

>   and
> black is of course open most of twilight things
>   and
> if everyone is enough darling
> every star holds a violet carefully in its mouth
>   and
> several B flat A's press erotic hollows into the tender where
> arms of the sky join the
> body of sky
> to the legs of sky
>   and
> the tree of twilight pressed deep against eyes
>   and
> opens them to death
>   and
> the (i) wishes to walk under all the several precious waters of man
> the way every moon walks softly under the seventh soul of an
>   ocean.[19]

Another poem written three days later was even more explicit in its sexual references, and more surreal in its imagery (i.e., "a box of confetti-murmured roller skates"):

> the coming of you is as slender specific as one precise polar
>   vein bearling [sic] moonlight
> the coming of you holds the smallest space there is
> holds the alto absolute axis of air
>   and
> time kisses over it 24 times but never gets in
>   *
> i would love to split you tissue by tissue
> the way moon pushes earth mud ray by ray
>   and
> the skin of your eyes might break to let the dark god rise in
>   their surface
>   and this
> microscopically solftly [sic] so the sound of loving would show
>   *
> when sunlight stretches its body onto the world
>   and
> sky closes its veil over him glowing
>   and
> leaves stand up naked and white for the sun

>   and
>   the nerve of smell grows complex for april
>   and
>   the black green angel sings inside the mud
>   (if you would be my young and now now my love)
>   i would give you a box of confetti-murmured roller skates
>   and
>   the space of spring to use them[20]

Three days later, she wrote another erotic poem for Hawkins, and called it "Metaphysic in the Earth of Twilight," which blurred the boundaries between the lovers' identities:

>   did i hold the form of snow in my mouth
>   for you
>   and
>   hide one exquisite special seed of wet wind
>   in some loop of my breathing
>   and
>   carry darkness in my palest skin for you
>   all day
>   and finally
>   divide my limbs with the tender glass
>   in silence
>   or did you do me[21]

Two months later, Hawkins wrote to a friend suggesting that a romance with Dlugoszewski had begun—and also contradicted her later claim that she never studied with Cage: "Lucille is writing music for the four dances. You know she studies with John Cage. She has prepared the piano this week. It is terribly beautiful. Just unearthly sounds, screws, wooden wedges, rubber hose, brass strips, etc. Will use flute and several percussions. Believe she can get something lovely. She is lovely! It has been wonderful to have her at this time. Have made a step forward in my internal life."[22] Dlugoszewski's experimentation with the piano, and her work on the "four dances," indicate that they had already begun work on their first collaboration. A few weeks later, Hawkins again reported to his friend: "Lucille has taught me a great deal. Her love for me has been absolutely wonderful."[23] On that same day, Dlugoszewski wrote to her mother about a "series of four ballets that I'm writing for prepared piano, flute, and percussion." According to Hawkins scholar Julia Keefer, who interviewed Dlugoszewski in 1977, the composer was not well acquainted with the world of dance when she started working with Hawkins, but her "eye for movement later impressed Hawkins a great deal."[24]

In late March 1951, Dlugoszewski began exploring how to draw sound out of a grand piano—a technique that she originally referred to as a "prepared piano" and which was later dubbed "timbre piano" by Robert Sabin, a music critic who served as the editor of *Musical America* from 1960 to 1962.[25] The timbre piano technique, like John Cage's prepared piano invented around 1940, aimed to elicit sounds from the piano by applying different external materials directly onto the strings. Unlike Cage's screws, bolts, and weather stripping inserted between the strings to act as mutes and dampers, Dlugoszewski played directly on the (mostly) unaltered strings using a variety of bows and plectra made from the widest possible source of materials: wood, plastic, metal, glass, string, wire, bone, porcelain, paper, hair combs, fingernails, brushes, and so on.[26] Her performance technique for the timbre piano was theatrical, as it necessitated her leaning into the body of the piano and gesturing with dramatic sweeps of the arms, and photographs of her playing it give the impression of a physical presence that must have been captivating, a quality noted by critics who wrote about her performances.

Dlugoszewski continued writing erotic poetry and letters to Hawkins throughout 1951; occasionally, she even scribbled romantic haiku on the small squares of her day calendar, as she did in October and November 1951. In August of that year, she traveled home to Michigan, where she wrote a breathless ("utterly tongue-tied"), stream-of-consciousness love letter to Hawkins: "I remember now that the sun was always my first lover and I remember how I used to be very still and let him cover me with his warmth and press down his radiance into me and all the time I was learning how to behave properly for you, the more radiant lover."[27] Throughout the fall, as her passion for Hawkins grew, they rehearsed for their first public performance together. Many of her letters and poems written during these months referred to the Greek themes of their new piece, and later explanations of the piece itself contained overt references to their new love. The final version of the piece was in five parts (instead of the "four dances" originally planned):[28]

i. Discovery of the Minotaur
ii. Disconsolate Chimera
iii. Ritual of the Descent
iv. Goat of the God
v. Eros, the Firstborn

Dlugoszewski's trio score for *openings of the (eye)* exists today as a precisely notated, eighty-six-page score.[29] As the titles of the movements suggest, the dances explored themes of Greek mythology, which Hawkins had studied at Harvard. Ralph Dorazio contributed all the visual material; this would be the first of many collaborations between the three artists over the next several decades. Dorazio's costumes included richly colored and textured felt, balsa wood for the wings of Eros and the hooves of the Goat of the God, and horsehair, wire, and string for the Goat's mask.[30]

The music for *openings of the (eye)* was fairly conventional for the time, in terms of notation, texture, and sound, with the flute part seeming secondary to the piano and percussion writing. Dlugoszewski oscillated between amorphous sound-effect passages and more traditionally flashy sections that demanded technical virtuosity in the piano part, which moved among clusters, tremolos, trills, and glissandi. Throughout the piece, the percussionist was asked to pluck the piano's open strings, to throw wire springs on them, or to strike or rub them with a wire rods, wire brushes, spoons, or slivers of bone. The percussionist was also instructed to drop "deer hooves" on the timpani, to shake and rotate cocoons like rattles, and to maneuver between logs, bones, gourds, and bells.

Many years later, in a lecture given at the Smithsonian Institute, Hawkins reflected on his "small scale" intentions in this early work: "They were a progression of metaphors of states of metaphysical knowledge. [...] But I was too far ahead of my time, and few people were aware of the metaphors and how to read them."[31] "Ahead of his time" or not, decades later, Hawkins would tell a *New York Times* dance writer that he felt that the most important aspects of his work came together for the first time with *openings of the (eye)*, stating that with it he succeeded in creating "a metaphor of important ideas of the spirit put into sensuous form."[32]

In January 1952, choreographers Cunningham, Hawkins, and Jean Erdman rented New York's Hunter Playhouse in order to present their newest work, including the premiere of *openings of the (eye)* on a program that also included Hawkins's dances *Bridegroom of the Moon* (with music by Wallingford Riegger) and his *Lives of Five or Six Swords* (with music by Lou Harrison).[33] These performances were part of a weekend-long mini-dance festival that also included dances by Erdman (with music by Cage, Debussy, Feldman, Harrison, and Hovhaness), and Cunningham (with music by Cage). The Sunday *New York Times* listing for the festival was probably the first time Dlugoszewski's name appeared in that publication.[34] *Musical America* critic Robert Sabin offered a confusing account of how many dances were actually performed in his review of the Hawkins performance on 19 January 1952: "The four [dances] that followed the intermission were preceded by a cryptic note: 'openings of the (eye).' Of the seven dances, only one—Disconsolate Chimera—was choreographically sustained and interesting. This owed much to Martha Graham's *Herodiade* and *Cave of the Heart*, but it had original touches and it was performed with considerable virtuosity. The Chimera costume by Dorazio was handsome and the music by Dlugoszewski was properly vague and dissonantly atmospheric."[35] Actress and Living Theatre director Judith Malina (1926–2015) attended the premiere of *openings of the (eye)*, and described the performance in her diary the following day: "Erick Hawkins' dances create a world which we recognize as having lived in long before we met this one. Primeval symbols awaken responses whose origins are lost but whose evocations retain an inexplicable power. The goat, the single eye, the sword, the winged child, the gestures of the unremembered. Lucia Dlugoszewski creates a startling, inventive percussion score for *Openings of the Eye*. Dorazio designs devices in which, and through which, Hawkins moves with an unhurried walklike tread."[36]

Decades later, Dlugoszewski reflected on her intentions in some of her early work, including the distinction between Logos (logic) and Eros (feeling)—a mind-body dichotomy that occupied her thoughts at this time—and her focus on the concept of *radical empirical immediacy*:

> Musically, an analysis of the problem of artificiality caused me in 1951 to write OPENINGS OF THE (EYE) [1952], repudiating Logos for a pure Eros music that was also non-melodic, non-emotional—the sheer "beautiful sound," music as a miracle of unintelligibility. This music attempted a wider Eros experience than the self-expression of petty human hopes and fears. Notice how quickly pitch-interval, melodic juxtapositions (movie and TV music) recede from the open aired largeness of immediate hearing into the egocentric, cramped interiors of our emotional life. Another effort to counteract this was STRUCTURE FOR THE POETRY OF EVERYDAY SOUNDS. But how quickly noises escaped the ineffable act of hearing to become the denotative pointer readings of our practical common-sense life!

She went on to obliquely reference Cage: "When I defended the alive, egoless, non-emotional immediacy of the 'beautiful sound,' other composers and critics hastened to assure me that what I think is beautiful may not be what you think is beautiful." Such cynical views left her asking why one should bother trying to create something sensuously beautiful. "This is the destructive dilemma of relativistic radical empirical immediacy," she concluded.[37]

THE LIVING THEATRE AND THE POETRY OF EVERYDAY SOUNDS

Along with the Hunter Playhouse and the 92nd Street Y, where Dlugoszewski and Hawkins had participated in a "choreographer's workshop" on 13 January 1952, a new entity called the Living Theatre offered another outlet for performance and creative support. The first performances of the Living Theatre, founded by Judith Malina and her husband Julian Beck (1925–85), took place in their New York City apartment on 15 August 1951.[38] By early 1952, Dlugoszewski and Hawkins joined the social and professional circle of Beck and Malina, which included other artists and intellectuals like Jean Erdman and Joseph Campbell, and Alan and Serafina Hovhaness. Near the beginning of spring 1952, Malina described a party she and her friends attended: "We walked coatless in the new spring air to a gathering at Alan and Serafina's home. The Hovhanesses have a room full of enigmas. Here Alan is strikingly gaunt and [Serafina] an Egyptian princess.... Everyone present has his magical function: Serafina, the princess; Alan, the Oak King; Judith, the victim; Julian, the agnostic priest; Frances [Clark], Circe, the enchantress; Lucia, the muse; Philip [Smith], the prince of the waxing moon."[39]

Dlugoszewski "the muse" enchanted Malina, and they became friends. In February 1952 Dlugoszewski worked with Malina on a Living Theatre production of Pablo Picasso's absurdist play *Desire Trapped by the Tail*, which was to be premiered by the Living Theatre on 2 March 1952 at the Cherry Lane Theatre, in only the fourth public performance given by that group. During their preparations, Malina noted: "Lucia has an especially witty ear."[40] She also observed: "Lucia has a very personal way of speaking. She gets involved immediately and there is nothing I admire more. She is involved in art through people. Speaks intimately of Erick Hawkins and of his relation to Martha Graham."[41] Malina's delight in Dlugoszewski's contributions continued, as she noted a few days later: "Lucia's sounds make the [Picasso] play move as I had hoped: a farce ritual and the story of Pandora's bee of hope."[42] For the Picasso piece, Dlugoszewski employed the timbre piano technique and her own voice. *Desire Trapped by the Tail* was presented in a performance called "An Evening of Bohemian Theatre" along with Gertrude Stein's *Ladies Voices* (1916) and T. S. Eliot's *Sweeney Agonistes* (1926–7/1932). *Theatre Arts* magazine reviewed *Desire Trapped by the Tail*, and mentioned (in passing) Dlugoszewski's "uninterrupted musical score" for the six-act play.[43] According to Living Theatre historian Pierre Biner, the evening was the company's first real success, and as a result, Beck and Malina were able to begin paying their actors, who, in this production, included Frank O'Hara and John Ashbery.[44] Visual artist Grace Hartigan, who attended a performance of *Desire Trapped by the Tail* on 13 March 1952, characterized the show as "a real sex circus, a lot of fun."[45]

On 5 May 1952, Beck and Malina presented a concert of new music at the Cherry Lane Theatre, which included selections from Cage's *Sonatas and Interludes* for prepared piano, *Four Trumpets and Muted Piano* by Cowell, *Khaldis (Ancient God of the Universe)* by Hovhaness, *Music for Trumpets* by Vanig Hovsepian, *Round Dance* by Lou Harrison, and a solo timbre piano piece by Dlugoszewski that she played herself, called *The Space of March and April and May Has Turned the Ground on Its Tender Side and Everyone Has to Turn the Same Way*.[46] Malina observed in her diary: "Lucia plays a loose piece—formless, yet nonetheless carefully drawn; the audience is small but responsive."[47] Writing again for *Musical America*, Robert Sabin reviewed the Living Theatre–sponsored concert at length, which, he wrote, took him "back to the balmy days of the Greenwich Village American revolution of the arts." He called Dlugoszewski's oddly titled piece "the most unusual of the evening's offerings," and drew a distinction between the intimate yet informal surroundings of the "somewhat unkempt but wildly enthusiastic" downtown scene and the "decorous and more or less stereotypical" uptown one. The concert began after 9:30 p.m. and went on until after midnight. By the time Dlugoszewski's piece began, late in the program, the critic seems to have lost interest in the event: "The composer emerged, with a formidable-looking manuscript, and proceeded to produce weird wails by rubbing a water glass up and down the piano strings, pluck the strings, use the sustaining pedal for sympathetic vibrations, and perform other painstaking experiments in sonority. She was in the midst of page three when I left, it being close on midnight and the piece showing no signs of developing into coherent music."[48] Sabin had nothing to say about Cage's *Sonatas and Interludes*. He considered Cowell's trumpet piece a "disappointment," and wrote that Hovhaness's *Khaldis* "was not up to his customary standards of orchestration and texture." Hovsepian's *Music for Trumpets* "revealed little originality of invention or ability to sustain a texture." Harrison's work, though a premiere, received neither praise nor criticism. A brief review of the concert titled "Living Theatre Gives Concert of the Moderns" published on 6 May 1952 in the *New York Times* listed Dlugoszewski as one of the featured composers, but neglected to comment on her piece.

On Friday, 21 November 1952, Dlugoszewski presented a work called *The Structure for the Poetry of Everyday Sounds* at Ralph Dorazio's 23rd Street studio.[49] She sent "Mr. Hawkins" a provocative invitation on a postcard: "We would like your lovely structure to give a beautiful flavor to our structure and your ears will be delighted also."[50] Dlugoszewski later discussed this particular performance, and contradicted herself again with regard to Cage:

> *The Structure for the Poetry of Everyday Sounds* was an extreme experiment in what Zen Buddhism calls "suchness." The New York piece was performed in the loft of a wonderful sculptor, Ralph Dorazio, and the whole New York school of painters and poets and composers were there, including John Cage and Morton Feldman. John loved it and said I created a whole new kind of theater. That "everyday" stuff really made John flip. In fact, he and Morty had a fight over it that night, because they both came and Morty obviously was very possessive about John and was determined to put me down, and John just argued with him all night long about that, and kept telling him he was wrong about me.[51]

A few days after Dlugoszewski's performance of *The Structure for the Poetry of Everyday Sounds*, Malina reported in her diary that Cage seemed to have enjoyed Dlugoszewski's approach toward ambient sound, an account that provides further evidence against Dlugoszewski's later claim that Cage did not take her seriously: "Lucia Dlugoszewski plays the *Music of Everyday Sounds*—her music for *Ubu* [*the King*] a play by Alfred Jarry], in Ralph Dorazio's studio, behind a screen of newspapers. In this congregation there is neither the hush of undue reverence nor indifference. Lucia's orchestration of everyday sounds confounds the concert ear. We hear the clatter of teacups, the turning of the doorknob, breaking glass. John Cage listens better than anyone because he exalts the very faculty of hearing."[52] Ralph Dorazio and Mary Norton performed Dlugoszewski's piece behind screens intended to obscure the audience's view. The piece was allegedly written out, with nothing left to chance, though the performers mostly engaged in "tearing paper, hitting hammers on nails, making a tea kettle whistle on a hot plate, tapping blocks or wood, lighting matches, pounding on a typewriter, and playing a radio."[53] Dlugoszewski claimed that after the performance concluded, Cage requested that they remove the screens and perform it again.[54]

Between 1951 and 1952 Dlugoszewski seems to have composed a number of interrelated pieces, about which almost nothing is known. The following titles appear on various work lists created by the composer and others:

Transparencies for Everyday Sounds 1–50 [1951]
Transparencies for String Quartet [1952]
Orchestra Structure for the Poetry of Everyday Sounds [1952]
Transparencies for Harp [1952]
Transparencies for Flute [1952]
Transparencies for Harp and Violin [1952]
Everyday Sounds for e.e. cummings with Transparencies [1952]

In 1952, Dlugoszewski created a score for the Living Theatre's production of *Ubu the King*, which premiered at the Cherry Lane Theatre on 5 August 1952. Musician and instrument builder Hal Rammel later wrote that Dlugoszewski's incidental music for this production of *Ubu* "drew upon this collection of everyday sounds, . . . as did her music for Marie Menken's film *Visual Variations on Noguchi* (1953)."[55] These early performances drew praise and support from poets Frank O'Hara and John Ashbery, sculptor David Smith, and painter Robert Motherwell, and soon Dlugoszewski became active in the Eighth Street Artist's Club and among the art and literary crowd that frequented the nearby Cedar Tavern.

Dlugoszewski's music cues for *Ubu the King* offer a glimpse into what kinds of instruments and other noisemakers she employed in the creation of this score, and during this period of composition in general:

Scene I Blackout	Silence
Scene II Blackout	honk
Scene III Blackout	drop saw
Scene IV Blackout	silence
Scene V Blackout	glass bells>>>hit metal gong
Scene VI Blackout	Catholic bell
Scene VII Blackout	metal gong
Scene VIII Blackout	drop lid
Scene IX Blackout	tea kettle whistle alone
Scene X Blackout	2 hits of metal gong
Scene XI Blackout	tea kettle whistle alone
Scene XII Blackout	P.A. shriek
Scene XIII Blackout	4 honk
Scene XIV Blackout	Catholic Bell
Scene XV Blackout	3 metal gongs

Scene XVI Blackout	typewriter all alone
Scene XVII Blackout	rattle thunder sheet
Scene XVIII Blackout	hit metal gong 3 times
Scene XIX Blackout	5 honks
Scene XX Blackout	Catholic bell
Scene XXI Blackout	2 bells

A second page included a chart-like list of numbers, with additional instructions or descriptions penciled in, including: "beans rattled in jar"; "water on oil can"; "water into pan from bottle"; "beans slowly irregularly on copper sheet"; "type"; "water poured into oil can"; "use p.a. clock"; and "water bubbles."[56] This kind of soundscape, though not unheard of in experimental theater at the time, foreshadowed the Fluxus-flavored infatuation with "everyday" materials of some ten years later.

In a 1975 essay, critic and composer Tom Johnson described a New York loft performance of Dlugoszewski's music that drew upon the sounds of "bouncing balls, crashing glass, pouring water, a whistling teakettle, and just about every sound possible with pieces of papers." He added: "A screen was placed between the performers and the audience, so that the listeners were forced to deal with the sound itself, without visual distraction."[57] Likewise, conductor Joel Thome later recalled hearing about a loft performance—attended by Alexander Calder and Edgard Varèse, among others—during which Dlugoszewski performed near a kitchen from which she borrowed pots and pans and other materials for making her "everyday sounds." Thome recalled that she was particularly fond of paper as a sonic source: "What she did with paper was a very spiritual statement as well, because she was very drawn to Zen," he said.[58]

In August 1952, following the production and performances of *Ubu the King*, Dlugoszewski traveled on "The Wolverine" train line back to Detroit to visit her parents. From there she wrote Hawkins an erotic love letter in which she reminisced about a trip they had taken to Nantucket Island in the early days of their courtship, and vividly described the anguished physical longing she felt for him in his absence, concluding that "a woman loses so quickly that precious radiance that is her only life without a beautiful man to unfold her."[59]

Back in New York a week later, Dlugoszewski embarked on a new collaboration, this time with filmmaker Marie Menken (1910–70), who invited Dlugoszewski to create a soundtrack for her 1945 abstract film titled *Visual*

Variations on Noguchi. The four-minute, black-and-white film, the first ever made by Menken, showcased the experimental sculpture of Japanese American artist Isamu Noguchi (1904–88). With the assistance of Dorazio and a few others, Dlugoszewski created a soundscape that was as close as she ever got to the sound of the tape-manipulation-based compositional technique of musique concrète: an array of crashes, vocalizations, percussion sounds and inside-of-the-piano effects assault the ear with cacophonous force.[60] Dlugoszewski created and recorded her score in the Barron Sound Studios of Louis and Bebe Barron, the same site where Cage assembled his revolutionary tape piece *Williams Mix* (1952) alongside similar tape works by Earle Brown, Morton Feldman, and Christian Wolff. (Just a few years later the Barrons would become famous for their electronic score for the science fiction film classic *Forbidden Planet* of 1956.)

A promotional flyer put out by the New York company that produced *Visual Variations on Noguchi*, Gryphon Productions, included a statement by Dlugoszewski that introduced the notion of Joycean "suchness" or a Zen "beginner's mind": "Every sound in the score is the magic of its bewilderment and exists only as its timbre and so the ear will be shocked into listening to paper because it has probably never heard it before.... If the listening is innocent enough it will see that bewilderment is glorious because it alone is true." The filmmaker added a (less lofty) blurb of her own: "My camera and I took a turn about Noguchi's studio and the camera-eye recorded the happy journey and when Lucille saw what the camera had seen she too took a happy journey and together it is all happiness."[61] A photograph of the musicians recording the music for *Visual Variations on Noguchi* included on the promotional flyer showed Dlugoszewski leaning over the strings of an open grand piano, Ralph Dorazio scraping what looks like a large gong, a woman (possibly Mary Norton) singing, and two other men holding noisemakers. An unattributed description of the project included in the promotional material highlighted Dlugoszewski's use of "everyday sound," which would "no doubt, (as it has at its previews) create violent reactions among those not too familiar with avant-garde music, but the unprejudiced will be loudly grateful (as they have at its previews) for this audacious experiment. It is music where structure emphasizes timbre, using percussion, 'the poetry of natural sound' (matches being lit, paper torn, books dropped), the human voice and techniques in the piano strings. It is, as composer John Cage suggests, 'a jungle of sounds' which the willing will 'explore!'"

· · · · ·

Dlugoszewski and Hawkins's first collaboration *openings of the (eye)* was performed again at the Hunter Playhouse, one year after its premiere, on 24 January 1953. The second page of the program for this performance included a fanciful (and unattributed) note, with bracketed numbers highlighting references to the five movements. The manifesto-like essay began with what seemed like an affirmation of Dlugoszewski and Hawkins's relationship: "because there is nothing to keep us away from each other everything with a voice tells us to / look and delight / (look with your muscles and delight) / (look with your ears and delight)." After a rambling, poetic description of the sections of the piece, the note ended with another overt reference to romantic ecstasy, as well as a hint of the "us against the world" attitude—"because you and i know what everyone else does not know"—that would later come to symbolize a kind of creative isolation for the pair:

> you are here and i am here only for one reason, because we love.
> supposing movement were a miracle of unintelligibility, we would be so fortunate to have no egotistical intellect of wall between you and me when we touch each other with our child's mouths
> because you and i know what everyone else does not know that the natural state of man's mind is delight.[62]

In an essay written in 1991 for his collection *The Body Is a Clear Place and Other Statements on Dance* (1992), Hawkins tried to explain—not any less cryptically—how he had hoped to use metaphor as a way to communicate a spiritual idea. These ideas culminated in the final movement, "Eros, the Firstborn," in which "the insight arrives at the metaphor of love—the love, which pervades the world, and is available to every creature, showing the strange principle that it is there, if one recognizes it." Describing Dorazio's artistic representation of a third eye, which Hawkins taped to his forehead, the dancer explained the meaning of the title of the piece: "I used a metaphor of opening the third eye, the eye of enlightenment, of seeing things as they are."[63]

Judith Malina attended the January 1953 repeat performance of *openings of the (eye)*, and described the event in her diary: "Erick Hawkins' concert. But once a year he performs his rituals and still there are only some 800 persons to see them! . . . Lucia's sounds challenge music. Surpassing its logic. Ralph's masterful settings. John Cage and Merce Cunningham and Lou Harrison were not there. Who will love us if we do not love each other? Backstage, Alan Hovhaness praises Lucia, 'You are a great composer.'... 'Where are John and Lou?' asks Lucia."[64] Malina's question—"Who will love us if we do not love each other?"—echoed art critic Irving Sandler's summary of New York's downtown scene in the mid-1950s, in which poets, musicians, and dancers looked to visual artists for a sympathetic audience:

> Because they got to know artists who came to their readings, poets became critics: Frank O'Hara, who was a curator at the Museum of Modern Art, John Ashbery, who was writing in *Art News*, Barbara Guest in *Arts*.... And because of the closeness of artists to dancers and musicians like Merce Cunningham and John Cage—and both were very important in the art world—Meryl Marsicano, married to painter Nick Marsicano, choreographer Erick Hawkins, Lucia Dlugoszewski, the composer for Hawkins, Morty Feldman—*they* were invited to speak or perform at The Club. Avant-garde painters and sculptors became the primary audience for all of *these* arts. They were the critical mass, the 250 of them plus spouses and friends.[65]

Sandler recalled Cage telling him that if the poets and artists weren't there, despite their reservations about his work, there would be "nobody there": "It was just one avant-garde supporting another," Cage claimed matter-of-factly.[66] (Malina herself wrote in her diary after a concert of Cage's: "Everyone in the audience has seen our plays and we have seen their pictures, dances, concerts, lectures, books, soirées, openings, mailings, posters, crafts, songs, parties.")[67] But Malina and Dlugoszewski's bewilderment about Cage, Cunningham, and Harrison's absence is poignant and bleak, as if an unspoken "we are all in this together" understanding alluded to by Sandler had been betrayed. Though there continued to be points of contact and shared performances in the future, by 1953, alliances had been established. Dlugoszewski and Hawkins, committed to one another and to their shared idiosyncratic ideologies, moved on together.

Baby book photographs, ca. 1931. Photographer unknown. Used by permission of the Erick Hawkins Dance Company.

Family portrait, ca. 1931. Photographer unknown. Used by permission of the Erick Hawkins Dance Company.

The *Detroit News*, 1939. The caption accompanying the photograph stated: "Lucille Dlugoszewski, whom many will recognize as one of our Young Writers and pianists, gave a recital Sunday, January 15, at the Carl Beutel Studio on West Grand Blvd."

School portrait, ca. 1939. Photographer unknown. Used by permission of the Erick Hawkins Dance Company.

"Officers' Club" High School Photograph, ca. 1941. Photographer unknown. Used by permission of the Erick Hawkins Dance Company.

Lucille relaxing under a tree (date unknown). Photographer unknown. Used by permission of the Erick Hawkins Dance Company.

Lucille posing for the camera (date unknown). Photographer unknown. Used by permission of the Erick Hawkins Dance Company.

WAYNE UNIVERSITY

Division of Student Personnel
Record of
Detroit, Michigan

134 Brooklyn, Brooklyn 13, N.Y.
Entrance

Lucille Ruth DLUGOSZEWSKI

706611

Admitted on 2-42 to College of Liberal Arts	**** Units	Units Deficient / Removed
High School Northeastern, Detroit	English 3, Electives 4	
By Certificate X Examination... With advanced standing	For. Lang. Latin 2	
To matriculated division Fr. X So. ... Jr. ... Sr. ... Class	History 2, Other Soc. Sci. 1	
Matric. Fee paid... Not paid X * On trial	Alg. 2, Geom. 1, Trig. ½	
Date of birth 6-16-25 Curriculum B.B.S. (Premed)	Science Biol. 1, Chem. 1, Phys. 1	
Father's name Chester Dlugoszewski	Total 18½	

University

No. of Weeks Ending	Course number and description	Eng.	Lang.	Sci.	Soc. Sci.	Other	Pro. Pts.	Lab. Hrs.	Total Semester Hours	Status, Relations, Adjustment
18 6-42	Engl. 1 - Fresh. Comp.	A3					12			
	Germ. 1 - Elem.		A4				16			
	Chem. 3 - Gen'l			B4			12	72		
	Hist. 1 - Western Civiliz.				A3		12			
	Hist. 1L - Lect.West.Civiliz.				A1		4			
	Orient.					Cr	-			
	P.Ed. 41 - Swim. I					B1	3			
	Total to date	3	4	4	4	1	59	16		
2-43	Engl. 2 - Freshman Comp.	B3					9			*Matric. Fee Paid
	Germ. 2 - Elem.		B4				12			
	Chem. 12 - Qual. Anal.			A5			20	144		
	Hist. 2 - West. Civiliz.				A3		12			
	Hist. 2L - Lectures-West.Civiliz.				A1		4			
	P.Ed. 31 - Field Hock., Badminton					C1	2			
	Total to date	6	8	9	8	2	118	33		
6-43	Engl. 150 - Intr. Engl. Lit.	B3					9			
	Chem. 116 - Quant. Anal.			W			-	144		
	Zool. 1 - Gen'l			C4			8	108		
	French 1 - Elem.		A4				16			
12 9-43	Withdrew 6-30-43									0
18 2-44	French 2 - Elem.		B4				12			
	Germ. 104 - Intermed.		C4				8			
	Chem. 121 - Org.			A4			16			
	Math. 107 - Col.Alg.					W	0			
	Total to date	9	20	17	8	2	187	56		
6-44	Engl. 167:2 - Modern Novel	A3					12			Major: Chemistry
	Engl. 202 - Creative Writing	A2					8			Adv.: Bird
	Chem. 121L - Organ.Chem.Lab.			W			-	144		
	Math. 144 - Anal.Geom.&Calculus					E(4)	0			
	Zool. 151 - Compar.Vert.Zool.			W			-	108		
	Phil. 201 - Intro.				W		-			
	P.Ed. 36 - Tap Dancing I					E(1)	(0)			Has max.
	Total to date	14	20	17	8	2	207	61	(65 hrs.h.pt.base)	

The last entry is on line............ This is an official transcript only when it bears the imprint of the University Seal and the Recorder's signature.

Continued on Page #2

Honorable dismissal is...
A fee of $1.00 is required for each official transcript after the second.

Date..

Form 1208 M 12-41 4M DV-LK

Recorder.

Dlugoszewski's Wayne State University Transcripts, page 1. Courtesy of the Office of Alumni Relations Records, Wayne State University.

Publicity portraits of Dlugoszewski with some of her invented percussion instruments (ca. 1962). © Daniel Kramer.

Posed portrait with instruments (date unknown; ca. 1960). Photographer unknown. Used by permission of the Erick Hawkins Dance Company.

Dlugoszewski with sculptor Ralph Dorazio, builder of her instrument designs (ca. 1962). © Daniel Kramer.

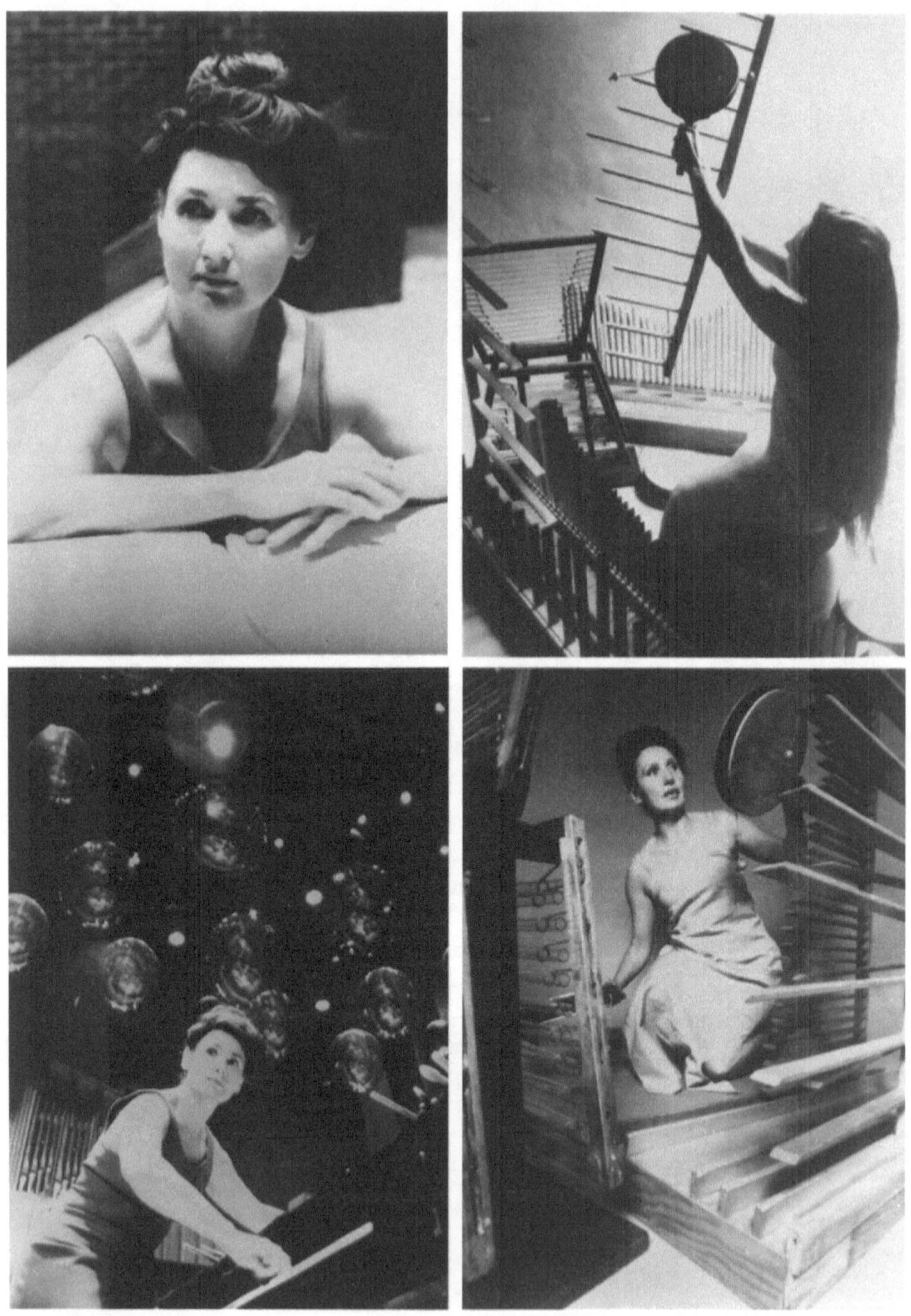

Composite of publicity photographs (date unknown; ca. 1960). Right side photographer unknown; used by permission of the Erick Hawkins Dance Company. Left side photography by Robert Lightfoot III; used by permission.

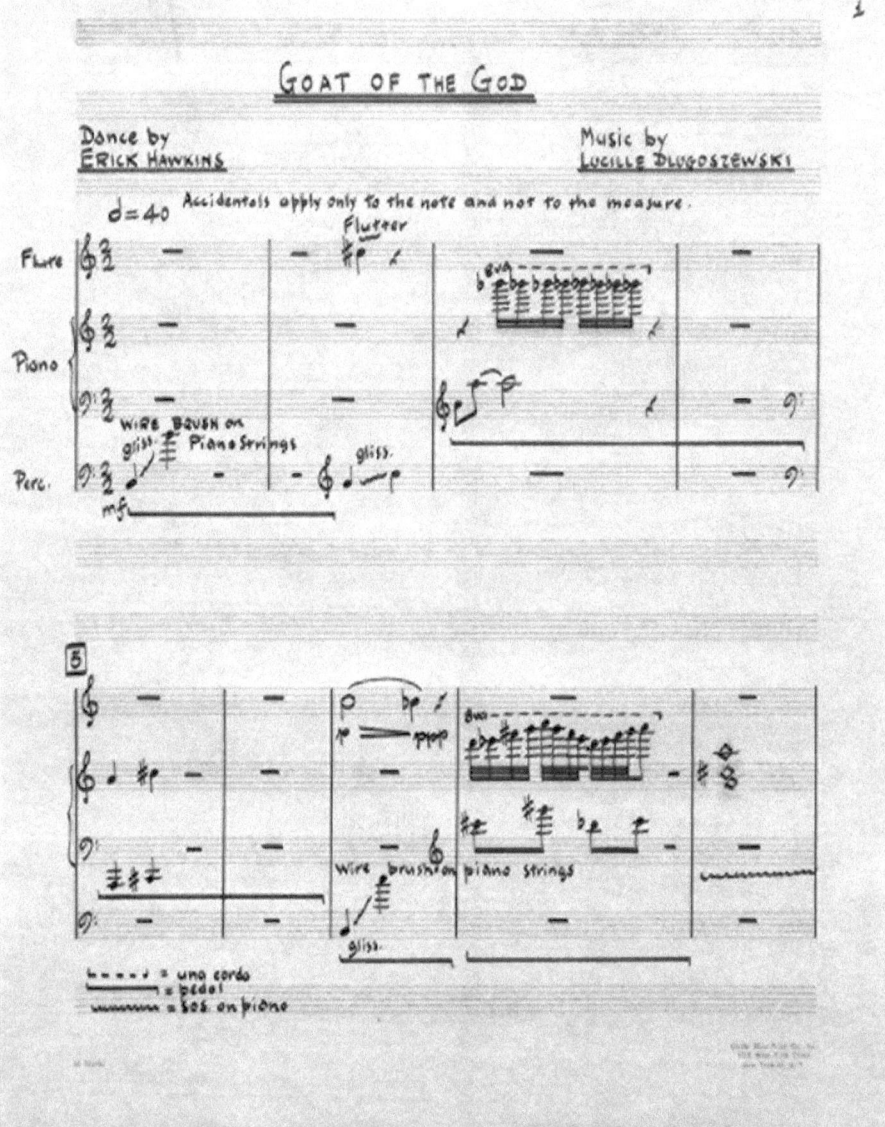

Page one of "Goat of the God," from *openings of the (eye)*, 1952–53. Used by permission of the Erick Hawkins Dance Company.

THE LIVING THEATRE, Inc.

JUDITH MALINA & JULIAN BECK, DIRECTORS

PRESENTS

A CONCERT OF NEW MUSIC
MONDAY EVENING, MAY 5, 1952, AT 9:30 P.M.
CHERRY LANE THEATRE

PROGRAM

SELECTIONS FROM SONATAS AND INTERLUDES	JOHN CAGE
*FOUR TRUMPETS AND MUTED PIANO	HENRY COWELL
*KHALDIS — (ANCIENT GOD OF THE UNIVERSE)	
CONCERTO FOR PIANO, 4 TRUMPETS AND PERCUSSION	

    SHARAGAN (HYMN)
    TRANSMUTATION
    KINI (DRINKING SONG)
    BALLATA
    THREE TONES
    BHAJANA (ADORATION)
    CANZO
    CANZONA
    TAPOR (PROCESSIONAL)
    DANCE
    POVADA (HEROIC)   ALAN HOVHANESS

— INTERMISSION —

*MUSIC FOR TRUMPETS
    OVERTURE
    CHORALE   VANIG HOVSEPIAN

*THE SPACE OF MARCH AND APRIL AND MAY
HAS TURNED THE GROUND ON ITS TENDER SIDE
AND EVERYONE HAS TO TURN THE SAME WAY   LUCILLE DLUGOSZEWSKI
    (Played by the Composer)

*ROUND DANCE   LOU HARRISON

(*first performance)

PIANIST	SHOGHER MARKARIAN
	JAMES SMITH
	NORTON KRASNOFF
TRUMPET ENSEMBLE	JOHN FALLSTICH
	ARTHUR STATER
TIMPANI AND PERCUSSION	GEORGE GABER

Program for concert presented by the Living Theatre, 1952. Used by permission of the Erick Hawkins Dance Company.

> New Directions in Movement, Music, and Design for Theatre Dance
>
> **ERICK HAWKINS** choreography and dance
> **LUCIA DLUGOSZEWSKI** music
> **NANCY LANG** dance
> **RALPH DORAZIO** designs
>
> in a new work
>
> # HERE AND NOW WITH WATCHERS
>
> **HUNTER PLAYHOUSE**
> 68th St. between Park & Lexington
>
> All seats reserved: $2.30
> Mail orders from Fern McGrath
> 24 Horatio St.
> Window sale Carl Fischer, 175 W. 57th St.
> from Nov 18 thru 23. At Hunter Playhouse
> box office Nov 24. RE 7-4782
>
> **SUNDAY EVE**
> **NOV 24**
> at 9 pm

Musical America advertisement for the premiere of *Here and Now with Watchers*, November 1957. Used by permission of the Erick Hawkins Dance Company.

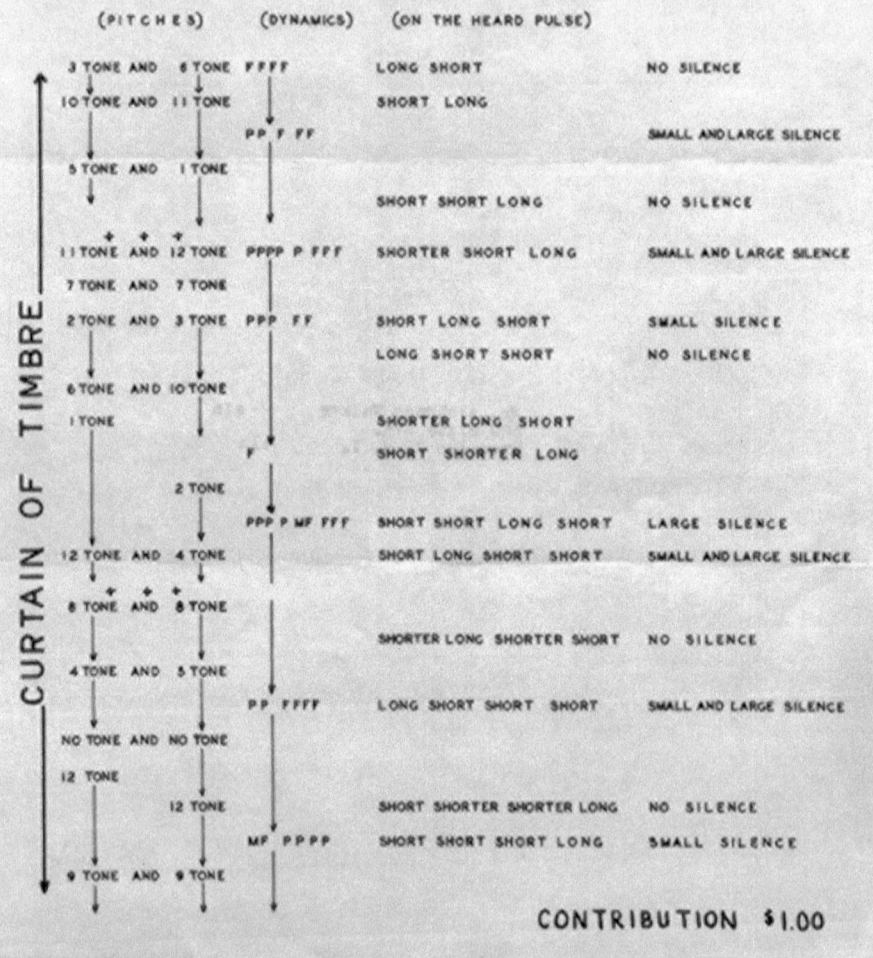

Dlugoszewski's "Curtain of Timbre" program for the Five Spot Cafe concert, 1958. Used by permission of the Erick Hawkins Dance Company.

COMPOSERS' SHOWCASE

Monthly Series   SEVENTH CONCERT 1958-1959   Charles Schwartz-Director
Monday, May 18, 1959   8:40 P.M.

MUSIC OF NETTY SIMONS

1. THREE SONGS (Texts by Hilda Morley)   (1950)
    a) Early Ballad
    b) Sleep Song
    c) Aubade
   Shirley Sudock-mezzo soprano   Robert Parris - Piano

2. PIANO WORK (1952)
    Allegro
    Poco adagio; presto
    Allegro molto rhytmico e staccato   Robert Parris - Piano

3. TWO VIOLIN SONATA (1954)
         (first performance)
    Allegro
    Lento
    Poco allegro
    Presto   Matthew Raimondi and Joseph Rabushka - violins

INTERMISSION

MUSIC OF LUCIA DLUGOSZEWSKI

1. RITUAL OF THE DESCENT (1952)
         John Perras-flute   Composer-piano and tympany

2. EVERYDAY SOUNDS for bright by e. e. cummings (1953)
         Beatrice Allen, Barbara Tucker-percussion   and the Composer

3. like DARLING (1957)
         12 tone and 12 tone   mf and pppp   short short short long
              into
         9 tone and 9 tone   Composer - piano

4. INSIDE WONDER   OR WHALES   (1954)
         10 tone and 11 tone   ffff   short long
              into   into   into
         5 tone and 1 tone   pp and f and ff   short short long   Composer-pia

5. THE (1958)
         3 tone and 6 tone   ffff   long short   Composer-pia
   (3, 4, and 5 are from "HERE AND NOW WITH WATCHERS")

6. SEPARATED MUSIC (1958)
    a) for rates of speed
    b) for delicate accidents
       (Instruments constructed by Ralph Dorazio)
       Beatrice Allen, Barbara Tucker, and Composer - percussion

7. MUSIC FOR LEFT EAR IN A SMALL ROOM (1959)   Composer - piano

DISCUSSION

Guest Composers: Netty Simons   Lucia Dlugoszewski

Moderator: Charles Schwartz

CIRCLE IN THE SQUARE   5 Sheridan Square, New York 14, N.Y.   ORegon 5-9437

Program for Composers' Showcase concert (shared with Netty Simons), 1959. Used by permission of the Erick Hawkins Dance Company.

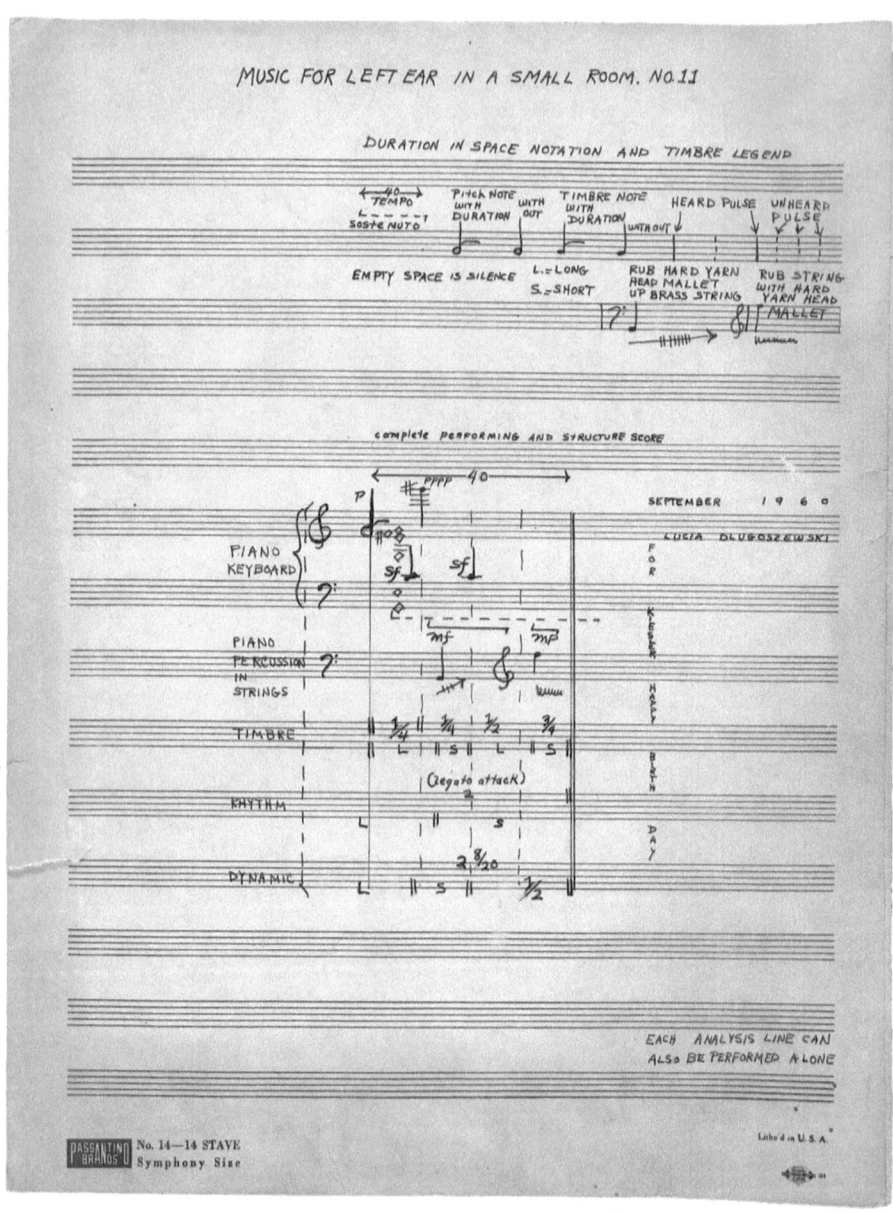

Complete score for *Music for Left Ear in a Small Room*, 1960. Used by permission of the Erick Hawkins Dance Company.

Erick Hawkins and Lucia Dlugoszewski wedding portrait, 1 September 1962. Photographer unknown. Used by permission of the Erick Hawkins Dance Company.

[From left] Hawkins, Dlugoszewski, Jennie ("Jolas") Dlugoszewski, and Chester ("Czesio") Dlugoszewski, wedding day family portrait, 1 September 1962. Used by permission of the Erick Hawkins Dance Company.

First page of *Densities: Supernova/Corona/Clear Core* (music for Hawkins's dance titled *Angels of the Inmost Heaven*), 1972. Used by permission of the Erick Hawkins Dance Company.

Advertisement for Erick Hawkins's dance classes (date unknown). Used by permission of the Erick Hawkins Dance Company.

PROSPECTIVE ENCOUNTERS

Presented by the
New York Philharmonic
PIERRE BOULEZ, *Music Director*

Friday Evening, December 5, 1975 at 8:00
The Great Hall, Cooper Union

Pierre Boulez, *Conductor*

LUCIA DLUGOSZEWSKI   "Abyss and Caress" (world premiere)
               GERARD SCHWARZ, *trumpet*

flute, piccolo
Renée Siebert
Trudy Kane

oboe
Albert Goltzer
Eugene Box

clarinet, bass clarinet
William Shadel

French horn
John Cerminaro

trombone
David Langlitz

violin
Kenneth Gordon
Sanford Allen
Hanna Lachert
Barry Finclair

cello
Gerald Appleman
Evangeline Benedetti
Kermit Moore

piano
Paul Jacobs

bass trombone
David Taylor

DONALD MARTINO   "Notturno"

Renée Siebert *flute, piccolo, alto flute*
Peter Simenauer *clarinet*
William Shadel *bass clarinet*
Kenneth Gordon *violin*

Ralph Mendelson *viola*
Gerald Appleman *cello*
Richard Fitz *percussion*
Paul Jacobs *piano*

HARRISON BIRTWISTLE   "Verses for Ensembles"

flute, piccolo, alto flute
Renée Siebert

oboe, English horn
Albert Goltzer

clarinet
Peter Simenauer
William Shadel

bassoon, contrabassoon
Leonard Hindell

French horn
John Cerminaro

trumpet
Gerard Schwarz
Mark Gould

trombone
David Langlitz
David Taylor

percussion
Gordon Gottlieb
Richard Fitz
Joseph Passaro

James Chambers, *Orchestra Personnel Manager*

This project is made possible in part with public funds from the New York State Council on the Arts and the National Endowment for the Arts, Washington, D. C., a Federal agency.

Next Prospective Encounter: Friday, May 14 at 8:00
                Pierre Boulez, Conductor
                JON DEAK "Dire Expectations" (world premiere)
                EARLE BROWN "Centering"
                GEORGE ROCHBERG "Tableaux"

Steinway Piano   Columbia Records

New York Philharmonic program for premiere performance of *Abyss and Caress*, 1975. Courtesy of the New York Philharmonic, Leon Levy Digital Archives. Used by permission.

Composers assembled in Avery Fisher Hall, New York, on the occasion of conductor Pierre Boulez's retirement, 12 May 1977. Pictured are Milton Babbitt, Pierre Boulez, Earle Brown, John Cage, Elliott Carter, Aaron Copland, Mario Davidovsky, David Del Tredici, LD, Jacob Druckman, Harley Gaber, David Gilbert, Donald Harris, Roy Harris, Sydney Hodkinson, Steve Jablonsky, Ulysses Kay, Donald Martino, Carman Moore, Vincent Persichetti, Daniel Plante, George Rochberg, William Schuman, Roger Sessions, Stanley Silverman, and Charles Wuorinen. Photographed by Peter Schaaf. Used by permission.

First page of notation for introductory percussion cadenza, *Tender Theatre Flight Nageire*, 1978. Used by permission of the Erick Hawkins Dance Company.

Poster for Carnegie Recital Hall premiere of *Cicada Terrible Freedom*, 1982. Used by permission of the Erick Hawkins Dance Company.

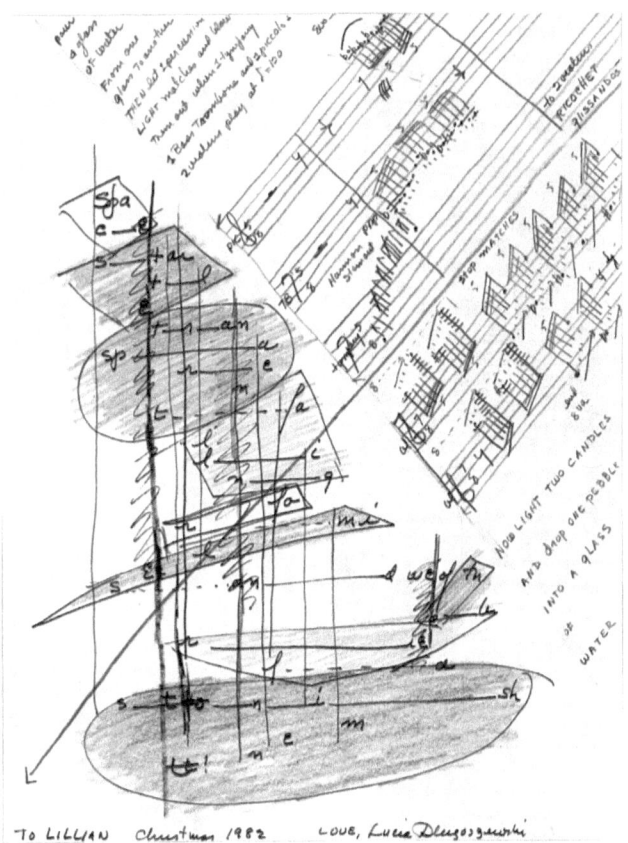

"To Lillian, Christmas 1982," graphic poem by Dlugoszewski. Diagonal text from upper left to lower right: "pour / a glass / of water / from one / glass to another / THEN let 1 percussion / LIGHT matches and blow / them out when 1 tympany [*sic*]/ 1 Bass trombone and 1 piccolo and / 2 violins play at quarter note = 120/NOW LIGHT TWO CANDLES / AND drop ONE PEBBLE / INTO A GLASS / OF / WATER. Used by permission of the Erick Hawkins Dance Company.

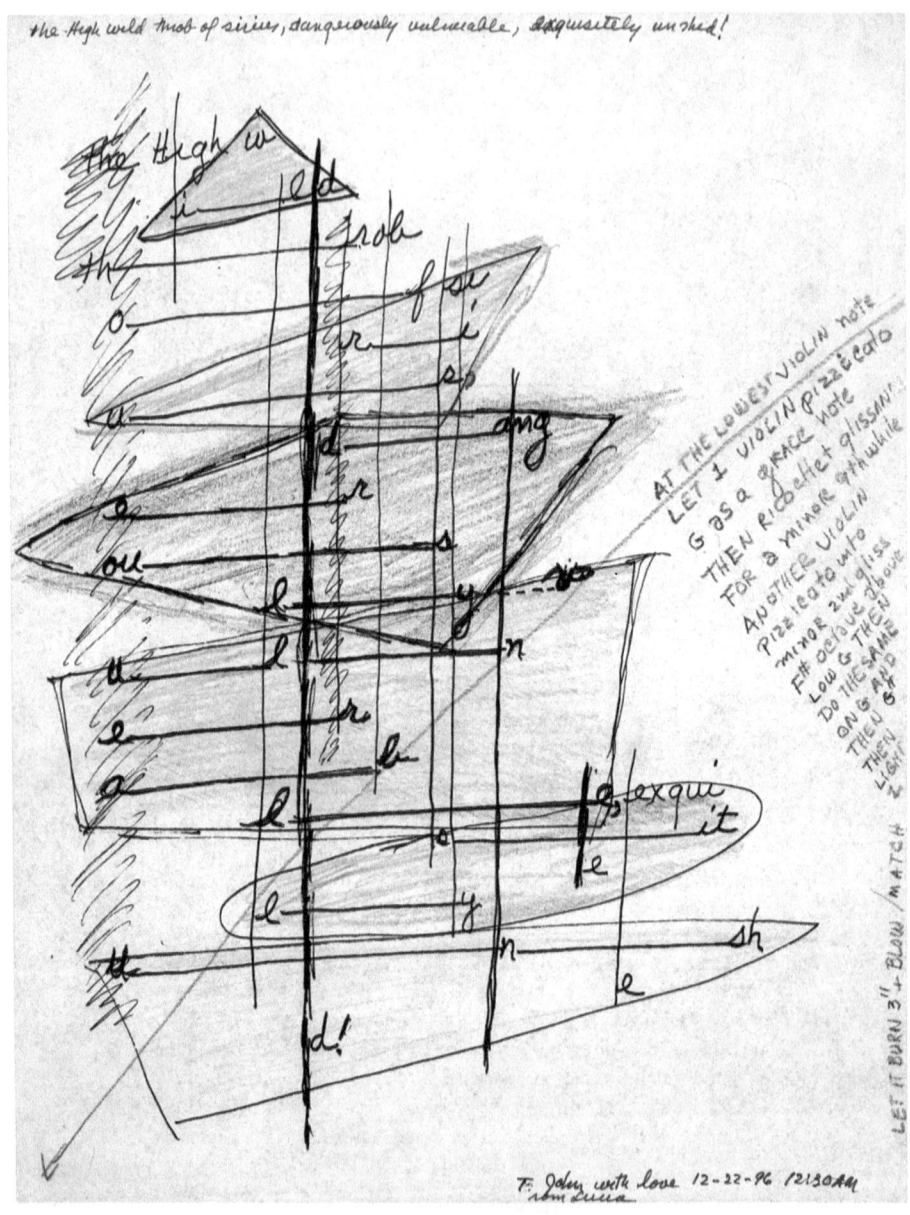

"The high wild throb of sirius, dangerously vulnerable, exquisitely unshed!" Graphic poem for John Ransom Phillips, 22 December 1996. Used by permission of John Ransom Phillips.

Private diary writings ("duende scream"), 1987. Used by permission of the Erick Hawkins Dance Company.

Private diary writings ("gauntlet of courage"), 1992. Used by permission of the Erick Hawkins Dance Company.

FOUR

Expanding Creativity and Collaboration (1953–60)

Torch Song
whole world: doing-like-mad
        and i-don't-caring
take away my i-don't-caring
take away my doing-like-mad
nobody knows how the world goes
nobody knows the i-don't-caring
nobody knows the doing-like-mad
this nobody must be pretty damn
       good to unafraid me of
           myself
(signed)
      anonymous
          (pseudonym)[1]

DLUGOSZEWSKI REMAINED CLOSE TO Julian Beck and Judith Malina and others in their circle throughout the 1950s. In October 1953, Malina wrote in her diary about attending a film symposium whose participants she described as "four vibrant personalities bored to death" (filmmaker Maya Deren and writers Dylan Thomas, Parker Tyler, and Arthur Miller). Afterward, Malina, Dlugoszewski, and others debated the subject of modern film at Ralph Dorazio's studio before heading to the White Horse Tavern on Hudson Street in the West Village "to hear Dylan carry on."[2] (Dylan Thomas died of pneumonia just ten days later; Malina wrote about attending his funeral on 13 November, an event Dlugoszewski might also have attended.)[3] Dlugoszewski continued to enjoy her friendships with writers, actors, and artists in the Greenwich Village arts scene. Several years later, when asked by an interviewer, "Do you tire of being called avant-garde?" she responded, "As the brave and beautiful painter Ad Reinhardt says, 'It depends on who are the other guys in the gang.'"[4]

Once a central figure in that gang, composer Lou Harrison had left New York for California around 1953. (According to Malina, Harrison had provided the original introductions between Beck and herself, and Cage and Cunningham.[5]) Dlugoszewski wrote to him of her enthusiasm following a performance she saw of his *Mass* (probably the *Mass to Saint Anthony*, 1939, rev. 1952). In her usual effusive manner, which might have pleased Harrison with its enthusiasm and its attention to musical detail ("the counterpoint throughout was like the delicate poetry of Walther von der Vogelweide or the imagery of St. Teresa the little flower"), she wrote of the deep impression his piece had on her ("it was clean as pure and very real water"), and her desire to hear the piece again: "And the trumpet was such a mystery with the voices and the cello-harp unisons and octaves at the end reminded me of the beautiful work of yours I heard years ago for flute harp and cello long before I knew the you of you but I did recognize the magic."[6] Though Dlugoszewski's letters sometimes sound self-serving in their copious praise for the more established composers to whom she wrote, they also demonstrate a sincere engagement with their music.

Around this time Dlugoszewski received a letter from Beck and Malina suggesting a further collaboration: they referred to her works as "masterpieces." Asking, "Where have you been hiding?" they implied that she might have withdrawn into a world where there was only room for Hawkins. Inviting her to write "one of your healthy long scores" for the Living Theatre's upcoming production of Paul Goodman's new play, *The Young Disciple*, they requested a piece of musique concrète.[7] Dlugoszewski turned down this offer, perhaps because she was not experienced in creating tape music, or perhaps because she was immersed in her collaborations with Hawkins, who shared her preference for live instrumental music instead of fixed media using tape or electronics.[8] *The Young Disciple* premiered on 12 October 1955 with choreography by Merce Cunningham and music by Pierre Schaeffer (with contributions from Pierre Henry and Ned Rorem).[9] This declined invitation might seem like a missed opportunity—one that would have brought more attention to Dlugoszewski, given the increasing visibility of The Living Theatre. Perhaps it was just a clear choice by an artist who knew exactly what she wanted. Around this time Dlugoszewski attended the Living Theatre's production of Jean Cocteau's *Orpheus*, which premiered at The Studio on 30 September 1954. Dlugoszewski told her friends about her reaction to the performance: "I was moved by the play to such a state of perfect quietness," she wrote.[10] She also invited them to attend one the many rehearsals of

"Noguchi music," her composition for Marie Menken's film *Visual Variations on Noguchi*.

HERE AND NOW WITH WATCHERS

By 1954, Dlugoszewski and Hawkins had begun working on their second collaboration, which would culminate in a seventy-five-minute dance duet for male and female dancer with Dlugoszewski's timbre piano accompaniment and Ralph Dorazio's designs. They presented an early version of the piece, called *Double and Single Labyrinths*, at the NYU School of Education Auditorium on 28 January 1955, with dancer Eva Raining in the role of the female dancer. (Another early title for the piece might have been *Threshold of Changing Twins*.)[11] In the planning for *Double and Single Labyrinths* Dlugoszewski started using a scoring technique she later called a "Curtain of Timbre."[12] The developmental work on *Here and Now with Watchers*, which went on for several years (approx. 1954–57), overlapped with Dlugoszewski's work on a solo timbre piano piece she called *Archaic Timbre Piano Music*, which also served as the music for the dance. Typescript notes for *Here and Now with Watchers* noted that "the choreography was composed in silence."

Dlugoszewski examined her relationship to the piano in extensive (undated) notes, kept in one of her many compositional notebooks. Five pages of "piano insight," as she labeled them, hinted at her concerns as a composer for an instrument she increasingly considered an "anachronism." Her notes explored what she considered to be "the main challenge and stumbling block," namely, the eighty-eight equidistant pitches that comprised the conventional piano keyboard: "Arbitrary divisions not beautiful," she concluded. She felt that the distinct registers of the keyboard might hold the secret to the piano's meaning or beauty, and that both the touch of the depressed keys and the lack of sustained sound presented particular compositional challenges.

Interrupting her work on *Here and Now with Watchers* during August 1955, Dlugoszewski traveled back to Detroit for her annual summer visit with her parents. In a letter written after a difficult phone conversation with Hawkins, she expressed distress at his aloofness, but quickly turned to a happier memory about his creative process and how it intermingled with her passion for him. Referencing a night they spent in Provo, Utah, she recalled how Hawkins "did some of the leaps for me and your eyes were shining and even thru the street clothes I could see how extraordinary the movements were and your voice telling about it was the sweetest voice in the world full of wondrousness and I knew there was no one like you." A month later, Judith Malina, who sometimes took dance classes with Hawkins, wrote in her diary: "Class with Erick. His devotion is also a form of fanaticism. But what art is there without some madness?"[13] A few months later, Dlugoszewski wrote a note to Hawkins, brimming with her own "fanaticism" about the music she was working on for *Here and Now with Watchers*: "I could just put all my pure feeling into it and not struggle so with structure and form and anyway I'm on fire with it and would like to explode all over you about it."[14] Clearly the lovers stimulated one another's creativity.

Here and Now with Watchers was premiered on 24 November 1957 at the Hunter Playhouse; alongside Hawkins, Nancy Lang danced the female role. The *New York Times* calendar announcing the premiere of *Here and Now with Watchers* also listed a performance by Merce Cunningham and his company of seven dancers at the Brooklyn Academy of Music the following night, with a program that included music by Earle Brown, Louis Moreau Gottschalk, Josef Mattias Hauer, Erik Satie, and Christian Wolff.[15] Both the Hawkins and the Cunningham events might have been overshadowed by the premiere of *Agon*, a new collaboration between George Balanchine and Igor Stravinsky, at the New York City Ballet on the first of December.

Before the premiere of *Here and Now with Watchers*, *Dance Observer* magazine published an article by Dlugoszewski called "Notes on New Music for the Dance." She began her article by stating that dancers and composers were currently "confronted with two momentous trends," namely "the unknown quantity of magnetic tape," and "a constant barrage of every conceivable culture other than our own." She mentioned as examples recent performers seen in New York City, including the Indian Bharatanatyam dancer Shanta Rao, and a group of Balinese dancers. She discussed various approaches to dealing with an abundance of source material: "It seems the truest direction of music and dance art in 1957 is a sensitive search for *what is* which is an archaic position—the position of beginning—a most exciting position in the arts of any time." Echoing a "Beginner's Mind" attitude that would come to be associated with Cage—but insisting on calling it "the archaic position"—she continued: "In the archaic position every element is used for the discovery and illumination of *what it is* and for no other reason."[16]

Discussing dance's history of subservience to music, Dlugoszewski's article referred indirectly to Hawkins's practice: "The modern dance did the bold unprecedented thing—composed complete movement structures in silence." So, she wrote, as an independent art of dance was born, "so, too, was born the still persisting problem of what music structure would be acceptable to this new dance." This was an important aspect of their work during this time—allowing the dance to develop independently from musical structures. She summarized by listing various "solutions that music has proposed in the recent history of new dance," naming the full gamut of available options: "Western classical music, western romantic music, various 'ethnic' music, jazz, music of the rhythmic structure, twelve-tone, modal, and atonal music, involving mathematics, tape sound, structures of chance, ostinato structures, music of near silence, pure silence, and the structure of the heard pulse."[17] Going on, she explained her compositional goals, and why her focus on timbre as musical material won out over inferior solutions, even though, she claimed, "Western musical development has always suspected timbre of lacking sophisticated possibilities of structure." Timbre was, in her definition, sound for sound's sake. She placed this idea into a cerebral-intuitive dichotomy with gendered connotations, pitting the "cerebral" (i.e., male) use of timbre as a structural or architectural element against "an intuitional hearing—instant by instant," that, according to Dlugoszewski, thinkers like F. S. C. Northrop and Virginia Woolf would consider "the feminine component of art—the component so often lacking in western culture."[18] Equating intuitional hearing with "qualitative discipline," she recommended a listening exercise: "I suggest a New York City garbage truck. How long can you hear instant by instant, undenotationally, and how long can you therefore create this pure theatre of the ear? The longer you can do this the better you will be equipped to face that new monster: tape, to experience the dancer's kinesthetic material, to appreciate the music and dance of any culture. It is then truly the archaic position that one will achieve, what so beautifully James Joyce calls the 'epiphany.'"[19] This attitude ("listen to a garbage truck") might again seem similar to Cage's attitude—that is, "which is more musical, a truck passing by a factory or a truck passing by a music school?"[20] But Dlugoszewski's emphasis on intuition as a "feminine component" implies an argument against the methodical nature of Cage's compositional choices, which were by now wholly invested in chance operations.

Like *openings of the (eye)*, Dlugoszewski and Hawkins divided *Here and Now with Watchers* into several continuous sections, displayed on the program with E. E. Cummings-like spacing, punctuation, and self-conscious ambiguity:

i. now:	THE	
ii. now:	INSIDE WONDER OR WHALES	
	(says my body of things)	
iii.	(vulnerable male is magic)	
iv. now:	HERE MADE OF FALLING	
	(and my body)	
v.	(invisible house is female)	
vi. now:	MULTIPLICIY (or flowers)	
vii.	(clown is everyone's ending)	
viii.	the (effortless) now: like DARLING	
	(shouts my body and shouts itself transparent)	

Unlike *openings of the (eye)*, the eight sections of *Here and Now with Watchers* were meant to be poetic instead of metaphoric. As one reviewer of a performance in 1959 put it: "Hawkins, in a printed program note, relieved his audience at once of the burden of seeking a story, communication of emotion, or any other elements than pure movement in his performance."[21] One section of the program notes for *Here and Now with Watchers* attempted to describe the musical method employed by Dlugoszewski, which was meant to reveal "every element of sound clearly, independently, and for its own sake":

- through bracketing (timbre, dynamic, 88 pitches, etc.) into spectrum of range including the wild timbre of 88 simultaneously resonating pitches and the extreme attentuation [*sic*] of a one tone scale;
- through counterpoint for aspects of sound other than pitch such as the delicate "imaginary melodies" of dynamic, *pp, p, ppp*, proposed against "melodies" of *ffff, p, mf*;
- through the device of the single performer as supreme qualitative entity;
- through the heard pulse as both musical ruler and a poetry in itself;
- through the occurring, simultaneous 10 counterpoints instant-by-instant in a constantly shifting new envelope of timbre, with the true music of the work happening not in the past or future but in the moment and therefore defining music as a form of pure theatre;
- through the curtain of timbre veiling the 10 counterparts (including every nuance and noise) and so defining music finally as the making and hearing of a sound.

In the absence of a score, these strategies are difficult to imagine as specific musical gestures, and the ideas she listed might have functioned as a framework for some sort of structured improvisation during the performance. For the section titled "(vulnerable male is magic)," for instance, Dlugoszewski sketched out more precise parameters for musical content, technique, and effect:

> scales: 1 tone
> 11 tone (stepwise)
> 12 tone (stepwise, 1/2 beneath 11 tone)
> 7 tone (diatonic major D)
> 7 tone (minor g#)
>
> dynamics: *fff, pppp, p.*
> (dramatic silences)
>
> pulse: x3
>
> timbre techniques: (medium and high)
> (very slow
> startling texture)
> 1 hits: (sound board, finger mute, finger mute slide like Japanese drum, finger mute on clip
> mallet on 2nd stringing
> 2 scrapes: comb on clip, comb on 2nd stringing, screw on 2nd stringing like motor moan[22]

In many of her later writings Dlugoszewski described the years of working on *Here and Now with Watchers* as a "first development" of her compositional ideas in which she was preoccupied with the idea of "pure radical empirical immediacy." One such writing, a fourteen-page undated document titled "Theatre, Timbre, Time, and Transparency," announced that it had been "written before the composing of music for HERE AND NOW WITH WATCHERS (1955)." Here she explained the intended immediacy of the music, which proposed "discovering and revealing all elements of sound equally, separately, and clearly; of treating them as epiphanies." Putting into prose the content of the chart listed above, she elaborated:

> The music, then, is a paradox of no continuity and constant continuity. It is simultaneously a pitch construct and a time construct. Two independent areas of sound move independently forward. In each one are clear levels of a distinct melodic line of dynamic, a melody of emotion, a melody of timbre, a melody of happening or rhythm, and a melody of pitch in such contrapuntal relation to the rest that each could possibly be performed separately....

The eighty-eight piano keys are divided, in each pitch layer, into twelve pitch situations (or scales, or gamuts, or rows) ranging from a one tone to twelve tones. They are never repeated or transposed. Each pitch community is also chosen for certain qualitative uniqueness—like the extreme "white on white" interval transparency of 8 A's and 8 B flats. Rhythm polarities of long and short are differently fixed in each segment. Each fixed ratio is then expressed in constantly changing variations of duration. Thus the rhythm structure is completed and total at each moment or instant the ear is listening.[23]

Though Dlugoszewski's emphasis on the isolation of musical parameters might seem akin to serial techniques being explored by Milton Babbitt, Pierre Boulez, Karlheinz Stockhausen, and other composers at the time, this elliptical document's second part, titled "Possible Motives and Manifestos," featured short aphoristic statements about sound and experience that showed her compositional ideas moving in different directions. A section called "Texts without Comment" included short quotes by philosophers F. S. C. Northrop ("One can look at a blue for hours and not quite intuit all its depth and richness"), Gabriel Marcel ("Time is the very form of experimental activity"), and others. The final part of the document offered even briefer philosophical statements of her own, including: "All sound is beautiful"; "Duration is not an image"; "The revolution is in perception rather than conception"; "The real now is seldom here"; and "Remember our ears are on either side of the head."

One of the philosophers Dlugoszewski was fond of quoting, F. S. C. Northrop (1893–1992), had become famous for his book *The Meeting of East and West* (1946) and taught philosophy at Yale University. Northrop attended the premiere of *Here and Now with Watchers* and soon became both a friend and a champion of Dlugoszewski and Hawkins's work.[24] A week before the premiere, Hawkins invited Northrop to the performance: "Of all people in the world, Lucia Dlugoszewski, the composer, and I would have as our greatest heart's desire that you should see our work."[25] In Northrop, Hawkins and Dlugoszewski found an attentive, thoughtful advocate willing to engage with their art. A few days after the performance, Northrop wrote to Hawkins, admitting that he found the music "easier to grasp" than the dancing:

> The way in which Lucia has broken the sounds apart so that each is immediately apprehended in and for itself was truly art in its first function. At times I got the impression that you have conceived of the dance in this manner also. This occurred when, at times, the movements suggested a discontinuous sequence of stills rather than a continuous flow. Yet there was more than this

discontinuity in both the music and the dancing. I had the impression that both of you know the classical art, with its control by the theoretic component, as thoroughly as you appreciated and exhibit the aesthetic component in and for itself. More than this, both from your written comments and from the dancing, perhaps even more than from the music, the intuition was suggested at least that you were laying hold of the aesthetic component's creative formlessness as something ultimate in the nature of things.

In writing in this way it is, of course, difficult to know how much is truly yours and how much I am reading my own thoughts, intuitions and theories into what you are doing. The fact, however, that both you and Lucia regard my own intuition and reflections with respect to these matters as so relevant and important suggests that aesthetic theory and aesthetic creativity have come together. In any event, you can hardly appreciate what a joy and satisfaction it is to have something which one wrote several years ago taking on concrete, creative, aesthetic form in this way.[26]

Early in 1958 Hawkins lobbied Northrop to write an official endorsement of Dlugoszewski's work. As a result of the November premiere of *Here and Now with Watchers*, she had been invited by painter Leon Smith, who taught at the Mills College of Education in New York, to give a solo concert of the music for *Here and Now with Watchers* at that college.[27] Hawkins felt that an endorsement from Northrop would help sell tickets and fill the hall. "Even more than a question of money, it is of prestige," Hawkins wrote, while also expressing support for Dlugoszewski's music being experienced as something autonomous, separate from his own work:

> Since Lucy first came to work with me in 1951, she has devoted herself almost entirely to writing for the dances, in a way unprecedented in the history of the modern movement in dance which of course I have first-hand knowledge of from the beginning except for the very first years. No artist of first rank other than her has really collaborated with enough knowledge or love to fathom the problem of seeing and hearing at the same time.... After spending literally four years on *Here and Now* it is important that she make a dent from the music angle since our benighted criticism ignores music for dance. No one qualified or interested wrote about the music of the concert.... I have been working far longer than Lucy, but never before has anyone whom I respected or who I felt on principle could see what I have done either choreographing or dancing, had earned the right to see, ever voluntarily responded—except Lucy herself.[28]

Within a matter of days, Northrop responded that he would be delighted to write a note in support of Dlugoszewski's concert—essentially the first formal endorsement of her work. "You may use any of the following," Northrop wrote Hawkins:

> The music of Lucia Dlugoszewski is one of the unique and refreshing creations of our time. It is musical art for its own sake. By abruptly breaking the temporal sequence of the sounds, thereby freeing sound in its ineffable aesthetic immediacy from the ideas and associations suggested by an ordered march toward a climax, one experiences music in the *Here and Now* in and for itself.
>
> As if this in itself were not enough of an advance for one person, Miss Dlugoszewski has also done this with the immediately given aesthetic images of Erick Hawkins' art of the dance in mind. He, correspondingly, in his choreography has created the visual images of his art of the dance with the immediate auditory images of Lucia Dlugoszewski's musical art in mind. Thereby a solution is offered to the problem of the modern dance as first fully appreciated by Gertrude Stein—the problem namely of breaking down the dualistic parallelism between the dancing and the music to bring about a single art of ineffably immediate auditory-visual aesthetic experiences.[29]

Northrop added that Hawkins should share with Dlugoszewski his views on her "superb" article in *Dance Observer*: "The article is packed with philosophical insight and distinctions and is a real achievement in the field of aesthetic experience and theory," he applauded.[30]

Just a few years later, Northrop would publish a book called *Philosophical Anthropology and Practical Politics*. In chapter 18, titled "The Normative Ideals of a Free People," he featured Dlugoszewski and Hawkins as an example of aesthetic immediacy in the context of the simmering Cold War:

> For people thus trained to separate immediately experienced fact from theoretical inferences that transcend it, the standard for measuring achievement in the dance may well be something in addition to, or quite other than the theoretical combination of ancient Greek geometry and the physical culturalist's muscle building, always fighting gravitation, which, beautiful though it be, is the traditional ballet. The dance and music of Erick Hawkins and Lucia Dlugoszewski will be appreciated also as the much less muscularly artificial and the more immediately natural and beautiful standard of artistic measurement in the domain of the aesthetically immediate which it is. In short, concept by intuition contemporary dancing *as well as* the anti-gravitational Greek geometrically ordered dancing of medieval or modern Soviet bourgeois society will flourish.[31]

For her Mills College of Education performance on 29 March 1958, Dlugoszewski created a printed program for the audience that consisted entirely of the score of the piece, which she labeled "Curtain of Timbre" in vertical letters down the left side of the page. Across the top of the page she made columns for the different musical parameters: "Pitches" (3 Tone and 6 Tone; 10 Tone and 11 Tone; 5 Tone and 1 Tone; etc.), "Dynamics" (FFFF, PP F FF, PPPP P FFF, etc.), and "On the Heard Pulse" (Long Short; Short Long; Short Short Long; Shorter Short Long; etc.), and finally an unlabeled column (No Silence; Small and Large Silence; No Silence; Small and Large Silence; etc.). This is the scoring procedure she most likely first explored in the precursor of *Here and Now with Watchers*, *Double and Single Labyrinths*, and it represents a unique form of graphic-text notation unlike any other developed during the 1950s.

On 5 May 1958, Dlugoszewski typed up a course description for a class she proposed to teach, called "The Art of Listening, through Simple Experimental Composition," in which she hoped to welcome students of all backgrounds ("including having no background"). She explained that "the simplest of creative experiences with sound is the truest place to activate the listening orientation," and that "to listen without the creative experiencing of the musical materials is to listen without the composer's ear." She concluded her proposal with a promise that her course would set aside the "Western tradition of sound" in favor of an exploration of "the very nature of sound" in all its aspects: "not only pitch (melody, harmony), but duration (rhythm), timbre (harmony, percussion, natural sounds, magnetic tape), and dynamics—and the intelligence that uses them, and the ear that perceives them."

LEFT EARS IN SMALL ROOMS

Sponsored by Willem de Kooning, Robert Motherwell, and other New York School artists, Dlugoszewski gave a solo performance of the music from *Here and Now with Watchers (Archaic Timbre Piano Music)*, as well as a new piece called *Music for Small Centers*, at the Five Spot Cafe at Cooper Square on 8 June 1958. Primarily a jazz venue that had most recently hosted a six-month engagement of the Thelonious Monk Quartet featuring John Coltrane, this "Bowery dive" became a popular location for artists partial to the Cedar Tavern and the 8th Street Artists' Club, as those venues became overrun with tourists by the mid-1950s.[32] The *New York Times* announced Dlugoszewski's performance as a "concert of 'total piano timbres'"; the events calendar page even included a photo of the composer. The printed program for "New Music for Piano of Lucia Dlugoszewski" included a "Curtain of Timbre" chart like the one she created for her Mills College of Education performance a few months earlier. The program note for *Music for Small Centers* read: "The time structure is a heard pulse so slow that the human ear with its memory span cannot apprehend it and within this on an unheard pulse are unmathematically conceived, asymmetrical, immediately apprehended durations. The dynamic range is very small and only 3 pitches (D-flat, F, A-flat an octave above middle C) are used with the whole overtone series as their timbre shadow. Silence is part of the material of the timbre shadow."

A manuscript score for the piece consists of forty three-staff systems, divided by black and red vertical pencil lines, indicating some sort of slow time division.[33] Over the first "measure," Dlugoszewski wrote the number "42" bracketed by arrows, indicating that a particular equal division of each system—six sections in each system—was to take 42 seconds to perform. Simple math reveals that, if this assumption is correct, the forty systems of six "measures" each would take nearly three hours to perform. Furthermore, at the exact middle of the piece, systems 20–22 are completely blank, indicating that a period of almost thirteen minutes of total silence would occur before the music resumed. The dynamic range in the score ran from *ppp* to *ffff*, contradicting her claim that "the dynamic range is very small." The pitches do concur with her explanation that the harmonic anchor of the piece was a D-flat major triad. The texture was a combination of individual played or plucked pitches and widely spaced chords, with some *sostenuto* chords held with the pedal. A note—"mark dampers"—indicated that yellow chalk would help locate a two-and-a-half octave ranging D-flat triad inside the piano for quicker orientation. At the end of the score she wrote down the parameters for this piece:

3 tone

ffff

42

x 6

shorter

short

long

At the bottom of the one page of program notes for the Five Spot concert, Dlugoszewski added a list titled "Possible Motives or Manifestos," which she mailed to artist Ad Reinhardt and several other friends after the event. She may have intended to read her "manifestos" aloud at The Five Spot:

> To let a sense organ happen and not interfere with it.
> To activate a sense organ of time rather than space; therefore no image, no motif.
> To activate a sense organ of time; therefore true theatre.
> To hear unemotionally; therefore without barrier.
> To hear temporally and not spatially; therefore much more dangerously and contingently.
> Therefore a true theatre of the ear, the subtlest, most intimate of theatres.
> To remember that music is really the making and hearing of a sound.

Overlapping with her ongoing work on *Archaic Timbre Piano Music* and *Here and Now with Watchers,* and perhaps inspired by her investigations into the musical possibilities of "everyday sounds," Dlugoszewski became intrigued by the idea of the "left ear" and small performance spaces (and, increasingly, the notion of "suchness"), creating a number of works with interrelating titles over the next decade, not unlike the "Everyday Sounds" cluster of pieces she wrote around 1951–52:

> *Flower Music for Left Ear in a Small Room* [1956/58; for flute, clarinet, trumpet, trombone, violin, double bass, and two percussionists]
> *Music for Left Ear* [1958; piano]
> *Music for Left Ear in a Small Room Nos.* 1–20 [1959–60; timbre piano)
> *Violin Music for Left Ear in a Small Room* "for Donald Downs" [1965][34]
> *Clarinet Music for Left Ear in a Small Room* [1965]

Dlugoszewski created sketches and structural maps for at least one of the pieces called *Music for Left Ear in a Small Room*, including what looks like instructions for three players in sections labeled "velvet section," "thick section," "violent section," and so on. Her use of the word *flower* in connection with this series of pieces aligned with her wish to maintain an element of unpredictability in her music. Hawkins scholar Julia Keefer has written about Dlugoszewski's use of the metaphor of a "flower" as an unexpected moment, or a surprise, and the idea of "giving the audience a flower at the right time": "A change in pulse, meter, or matra [*sic*], an unusually delicate or strong dynamic register, an unusual use of space, a particularly vulnerable sensation can create a flower."[35]

In September 1960 Dlugoszewski wrote a piece she called *Music for Left Ear in a Small Room, No. 11*, with a dedication: "For Kiesler Happy Birth Day."[36] The one-page score offered an explanation of the "duration in space notation and timbre legend," along with a "complete performing and structure score." In this way, and perhaps coinciding with ideas found in her "Curtain of Timbre" scores, the structure and the material of the piece were identical. Another piece titled *Music for Left Ear in a Small Room No. 3*, dated September 1960, was dedicated to Mary Norton; this score is more graphic and unfinished looking. In a published interview, which reproduced a cleaner version of the same score, Dlugoszewski responded to the question "What does the title *Music for Left Ear in a Small Room* mean?": "It means, remember our ears are on either side of the head. It means, especially to be listened to by very close and beloved friends. It means, much sensitivity, perception and immediacy. Also the left ear might just be more talented to hear duration. Also it might be dedicated to J. D. Salinger."[37]

Dlugoszewski's everyday experiences stimulated her perception of sonic immediacy. Writing from Nantucket Island during the late summer of 1958, she expressed her enchantment with the area's feline inhabitants to her friend Lillian Kiesler (1911–2001), an artist and performer married to architect Frederick Kiesler: "The cats here enjoy rain—either they are extremely musical and delight in the delicacy of that percussion or else they are just arch sensualists and enjoy having small happenings strike their various nerves over and over and over and softly again. Anyway, they perch on fences and experience the drizzle by the hour."[38] She further described her experiences on the island, mixing her daily activities with philosophical musings:

> In my situation here I can't be ever really alone but one morning I was up at 4 A.M. and down at the deserted beach watching daylight creep through the gray. There was a deserted child's swing and my Krazy Kat soul got me on it and swinging all alone before the white and wicked edge of the stormy ocean and before the windy gray dawn I suddenly thought of Northrop and the lovely Buddhist swing as the play [illegible] in the world creation. I've just finished reading Artaud on theatre—stranger, exciting, mad, stupid and impossible but sometimes saying just what I did in *Here and Now*.

In the same letter she shared her observations about Nantucket's sonic landscape, in particular the "rustles" that appealed to her fascination with the sounds inherent in paper: "The sounds are my favorite here—all varieties of rustles, rain rustles, tree rustles, ocean wave rustles on a heard pulse that is carried each time just a little out of its fixed orbit. And then sometimes the frantic moth rustles—rustling to death against our human lights."[39]

Dlugoszewski's next major performance following her 1958 Five Spot event took place at the Circle in the Square Theater on 18 May 1959. Writing to pianist John Kirkpatrick, who had responded with enthusiasm to a performance of *Here and Now with Watchers*, she admitted that she was feeling "very hectic" in preparation for this performance, which would be part of the Composers' Showcase series.[40] The music of composer Netty Simons (1913–91) made up the first half of the concert. In the second half, Dlugoszewski presented sections from *openings of the (eye)* and *Here and Now with Watchers*:

1. RITUAL OF THE DESCENT (1952) flute, piano, tympany [sic]
2. EVERYDAY SOUNDS for bright by e.e. cummings (1953) percussion
3. like DARLING (1957) [from here and now with watchers]
4. INSIDE WONDER OR WHALES (1954) [from here and now with watchers]
5. The (1958) [from here and now with watchers][41]
SEPARATED MUSIC (1958)
   a) for rates of speed
   b) for delicate accidents

Composers' Showcase musical director Charles Schwartz moderated a discussion with Dlugoszewski and Simons following the concert. An unusually detailed review was featured in the *Village Voice* just over a week later:

> Miss Dlugoszewski's half of the program opened with "Ritual of the Descent," in which the flute part, ably played by John Perras, sustains a captivating melody punctuated by piano, drums, and occasional vocal intonations. Then followed the audio-visual "EVERYDAY SOUNDS for brIght [sic] by e.e. cummings," whose title is self-explanatory. Beatrice Allen and Barbara Tucker, percussion—listed thus in the program—tore paper, dropped marbles, moved glass plates, etc., while the poem was written out—and all to a *written* score devised by the composer. An interesting piece, it served to call attention to the beauty of sounds in our daily living—which we ignore or, at best, accept unthinkingly. "Like Darling," "Inside Wonder," and "The" were piano works which exploited the potential of the instrument. Keys were played in the traditional manner occasionally; more often, the strings themselves were plucked, brushed, hit, and otherwise vibrated by mallets, combs, jars of varying sizes, etc. The tonal colors were unlimited. The most musical piece (as we understand the term "musical") was "INSIDE WONDER," which gives hope that this experimental exploration will develop into truly great music. Incidentally, these three compositions are from a group of eight pieces, "Here

and Now With Watchers," written for dances created by Erick Hawkins; the unusual feat is that the music was composed after the choreography was completed. New instruments (slats of wood of varying lengths and separated) were constructed by Ralph Dorazio for "Separated Music." Here again the new sounds are interesting but can hardly be classified as *music*.[42]

On the same day as Dlugoszewski's Composers' Showcase concert, the Poindexter Gallery on 56th Street held an opening reception for an exhibition of work by artist Herman Cherry (1909–92). An advertising flyer for the event included a poetic blurb written by Dlugoszewski: "If it is sky that we desire . . . and when do we ever not desire sky . . . something clean and clear and unendingly unpredictable . . . the real 'floating life' . . . then this is the new beauty that HERMAN CHERRY understands very well . . . it hangs awkward and delicate with the brutality of the clean and clear with the transparent ambiguity of immediacy."

Around this time Dlugoszewski wrote the first letter of what would become an ongoing correspondence with composer-critic Virgil Thomson (1896–1989), another influential man, like Northrop, who became both a friend and an advocate. At a critical turning point later in Dlugoszewski's career, Thomson praised her work in his book *American Music Since 1910*, published in 1970: "Far-out music of great delicacy, originality, and beauty of sound, also ingenious with regard to instrumental virtuosities and of unusually high level in its intellectual and poetic aspects," he wrote.[43]

In the summer of 1959, Dlugoszewski wrote to Thomson about their initial meeting in Oregon on the 22nd of May of that year at a Pacific Arts Festival at Reed College—an occasion on which "he was sassy with me," she would later recall.[44] Aligning herself with Thomson's love of Satie and Gertrude Stein, Dlugoszewski emphasized the importance of humor and "fun" in music, while inviting him for a home-cooked "exotic Polish dinner" once they were both back in New York. She added: "I did discover, performing in San Francisco, that audiences *do* respond to fun! Even though . . . they considered the score of *Here and Now with Watchers* bristling with 'novelty' many of them saw it as novelty for the sake of delight and the poetry of possibility and that's in the best of a Satie tradition! Right?"[45]

Dlugoszewski's meeting Thomson came about during a West Coast tour with Hawkins, which included performances in California. A newspaper article published in the *Oakland Tribune* on 5 June 1959 reported that Dlugoszewski and Hawkins performed *Here and Now with Watchers* at the Contemporary Dancers' Center in San Francisco on 3–4 June to a "capacity audience." The article called the work "controversial," on the grounds that, "while described as dance, some thought it wasn't dance at all, and were in a degree of confusion over just what Hawkins was trying to do."[46] The reviewer described how "Miss Dlugoszewski, equipped with felt-tipped and rubber-tipped mallets, glass jars, metal jar-covers, combs, hairpins, a table knife, paper clips and other assorted hardware, produced an amazing variety of sounds from the piano, whose strings were labeled with bits of colored paper to promote accuracy in the various strummings, mutings, and hammerings."[47]

During the same West Coast engagement, the *San Francisco Chronicle* music reviewer Alfred Frankenstein also noted Dlugoszewski's use of "bottles, jars, paper clips, drumsticks, combs, table knives, and numerous other things," while praising her score as "a work of enormous rhythmic complexity, paralleling and counterpointing the rhythms of the dance, and full of enchanting novelties of sound, and to see her at work, with one hand on the keyboard, another hand flourishing a drumstick, and a comb in her teeth ready for the next assault on the instrument's bare strings, was a choreographic experience as important as that provided by the dancers."[48] Stating that "a modern dancer's face is a rigid mask," Frankenstein observed that Dlugoszewski's face, while performing, was "anything but." Back from the tour, the Erick Hawkins Dance Company published a press booklet that included quotations from critical praise *Here and Now with Watchers* had earned while traveling.[49] A section on Dlugoszewski's music included glowing statements by Frank O'Hara at New York's *Village Voice*, Rose MacDonald at Toronto's *Telegram*, Alfred Frankenstein at the *San Francisco Chronicle*, Robert Sabin at *Musical America*, and F. S. C. Northrop, among others.

In September 1959, Erick Hawkins and Martha Graham divorced after eleven years of marriage and nearly a decade of separation.[50] In December of that year, Dlugoszewski received a letter from her father. Referring to Hawkins as "Fred," Chester wrote: "It is good that you think that Fred is getting to the top in his line of work, he had worked hard and denied himself so many things in order to keep it up so surely he deserves all he may get out of it." "And we glory in his spunk in keeping it up," he added.[51]

THE FOLDER POETS

During the late 1950s Dlugoszewski developed a friendship with a woman named Daisy Aldan (1918–2001), who was planning to edit and publish a book of recent original artwork and poetry. (At the time, Aldan was working on a PhD thesis on contemporary literature.) Aldan solicited work from Dlugoszewski, who sent her friend at least six graphic poems. One was selected and published in Aldan's book, *A New Folder, Americans: Poems and Drawings*, in 1959. Dlugoszewski's poem posed a simple question: "can swallowing be as marvelous to me as falling is to rain"? Striking in its visual arrangement, the words were broken up in odd places and seemed to cascade down the page like raindrops. The fragmented words were surrounded and interrupted by straight vertical lines, horizontal dotted and straight line, squiggly spirals, and geometric shapes similar to parallelograms. The graphic aspect of the poem resembled her father's drafting exercises, which she would have observed when she was about ten years old. Over the next four decades Dlugoszewski would create dozens of similar graphic poems, mostly as gifts for friends.

The frontispiece for *A New Folder* featured an ink drawing by Jackson Pollock. Other drawings in the book were by Willem de Kooning, Helen Frankenthaler, Philip Guston, Grace Hartigan, Franz Kline, Joan Mitchell, Robert Motherwell, Larry Rivers, and many others. The featured poets included Daisy Aldan, John Ashbery, Gregory Corso, Robert Creeley, Allen Ginsberg, Barbara Guest, LeRoi Jones, Jack Kerouac, Kenneth Koch, Anaïs Nin, Frank O'Hara, Charles Olson, M. C. Richards, Larry Rivers, and others. The book also included work by two men who would remain lifelong friends of Dlugoszewski's: poet Charles Boultenhouse, and architect Friedrick Kiesler. Photographs of Dlugoszewski and other contributors appeared at the back of the book. Explaining that the drawings included in the book were not illustrations of the poems, Daisy Aldan included this statement: "This collection of Mid-Century Americans is a personal choice and not meant to represent all the currents in American poetry today. The poets are, for the most part, not new to American readers, but they are new in the sense that they continue to 'favor what the supercilious do not favor,' and they are not afraid to dare as they sing of what is brutal, real, sweet, sad, unforgiving, and mad in America today."[52]

In January 1960, *Mademoiselle* magazine published a short article with a photograph of seventeen of the artists and writers published in Aldan's volume, including the editor-poet herself, and a glamorous and elegantly dressed Dlugoszewski, who stood directly above and to the left of a seated Le Roi Jones (later Amiri Baraka); the group posed self-consciously in an upscale New York restaurant called The Brasserie. In connection with the release of this new volume, Aldan organized a midnight event hosted by The

Living Theatre for sixteen of the poets and nineteen of the artists. According to *Mademoiselle*, "the place was jammed" and "not a single customer walked out," though fifteen copies of *A New Folder* were allegedly stolen from the counter on which they were displayed.[53] The unnamed author of the article took this to be a sign of the success and appeal of the innovative publication.

· · · · ·

By the beginning of the nineteen-sixties, Dlugoszewski had established herself as a valued participant of an avant-garde community, contributing to the activities of the Living Theatre, The Five Spot, The Folder Poets, and other groups, venues, and institutions. At the same time, her compositional intentions, increasingly obscured by metaphor, became more elusive, as demonstrated by a description of her goals given in an interview around 1960: "To create an art as clear and inviolable as the impersonal affirmation of an elegant mathematical proof; and as personally vulnerable and immediate as a blow on the head and as adorably irreducible as pure suchness, and as ineffable as pure epiphany."[54]

In the following decade, her work would become more insulated by and dependent upon the world of the Erick Hawkins Dance Company, including touring the country with Hawkins frequently between 1959 and 1963, to the point that she later exclaimed: "Some of my friends feel I've wrecked my career."[55] But given the amount of collaborative work she undertook in New York in the mid-to-late 1950s— "doing-like-mad," as she put it—it is perplexing to learn that she claimed in an interview over ten years later that "Erick Hawkins was the only one, at the time, who took a chance on me; at the time I was not getting any music concerts at all, until 1968."[56] "I was underground, really underground," she insisted, recasting her own past as one of exclusion and isolation.[57]

FIVE

The Disparate Element (1960–70)

> This thusness suchness quidditas nakedness of sound enveloped my imagination through 1969.[1]

IN NOVEMBER 1960, Dlugoszewski visited her parents, who now lived in Pontiac, Michigan. There, she delighted in the local birds and natural beauty of her home state. Writing to Daisy Aldan, she raved about Hawkins's rising success following their recent national tours, and about his contributions to the advancement of modern dance. Foreshadowing a simmering tension that would increase during this decade, exacerbated by the interdependence of Hawkins and Dlugoszewski's collaborative process, the composer's head was "swimming with new musical ideas" while she pondered the importance of her own work: "I wonder whether I will make an equivalent contribution in music," she wrote her friend.[2] Her desire to be seen as a creative equal intensified over the course of the next few years, erupting in a personal crisis between Dlugoszewski and Hawkins in 1967.

Some ten years after the start of their romance, Dlugoszewski and Hawkins married before a justice of the peace in the garden of her parents' house, on 1 September 1962.[3] Snapshots taken the day of the wedding show the couple engaging in typical newlywed behavior: the laughing groom carrying his new wife over the house's threshold while her smiling parents look on; the bride, in a well-fitted, knee-length, satiny spaghetti-strapped white dress feeding her new husband a piece of wedding cake by hand. The marriage license, which listed Dlugoszewski's occupation as "Composer of Music," stated that neither of them had been married before, though Hawkins had been married to Martha Graham for some ten years. (As mentioned in chapter 2, Dlugoszewski had applied for a marriage license with Ralph Dorazio in the summer of 1950, but there is no evidence that they ever married.) Though Dlugoszewski and Hawkins decided to marry for some reason at this particular time, they kept their union a secret to anyone but close friends until Hawkins's death thirty-two years later. (Some friends and acquaintances suggested that the couple kept their marriage a secret out of fear of Martha Graham's wrath; others felt it was because Dlugoszewski wanted to be known as an artist in her own right, and not merely as Hawkins's wife.) Around the time of their marriage, Hawkins's praise for his new wife's work was abundant: "Lucia Dlugoszewski has made the most complete and inventive, most sensitive, most revolutionary, most future-opening and beautiful theoretical investigations and actual achievements of any composer collaborating with dance in recent years," he wrote.[4]

Encouraged by the success of their first collaborative works *openings of the (eye)* and *Here and Now with Watchers*, Dlugoszewski and Hawkins went on to create and premiere eleven new works together between 1960 and 1970: *8 Clear Places* (1960); *Sudden Snake Bird* (1961); *Early Floating* (1961); *Spring Azure* (1963); *Cantilever* (1963); *Geography of Noon* (1964); *To Everybody Out There* (1964); *Lords of Persia* (1965); *Dazzle on a Knife's Edge* (1966); *Tightrope* (1968/69); and *Black Lake* (1969). This decade of creativity intensified the "doing-like-mad" pace Dlugoszewski had established for herself since arriving in New York some ten years earlier. With the first of the works from this period, *8 Clear Places*, Dlugoszewski and Hawkins began orienting themselves toward a new concept that shaped their work for years to come, namely, "the disparate element." At the same time, Dlugoszewski turned her attention to the possibilities of percussion music, and, increasingly, its gendered interpretations and implications.

SUCHNESS CONCERT AND 8 CLEAR PLACES

In the late 1950s, Dlugoszewski created an evening-length solo work called *Suchness Concert*, for which she began designing approximately one hundred percussion instruments; Ralph Dorazio, a former student of sculptor José de Creeft, undertook their physical construction.[5] These instruments included "unsheltered (closed) rattles" made of skin and wood; "tangent rattles" made of wood, metal, skin, and glass; "square drums" made of wood and skin; and wooden and glass "ladder harps."[6] She favored the widest possibility of materials: paper, glass, plastic, wood, and metal—similar to her choice of materials for playing the timbre piano. She combined these invented instruments with other percussion, including bamboo, glass, and metal wind chimes, various types of gongs, woodblocks, timpani, xylophones, bongos, tom-toms, and other instruments. Speaking to a reporter some ten years later, Dlugoszewski explained her motivation to create new instruments: "I heard far-out sounds in my head—mysterious sounds, ethereal sounds—which were more beautiful than any existing instruments could produce."[7] The timbre piano and her cumulative percussion *batterie* would remain central to her own performance practice for the rest of her life.

Given that her former teacher Edgard Varèse had composed the influential percussion ensemble work *Ionisation* (1931)—which Dlugoszewski could have heard when it was performed at an ISCM concert at Juilliard on 25 January 1951—and used large and forceful percussion sections in most of his orchestral works, it is intriguing that she later expressed the view that traditional percussion instruments were "so masculine in the wrong sense." Referring to percussion textures as "aggressive," she told an interviewer: "It makes me think, the way they treat those drums, that they're really beating up women with their mallets."[8] Distinguishing herself from her former mentor's more noisy approach to percussion, she instead took his advice of going "to the direct exploration of sound" quite literally in her writing for percussion textures.[9] Dlugoszewski's reorientation of what percussion music could do remains one of her major contributions, and aligns her with Johanna Beyer, whose percussion ensemble works of the 1930s similarly explored the possibilities of subtlety over aggression.[10] Though she was surely aware of Cage and Varèse's contributions to the genre of percussion ensemble music, Dlugoszewski remained silent on the role of her former mentors within that history.[11]

In a program note for an event called "Suchness Concert/Otherness Concert," Dlugoszewski explained that this was the first time she "wanted to work in the purity and hush of luminous sound for its own sake without the interference of emotional jangle, without the deadening intellectual shortcuts that exclude our deepest life which only rest in the pure fact of the senses, and without the obtuseness of 'ordinary reality.'" Pursuing an ideal "pure sound," she embraced the abstract quality of her new instruments, which she celebrated for being "free of the intervallic melodic communication of emotion."[12] On another occasion, Dlugoszewski claimed that she began to invent percussion instruments once she felt that she could no longer write music in which her "piddling emotions would interfere with the dance."[13] In an undated letter to Daisy Aldan, Dlugoszewski further described her thoughts about percussion sound—albeit cryptically—as "probably the most mysterious in the world—unique—incapable of definition and therefore full of disarming naiveness."[14]

In an essay written for *Ballet Review* decades later, Dlugoszewski explained that in the creation of *Suchness Concert*, she was "uncompromisingly committed to the dangerous adventure of immediacy, the violent clarity of this time, this place, this season, in order to refine the mind to perfection," and that she wished "to provoke the uneasy anarchic sudden terrible ear, that strange risk of hearing whose moment in time is always daybreak."[15] *Suchness Concert* became the music for Hawkins's next dance, called *8 Clear Places*. Structurally similar to *Here and Now with Watchers*, *8 Clear Places* also had eight sections:

  i. north star
  ii. pine tree
  iii. rain, rain
  iv. cloud
  v. sheen on water
  vi. inner feet of the summer fly
  vii. they snowing
  viii. squash[16]

Originally set for four dancers, this series of dances was later reworked into a version for two solo performers.[17] (In the year or so following the premiere of *8 Clear Places*, Hawkins sought support for a possible four-person tour of the piece to India and East Asia.[18]) An undated typewritten program note explained that masks were used "to focus the attention on the whole moving body of the dancer instead of on the face." Describing *8 Clear Places* in an essay written in 1991, Hawkins compared it to his use of metaphor in *openings of the (eye)*. How could one dance a pine tree?

> I have danced this *pine tree* since 1960, and every time I come back to it, I see what a wonderful metaphor it is, and how bold; but it works. As I have danced it, I have felt that all of the movements metaphorically registered pine tree. There was nothing choreographically that I could do to "naive realistically" represent a pine tree. It had to be by metaphor.... The great part of the success of the metaphor comes from the costume. I have a very wide red sleeve for one arm, with a black leotard, and a green legging on one leg. For the face, Ralph Dorazio made an abstraction of pine needles, but they are in no way "naive realistic."[19]

According to dance historian Don McDonagh, *8 Clear Places*, like *Here and Now with Watchers*, was "ceremonial and suggest[ed] the unhurried passage of time that one encounters in the theater of the East."[20] Describing details of the music as "crystalline tinkling sounds," a sound that is "like heavy rain on a roof," the "light clatter" of pieces of wood, and "dry rustling," McDonagh concluded that the piece, essentially a "meditation on states of nature," had a "zany logic that brings the costuming, movement, and music together": the piece was both "very strange" and "very clear and obvious."[21] In his own book *The Body Is a Clear Place*, Hawkins explained what he had attempted to convey in the "ceremony of awareness" he called *8 Clear Places*: "violent clarity," "seeing the music," and "hearing 101 newly invented instruments of glass, wood, metal, skin, and paper."[22] Near the end of his life, Hawkins would name *8 Clear Places* as the work of which he was most proud.[23]

Dlugoszewski and Hawkins premiered *8 Clear Places* at the Hunter Playhouse on 8 October 1960 with an elaborate percussion setup that included mats, screens, gongs, and chimes, in addition to Dlugoszewski's many instruments. Like the program for her Five Spot performance, printed programs for later performances included a section titled "Manifestos on the Music and Dance of *8 Clear Places*" consisting of aphoristic statements by Dlugoszewski and Hawkins. One "manifesto" stated: "*8 Clear Places* is attention, perception, and pure time." A list of "Objectives" included "Suchness, not events." A "Postscript: Innuendoes" posed the questions: "Is all chance chance?" and "Why is there so much humility about not expressing or expressing and not humility about what is?" This was followed by "Why are composers calling each other liars?" A downtown art world newspaper called *New York's Finest*, edited by Anita Ventura and Sidney Geist, published these "Manifestos" in its 17 March 1961 issue. Not coincidentally, the first edition of John Cage's *Silence: Lectures and Writings*, which documented Cage's approach to chance operations and his view on the function of music, was published by Wesleyan University Press later that same year. Some of Dlugoszewski and Hawkins's "Manifesto" questions might have been aimed at Cage himself, and even seem to have been written in the style of his rhetorical questioning made infamous by his provocative Darmstadt lecture titled "Communication," of September 1958, also published in *Silence*.[24]

A Hunter College performance of *8 Clear Places* garnered substantial attention in an unlikely place, namely *Jubilee: A Magazine of the Church and Her People*, in 1962. That magazine's literary editor at the time, poet Ned O'Gorman, wrote eloquently of the performance:

Miss Dlugoszewski has fashioned music out of the sounds of paper being torn, sticks being run over other sticks, glass bars being struck by Chinese wind-bells and cymbals struck and then moved toward each other, not touching but producing a sheer, primitive timbre. She has observed that the perception of sound, like the perception of nature by a painter, or the use of language by a poet, must change with time, as the earth's crust has changed, as the body has. To hear is a difficult task for the music for the ear does not hear in an ordered and predictable way. We know that though there is a difference between Bach and Stravinsky we do not deny either of them beauty or greatness; in painting we delight in Giotto and Picasso; in the novel we praise Herman Melville and Joyce. Each time the world is perceived by an artist, each time it is given new form the world is changed and so is our perception of it. Dlugoszewski and Hawkins have taken portions of the world and a new "vision" of sound and movement and have created a holy, comic and graceful study of being. They have observed a pine tree, rain, a cloud, a summer fly, a squash, pared them down and by observing them anew with minds that take nothing for granted—melody, pitch, movement, sentiment—they have pointed out a certain shape of the world. They have created a beautiful and lyric meditation on how holy that encounter is that occurs when the body, ear, eye, mind and spirit meet and try to figure out what would be the best thing to do.[25]

In discussing *8 Clear Places* decades later, Dlugoszewski and Hawkins repeatedly used the phrase "the disparate element" to describe the work. When asked what it meant, Dlugoszewski explained: "It startles, confuses momentarily, pushes you off balance, and then opens to a whole new perception in your heart."[26] Like a physical or sonic non sequitur, or simply an unexpected juxtaposition, Dlugoszewski also frequently explained this idea by quoting Gertrude Stein: "You've got to put a little strangeness in a sentence to make the noun come alive."[27] On a later occasion she referred to "the disparate element" as "a significant juxtapositional tool."[28] This idea aligned with Dlugoszewski's frequently invoked structural strategy of "giving the audience a flower at the right time."

THOUGHTS ON SUCHNESS AND EPIPHANY; OTHER COLLABORATIONS

Dlugoszewski began writing extensively during this time, and kept a number of composition notebooks outlining the creation of *8 Clear Places*, including many colorful graphic "maps" of the structure of the piece, which showed her meticulous study of the placement and movement of the dance in relation to her sounds. Though immersed in the work of the Erick Hawkins Dance Company, her own compositional development was occurring in self-conscious stride with dominant trends in American experimental music. Handwritten notes regarding *8 Clear Places* include a page labeled "new compositional ideas." These included notes on "John," "tape," Varèse, and Webern, and the use of silence in composition ("remember a long silence is repetition too!" she observed), while she explained her own inspiration as coming from painting, dance, movement, and "percussion suchness." Many other pages of notes examined compositional ideas about continuity, melodic limitations of modes or scales, the emotional implications of certain intervals (in the work of Boulez, Cage, and Earle Brown), and the "exquisite sound complexes" of Varèse and Stravinsky. She also concluded that Elliott Carter was wrong when he asserted that "great art [is] always tied to a tradition."

In her private writings around this time Dlugozewski strove to articulate her own ideas about an enlightened, nonjudgmental ear, which she saw as the essence of Zen. Cage, in her view, failed to induce this state in his listeners. Further, Dlugoszewski became preoccupied with other artists' relationship to "the subtle distinction between suchness + epiphany." She categorized them accordingly in one of her many notebooks:

Shakespeare—no epiphany, much suchness
Bach suchness no epiphany
Haiku—epiphany and suchness
Webern epiphany, no suchness
Schoenberg—more suchness—no epiphany
Salinger—mostly suchness
Dickens—mostly suchness
Graves—sometimes suchness—same with Klee, mostly epiphany
Joyce no suchness lots epiphany
Proust some suchness lots epiphany

"*Must* have both in work," the end of the list demanded of its writer. Speculating further about her "revelation on the resonance of simplicity," she resolved that "John Cage has never achieved suchness / he has too categorical a temperament." Searching for something that defined her own unique perspective as a composer, she decided: "It is the suchness in Western music that interests me most": "suchness + epiphany / are *absolutely* overlooked / in our culture + treated / as nothing: people / practicing it alone are / social outcasts," she wrote. She explained to herself that suchness aligned with delight, which she considered "the natural state of man's mind," which in turn coincided with a state considered indulgent by the Western mind: innocence. She also critiqued "the cult of originality," singling out contemporaries Cage, Feldman, Stockhausen, and La Monte Young. She criticized Feldman in particular for relying on "the same aesthetic" for each piece, but Cage also, who "never has had the humility to practice a technique that many others practice for the sake of technique only." In her view, Cage "always has to have the unique technique to stand out—"Mamma's darling child prodigy type," she sneered, adding: "Thank god LD has gotten over that!"

Hawkins's next work following *8 Clear Places* was a dance called *Early Floating*, first performed in Portland, Oregon, on 30 June 1961. Dlugoszewski's solo timbre piano score for the piece, called *5 Radiant Grounds*, made use of her "Curtain of Timbre" performance structure. Despite Dlugoszewski's commitment to Hawkins's projects, she continued to be a presence in the wider New York School milieu. On 16 January 1961, The Living Theatre presented a benefit for *KULCHUR*, a magazine whose first issue had been published in spring of 1960. The event included Hawkins dancing two movements from *8 Clear Places* ("pine tree" and "she and he snowing") with Dlugoszewski accompanying; a reading from Paul Goodman's *The Young Disciple*; and additional readings by Allen Ginsberg and LeRoi Jones. On 8 April 1960, she joined sculptor Sidney Geist, painter Elaine de Kooning, and painter Paul Jenkins in a panel discussion at The Club called "What's Right, What's Wrong II." At this time Dlugoszewski also worked on a new score for a Living Theatre production of Ezra Pound's adaptation of Sophocles's *Women of Trachis*, which premiered on 22 June 1960 at the Living Theatre Playhouse. The guest list for the premiere included Daisy Aldan, John Cage, Remy Charlip, Earle and Carolyn Brown, Paul and Vera Goodman, Allan Kaprow, Richard Maxfield, Grete Sultan, and many others. Dlugoszewski reserved six complementary tickets for the premiere.[29] Nothing is known about the music for this production.

In 1961 experimental filmmaker Jonas Mekas (1922–2019) commissioned Dlugoszewski to create an original score for his feature-length film *Guns of the Trees*. The loose plot of the film concerned the existential crisis of two couples before and after the suicide of one of the women. The film's soundtrack featured a combination of folk songs (not composed by Dlugoszewski) and

Dlugoszewski's original music for two flutes, clarinet, oboe, bassoon, and cello. The film premiered in New York City in August 1961 at an invitation-only, midnight screening at the Bleecker Street Cinema. Public showings began in early December, and "the reception was brutal," according to film scholar David E. James.[30] A few years later, the *New York Times* published a review that mentioned Dlugoszewski's "discordant music" for this "frankly esoteric work" only in passing.[31] Though Dlugoszewski and Mekas were "good friends" according to an acquaintance, *Guns of the Trees* would remain their sole collaboration.[32]

In the early 1960s Dlugoszewski continued cultivating her friendship with Virgil Thomson, who frequently attended her and Hawkins's performances. She sent him her programs and writings, and tried to arrange for social meetings with him, usually with offers of a home-cooked Polish meal or dinner out at the Chelsea Hotel where Thomson lived. In June 1962, she sent him two of her recent articles, hoping that they might interest his "delightfully irrepressible and intellectually inquisitive temperament" due to their "sassy style and lively impertinent content."[33] One of the articles Dlugoszewski included in her letter might have been the essay titled "Is Music Sound," published in 1962. Here she argued that "music emphasizing the timbre aspect of sound maintains the clear emotional zero of a true nontonal music." She added: "Not having the emotional implications of pitch, it need not exploit the psychological aspects of sound but awaken the faculty of wonder to sound for its own sake."[34] Without directly referencing the connections, Dlugoszewski aligned herself here with Henry Cowell's notion of "getting rid of the glue," his metaphor for the New York School composers' preference for pieces filled with sparse, detached sounds that did not have structural connections to the sounds around them—"not objects but processes providing experience not burdened by psychological intentions on the part of the composer," as Cage explained Cowell's idea—as well as Cage's direct expression of "sound coming into its own."[35]

In addition to article writing, Dlugoszewski remained a prolific correspondent. In May 1962, she wrote to Irving Sandler, inviting him to hear some music at her house, while pleading for another engagement at the Artists' Club. She wished to share another evening with Sidney Geist, this time in a discussion "involving the aesthetics of the current concerts."[36] She suggested to Sandler an event title—"Can Art Be Necessary? F. S. C. Northrop, J. D. Salinger, and Erick Hawkins"—and provided him with a nine-page essay filled with philosophical musings as well as aesthetic critiques of many unnamed contemporaries: "Unfortunately, too few observers realize that even the fashionable cults of indeterminacy are conceptual methodologies," she grumbled to no one in particular.

In July 1962, Dlugoszewski sent dance writer Walter Sorell a letter that seems to have included an undated version of this same essay sent to Sandler. Typical of her letters to Virgil Thomson, in which she tried to underscore similarities between him and herself, Dlugoszewski also tried to emphasize common ground between herself and Sorell, whom she flattered as being "fearless and beautifully literate" while praising his "endless curiosity and open mind." Self-deprecatingly dismissing herself as "a rank amateur" in the face of "a superb professional like yourself," she "shyly" promoted her "first little excursion into dance aesthetics," hoping it might be "fun" for him to read: "Actually it is really my own search for my own aesthetic that prompted the writing of this article and the three men [Northrop, Salinger, and Hawkins] involved epitomize for me the most important considerations of modern art and the direction I would like to explore myself!"[37] After insisting that she and Sorell shared both "little philosophic quirks to our nature" as well as "endless speculations on aesthetics," she added in closing (as she was wont to do): "I am a fair cook and maybe I can tempt you with a Polish dinner."

After returning from a performance at Rice University in Houston in February 1963, Dlugoszewski applied for a job at Sarah Lawrence College. Increasingly proactive in promoting her own professional experience and apparently eager to land a secure teaching position, she described her qualifications in a letter to the Music Department, outlining her education and her "seven years experience teaching harmony, counterpoint, and composition privately," in addition to her professional and commissioned compositional work.[38] Nothing seems to have come from this appeal for a job. Perhaps craving the community of colleagues an academic job might have provided, Dlugoszewski continued seeking out the friendship of artists whom she felt were kindred spirits. Visual artist Ad Reinhardt was one of them. In June 1963, she sent him one of her graphic poems with a letter full of compliments—"the sensitive purity and poetry of your rare angelic pictures"—for his recent Museum of Modern Art show, which, in her view, "transcends everything, even museum stupidity!" She also congratulated him on the Paris opening of a new show, which she and Hawkins hoped to attend as soon as they arrived in Paris in late June; in turn, she hoped to see him at the Paris premiere of their new work, *Cantilever*. "We think you are the greatest painter today," she gushed, "you can quote us."[39]

TOURING

Hawkins and Dlugoszewski produced two new works during 1963: A piece for three dancers called *Spring Azure*, which premiered at the Hunter Playhouse in New York; and a sixteen-minute work for four dancers called *Cantilever*, which premiered at the Theatre Récamier during the Theatre des Nations Festival in Paris on 30 June 1963.[40] *Cantilever* was dedicated to "the love of architects who are building the exciting new American cities," specifically, American architect Frederick Kiesler, a friend and supporter of Dlugoszewski and Hawkins. (Daisy Aldan had included a drawing by Frederick Kiesler in her 1959 publication *A New Folder*.) As a structural element of a bridge or building, a cantilever had a supporting function, usually at some kind of an angle ("all that thrusts forth and hangs into the air," a program note explained)—an image of strength, balance, and collaboration that would have appealed to a choreographer. A program note for *Cantilever* described it as "a dance of excitement and celebration," and, perhaps poking fun at Martha Graham, the collaborators also called the piece's emotional state "passion without neurosis."

Between 1959 and 1963, Dlugoszewski and Hawkins performed *Here and Now with Watchers*, *8 Clear Places*, and other pieces while on a number of tours that had them crisscrossing the country, visiting both big cities and small regional colleges—some four-dozen locations from Miami to Seattle, Connecticut to San Francisco. (The Paris engagement for the premiere of *Cantilever* in 1963 was a rare occasion to present their work overseas.) In 1964, Dlugoszewski and Hawkins were on tour again, with dance performances and occasional speaking engagements for Dlugoszewski. During this trip, Dlugoszewski wrote to Daisy Aldan from Spartanburg, South Carolina, where the Company had performed at Converse College amid the "rich and sumptuous tenderness" of blossoming magnolia trees. Describing her struggle to write two orchestra pieces while traveling, she added: "This has been a season of much touring and much busyness."[41] Notebook entries from the summer of 1964 reveal that Dlugoszewski continued to envision new percussion instruments, and also continued to compare her ideas about piano and percussion music to Cage's, concluding that they both had a fundamentally different temperament: "The trouble with John Cage / is that he has turned / silence into a concept / (the treason of the artist)."

In early October 1964, on the recommendation of John Edmunds, former director of the Americana section of the New York Public Library's Music Division (and whom she met at a lecture-concert she gave at an International

Society for Contemporary Music meeting in San Francisco), Dlugoszewski wrote to composer and music critic Peter Yates in Los Angeles, announcing that she and Hawkins would be performing on 27 October at Occidental College and on 31 October at UCLA's Royce Auditorium. While praising Yates's writings for the journal *Arts and Architecture*, in particular the "sensitivity and insight [he] lavished on contemporary music," she invited him to attend their performance: "So few critics are really equipped to meet the challenge of new musical ideas with courage and skill and I feel you have done so much this way you are in a class by yourself."[42] An undated letter to Yates suggests that they did meet on this occasion, and that she also attended a lecture he gave during her time in California: "My most intimate delights and goals in music of my own are all tied up with the combination of just intonation and dissonance and your new ideas have inspired me in whole new ways," she wrote to her new friend.[43] Yates suggested that she should meet Lawrence Morton, director of the Monday Evening Concerts series in Los Angeles, fueling her hope for more West Coast engagements for her own music.

The 1964 West Coast tour also included performances in Albuquerque, where the local newspaper wrote that Hawkins, Dlugoszewski, and Dorazio had worked together for the past thirteen years to create "balance between sound, movement, and costumes."[44] In late November, Dlugoszewski sent Ad Reinhardt a postcard from Somerset, Pennsylvania, lamenting the fact that the past years of extensive touring had prevented her from seeing him recently.[45] An article published by an Oklahoma newspaper announcing a performance at the Oklahoma College for Women reported on Dlugoszewski and Hawkins's travels: "The current tour of the company takes them from Portland, Oregon (their third appearance there in five years), through California, Arizona, New Orleans, Oklahoma, and ends with a performance at the Fine Arts Conference at the University of Texas."[46]

Dlugoszewski and Hawkins created two major dance-music collaborations in 1964: *To Everybody Out There* (for eight dancers and chamber orchestra); and *Geography of Noon* (for four dancers and one hundred invented percussion instruments). Both works were premiered on 13 August 1964 during the American Dance Festival at Connecticut College in New London, and used sets by Ralph Dorazio. An undated program note from a performance of the work at Sacramento State University described the music for *Geography of Noon* as "a new departure from existing percussion music by emphasizing new bowing techniques and pianistic fingerings to achieve unusually delicate dynamic and remove the aggressive and brutal playing practices common among percussionists, in favor of perceptual and poetic values." A notebook containing Dlugoszewski's thoughts about the composition of *Geography of Noon* contained several ideas about percussion music: "Drumming will never make you cry / like melodic / but will give sex orgiastic triumph solemnity / the trouble with modern drumming it always sounds as if someone is being raped / What is drumming?"[47] Another entry, dated 7 June 1964, mused more directly about *Geography of Noon*: "What should *Geography* music be really? / What do you want to make of it? / The LD answer—in 20th century America / in sophisticated aristocratic musical / what is drumming + why do we want it / and why do I want it and why is it for Geog.? / Geog. is a drumming piece / not a percussion piece."[48] Dlugoszewski's association of drumming with rape—alongside her (aforementioned) comment about "aggressive" percussionists sounding like they were "beating up women with their mallets"—suggest that she felt deep ambivalence about the role percussion might play in her own work.

The Erick Hawkins Dance Company's 1964 and 1965 tours were reported on in a long, detailed typescript titled "The Erick Hawkins Dance Company: Newest American Touring Success Story," written by Charles E. Green, the Company's tour manager.[49] (Green had also been the tour manager for the Martha Graham Dance Company's European tour in 1950 during which time Hawkins and Graham's relationship unraveled.) Green described the cross-continental success of the tour in terms of "capacity houses, vociferous curtain calls, repeat engagements." Claiming that this unprecedented activity was being undertaken "entirely without subsidy," Green anointed the Erick Hawkins Dance Company as "the healthiest success story yet for American dance." With thinly veiled jabs toward the Merce Cunningham Dance Company, the Paul Taylor Dance Company, and perhaps others, Green emphasized Hawkins's success "with the other concert halls of America"—that is, presumably, beyond Lincoln Center—at colleges, universities, and museums. Citing administrators at institutions from UCLA to Wichita Falls, Texas, who invited the company back for additional performances, Green pointed to the appeal of "important new human values" and the "new degree of poetry [Hawkins] has brought to dance vocabulary." Making a public relations virtue out of Hawkins's "loner" appeal to non-metropolitan people, Green wrote:

> If New York seems to see Hawkins as a difficult outpost of subtlety, intellect, and experiment, Conway, Arkansas, Hammond, Louisiana, and Eau Claire, Wisconsin, with their lack of preconceived ideas simply delighted in what they saw and showed their delight by giving the company standing

ovations. Indeed, it was a dance buff as unusual as a professor of agriculture who started the bravos at California Polytech of San Luis Obispo where they have never had a dance concert before.... Several young architects drove all the way from Lubbock to Odessa, Texas, just to see the performance a second time. A sophomore Humanities student at River Falls, Wisconsin, drove all the way to Minneapolis to a second viewing. It got to be a pattern for fans to follow the Company to neighboring cities to see them perform more than once.... An automobile designer in Michigan seeing modern dance for the first time at the Hawkins concert confessed that he enjoyed being part of this audience stillness more than all the cheering variety shows and football games he usually attended.[50]

The long and detailed report went on to make an elaborate case for Hawkins's success being due to a shift in cultural values vis-à-vis a new generation of college students rebelling against a "comfortable middle-aged group waiting apprehensively for Pop Art to jolt them from their complacency." Alluding to postwar conformity, Green continued to profile this difficult-question-asking audience as "not the apathetic frivolously restless college generation of a decade ago, but some really strong, sophisticated, thinking people demanding fresh values." Rejecting the "Establishment" practices of Pop Art and "shock-Dada," these young audiences asked what to do "about boredom, about ugliness, about cruelty between men and women"? This twist on insider-versus-outsider art distorted the politics of the growing counterculture in an attempt to establish fifty-six-year-old Hawkins's relevance in the changing world of the 1960s—one in which people over thirty were proverbially not to be trusted:

> Current college students have already done their own experiments in masochism, their own happenings. They have already been exposed to considerable nudity, especially the kind without feeling. They know that shock will not cure their boredom, and that a puritanical desire to cause discomfort is not Zen. As one student put it, "So much Pop Art and shock type performances is like a creepy group therapy nobody needs. Hawkins is new, but he doesn't get his kicks out of making us angry."

Writing from the road, Dlugoszewski confirmed the impression that "the young kids have really made Erick their culture hero" in a letter to Virgil Thomson, adding modestly, "and they like the music, which is nice."[51] On another occasion she told Thomson: "These young kids have been so terrific to us," adding "we just can't get over the way its the *young kids* who passionately love Erick's work so much, and I always thought he would remain a choreographer's choreographer—a little precious—you know—but these young kids make him a *real star*."⁵² In another undated letter to Thomson, she commented with delight on the racial diversity—"white, black, Spanish-American"—of the enthusiastic young audiences for Hawkins's concerts.

Green's document concluded with a number of quotations from newspaper articles about the tour, many of which highlighted the accomplishments of the Company's composer: Los Angeles critic Peter Yates compared Dlugoszewski favorably to Varèse; San Diego critic-philosopher Alan Shields praised her music as "original, pristine, innocent"; Portland, Oregon, composer-critic Robert Crawley enjoyed the "loveliness of her arsenal," while claiming she made "a clean break away from traditional instruments instead of torturing them with music achieved [through] chance methods," making "the act of performing more demanding than ever instead of turning over sound production to electronic monsters." A critic for California's *Sacramento Bee*, William C. Glackin, also could not resist the comparison to Cage: "Where avant-gardist John Cage is an improviser and a humorist, Miss Dlugoszewski's music is carefully and exactly planned and in deep earnest." Green's report ended with what sounded like one last jab at Dlugoszewski and Hawkins's rivals: "Unlike the ivory tower and condescending avant-gardists, they sincerely like people and feel that to ignore the audience is to insult the audience."

The Merce Cunningham Dance Company's six-month-long world tour in 1964 had helped raise its international profile; clearly the Hawkins Company strove to make a case for its own *national* relevance as not gratuitously "avant-garde" but as something direct and beautiful—anti-elitist, even—that connected with average people around the country. In an undated letter to Walter Sorell, Dlugoszewski described her own feelings about what had happened during their tour, describing the mood of "the west" as "very receptive to new ideas and aesthetic and poetic directions":

> Can you imagine such a heavenly situation—sold out houses, 7 or 8 curtain calls, bravos and glowing reviews. In San Francisco we not only sold out but turned 200 people away. I was also able to do a lecture concert of my own in San Francisco to open their series of the International Society for Contemporary Music which was very exciting for me. In L.A. that marvelous music critic, Peter Yates came to my concert and flattered me to death because he felt that my direction in contemporary music is more sensitive than either

Stockhausen or Boulez. [. . .] At the Fine Arts Festival in the University of Texas the head of the drama department said we were the most success [sic] dance and music concert the university ever had. In San Diego the head of the philosophy department was so excited about our concert that he himself wrote a review in which he named Erick as the new important leader in the most recent American arts because he alone can fill the great vacuum caused by the modern aesthetic of the "ugly image of man" since he has contributed his new unique vision of beauty for contemporary man.[53]

Back in New York after their most recent tour, Dlugoszewski gave a concert titled "Swift Music and Beauty Music" of her new chamber music at NYU's La Maison Française on 29 April 1965. The program introduced a number of recent pieces, including *Swift Music* (timbre piano and percussion), *Music for Left Ear in a Small Room* (clarinet), *Percussion Flowers*, *Percussion Kitetails*, *Percussion Airplane Hetero* (timbre piano and percussion), *Suchness with Radiant Ground* (clarinet and percussion; a wedding present for Mr. and Mrs. Frederick Kiesler), and *Beauty Music* (clarinet, timbre piano, and percussion). As Dlugoszewski noted in several letters to friends, the NYU concert was sponsored by Virgil Thomson, and was recorded and broadcast on WBAI on 16 June—her fortieth birthday. The following evening, WBAI broadcast a discussion between Dlugoszewski, Hawkins, and Frederick Kiesler. Dlugoszewski wrote to Ad Reinhardt with news about the radio broadcast, and thanked him for specific suggestions he had offered after hearing the NYU performance.[54] She also invited Daisy Aldan to listen to the broadcast; she wrote of the broadcast to her friends Parker Tyler and Charles Boultenhouse on the same day.[55] She also wrote to William Schuman, with whom she had become acquainted during her early days in New York City, and took the opportunity to offer some flattery, in complementing the "passion, drama, and power" of his score for Martha Graham's *Judith*: "Only a *Wozzeck* is anything like its power," she marveled.[56] Never one to hold back praise for her friends, on the same day, she also wrote a letter full of flattery to Virgil Thomson about a recording she had received in the mail of his music. In particular, she was charmed by his *Sonata Da Chiesa* (1926), paying particular attention to his deployment of certain instruments: "The way you have the E-flat clarinet in its high impossible plateau at first and then later [the] low register viola and that beautiful following trombone passage and the mysterious way you mix the clarinet and the trumpet so that each one becomes more itself—wow!"[57]

MARITAL CRISIS

Despite the critical success of their national tours and the steady work that continued during the following years, Dlugoszewski's notebook entries starting around the beginning of 1967 indicate that she and Hawkins experienced a crisis in their relationship during that year. As Hawkins struggled to recover from a debilitating heel injury, Dlugoszewski wrote extensively about her loneliness and desperation. Her writing increasingly gained inspiration from other writers, and she included passages from the writings of Norman O. Brown, Albert Einstein, Ralph Waldo Emerson, Sigmund Freud, Johann Wolfgang von Goethe, Thomas Hardy, Georg Wilhelm Friedrich Hegel, Immanuel Kant, D. H. Lawrence, Friedrich Nietzsche, F. S. C. Northrop, Alfred North Whitehead, Ludwig Wittgenstein, and others in her own diaries. Some notebooks included extensive writings on musical topics (electronic music; twelve-tone methods), as well as candid thoughts on a wide range of composers: Milton Babbitt, Arthur Berger, Pierre Boulez, Aaron Copland, Ernst Krenek, George Perle, Charles Wuorinen, and Iannis Xenakis.

Her thoughts also tended to drift back to Cage. She wrote about his *Music of Changes* and his prepared piano, and criticized his approaches to composition—"all this austere baloney," she scoffed—as she ridiculed what she called "his science snobbism" and his rejection of "personal taste":

> personal taste
> what I think is beautiful may not be what you think is beautiful
> it is the supreme risk and gamble that we take
> on a human level
> [...]
> personal taste
> not a fence around myself
> but a bridge toward you
> operating on the faith that I am giving something beautiful to you.
>
> Cage personal taste
> personal taste unreliable
> I won't have it
> removed the question from the only arena where it can be answered
> like doctor kills the patient then no more disease

Parallel to her constant evaluation of the contemporary music scene and her place within it, Dlugoszewski's more immediate personal crisis started to dominate her writing in July 1967. The first page of a notebook labeled *8 Clear Places* included speculation about what happens "if two love / and there arises two deep needs that / are in conflict." She concluded that one of the two "must set aside his need to accommodate / the other / the one who sets it aside has / betrayed his own nature / the one who takes such indulgence / betrays his love / the question is who can best / survive the trauma." This passage exposes a profound dilemma for artistic couples whose ambition comes into direct conflict. Dlugoszewski seems to have sensed that her needs as a woman (and artist) were expected to be secondary to the needs of the male artist, and that on some level she was being taken advantage of, or at least taken for granted. This situation and its ensuing power struggle increasingly angered her, especially in light of what appears to have been a sexual transgression on Hawkins's part. Dlugoszewski determined that "a real man" was "a full human being" who "has the courage to hear what a woman needs." Making a comparison between men who understood what women needed and boys who did not, she concluded: "I do not see Erick as a man / I see him as a boy." Oddly, during the autumn of 1967, Hawkins wrote to a friend, the writer Sallie R. Wagner, about his "engagement" to Dlugoszewski, despite the fact that they had married five years earlier:

> I took Lucy away for a few days. I have relaxed a little from the driving I have done for years and we have had more time together. We are closer than ever in 16 years, and just today I started telling some of my close associates that we were "engaged." It has been a long struggle of keeping this out of publicity just so we could help each other better. But finally the time has come. I still want only really close people to know, so I wanted to tell you but keep it with you. At least for now.[58]

A few months later, in December 1967, Hawkins wrote an essay titled "My Love Affair with Music" (not published until 1992 in his collection of writings called *The Body Is a Clear Place*). This essay constituted the most substantial piece of writing Hawkins would produce concerning music, and was full of praise and admiration for Dlugoszewski's work.

Despite Hawkins's perception that he and Dlugoszewski were "closer than ever in 16 years," the crisis spilled over into the following year. Dlugoszewski's anger and injury were so powerful that she claimed "one kind of vulnerable love for EH / I will never have again / I will never ask / and I will never talk or reveal myself / to him again." Nearly seventy pages of writings in this vein followed, collectively labeled "1968 LD personal." She compared Hawkins to Herman Melville's Ahab and his obsessive pursuit of the White Whale, Moby Dick. At the same time, she worked to convince herself of her own artistic autonomy: "Tell no one about your own center / that aesthetic paradise / It is nobody's business / and *must be protected*." These kinds of directives to herself continued for the rest of her life, writings she sometimes labeled "LD personal" or, more often: "pure Lucia." Despite her private anguish, she prepared for major performances with Hawkins and Dorazio, including an engagement at the Brooklyn Academy of Music's 1968 Festival of Dance, where they performed *Geography of Noon*, *Cantilever*, and a new work called *Lords of Persia*, on 15 November.

Dlugoszewski increasingly questioned the assumption that men were entitled to "pure unselfish" and "all-forgiving" devotion—"as a constant at home to come back to." ("You *cannot* ask that of another human being!!!" she inserted as an exasperated afterthought into this section of writing.) She bristled at what she perceived to be an expectation that the woman would always "forget herself" in support of a man who was never to be neglected or upstaged. This kind of comparison became increasingly political, but also clearly personal, as she sensed that she had been "eroding and destroying" herself over a long period of time without noticing that this was indeed happening. Through her anger, she admitted that Hawkins was both manipulative and narcissistic, and described what she saw as two "big mistakes": "1. he encourages and thoroughly enjoys my slavery (he thinks he needs it for this Godlike image of himself as a free adventurous man); 2. he thinks I as woman do not need adventure—this is very terrible and where my bitterness resentment and envy is greatest."

As she elaborated on Hawkins's "mistakes," she exposed a contradiction between his need for her devotion ("slavery") and his simultaneous accusations of her possessiveness, which he saw as threatening his sexual freedom. Though some of her writing seems to indicate that Hawkins might have had an affair with a male dancer, she also wrote: "Erick—you go find all these other women and find out if I am the right one for you then when you do find out—grow up and honor it."[59] These writings seem to include the names of other lovers of both Dlugoszewski and Hawkins, and she continually alluded to Hawkins's apparent disinterest in satisfying her sexual hunger, a state she equated with a kind of immaturity and weakness on his part. She soon began copying out passages by Simone de Beauvoir, whose revolutionary book *The Second Sex*, first published in 1949, clearly had an influence on Dlugoszewski's thinking at this time. (Likewise, she soon came under the spell of Norman O.

Brown's post-Freudian *Love's Body*, first published in 1966.) She also alluded to a financial relationship that might have put her at a disadvantage: "You had the manhood privilege of doing exactly as you want / your work / and *no* money responsibility to me." Somehow, in the middle of a frank discussion of her own sexual anxieties, Dlugoszewski managed to bring her thoughts back to composition as a refuge for her own existence:

>   my freedom
>   my achievement
>   my work
>   my adventure
>   my sensuous openness
>   sensitivity
>   tenderness
>   all without fear
>   all this can only be achieved now through the brass quintet

Dlugoszewski's frustration about her lack of independence and Hawkins's treatment of her came to be expressed in increasingly dramatic language, as she wrote of him taking advantage of her devotion: "I put myself in constant artistic jeopardy to help you achieve that neurotic dream of success of being like Martha Graham." Most tragically, seeking an answer to the question "why our art is bad," Dlugoszewski declared: "I compose all of my work surrounded by your hate / You choreographed all your work surrounded by my love."

Eventually, Dlugoszewski took a deep breath and reminded herself of where she could find strength and comfort: "There is no one in the world I love as much as the haiku poets." Several diary entries written in November 1970 again professed her devotion to these writers: "As long as I am alive / it will never desert me / it will be with me in sickness / as well as health / when I am dying / I can have Basho on my right hand / and Mu'Chi on my left."[60] Finally, she resigned herself to a lonely existence, given meaning only through the poetic philosophy of what she labeled as "Haiku reality":

>   you will join Basho and the others
>   you will be in nonattachment
>   no attached love
>   no children
>   no career
>   no safe livelihood
>   no safe studio
>   the world will be your studio

TEACHING

Around the time of this crisis, Dlugoszewski began teaching composition classes to dancers, and started to develop an interest in teaching the craft of choreography from the point of view of a musician and composer, with her specialized understanding of timing and form. Insisting on her students' mastery of elements like rhythm, dynamics, and space, she urged them to steer clear of intellectual, emotional, or political narratives in their dance.[61] In her teaching of the principles of structure, she instructed her students to "give the audience a flower at the right time," an idea similar to her frequent repetition of Gertrude Stein's claim that "you've got to put a little strangeness in a sentence to make the noun come alive"—in other words, the "disparate element" she and Hawkins cherished in their work.[62]

In July 1967, and for several summers following, Dlugoszewski taught a composition class for dancers at Hunter College in New York. One of the students in the class, dancer Beverly Brown (1941–2002), kept detailed notes from these classes over several years, and they give a sense of Dlugoszewski's classroom behavior and pedagogical priorities.[63] Brown joined the Erick Hawkins Dance Company in 1967 and remained one of its principal dancers until 1974. On Monday, 10 July 1967, Brown attended one of Dlugoszewski's first classes. She noted her teacher's instruction that "composition must be equally 1. Poetic (creative), 2. Analytical," and that "the poetry is that special personal expression, different in each person; the teacher must try not to inhibit that element in the individual." Dlugoszewski's first assignment was a simple "time study" in which the student/composer needed to clearly show a pulse and meter, and to "have a kind of sound accompaniment." The following day, Dlugoszewski gave her students a reading list, which included Hubert Benoit's *The Supreme Doctrine: Psychological Studies in Zen Thought* (1955), R. H. Blyth's *Zen and Zen Classics* (1960), Norman O. Brown's *Life against Death* (1959), and F. S. C. Northrop's *Man, Nature, and God* (1962). (She also recommended which New York bookstores would be most likely to carry these books). Brown also noted a reading list offered by Hawkins in his parallel class, including Coomaraswamy's *The Dance of Shiva* (1918), Eugen Herrigel's *Zen and the Art of Archery* (1948), and Northrop's *Meeting of East and West* (1946), as well as a history of unexplainable phenomena like levitation.

A second "pure movement study" assignment given by Dlugoszewski called "To Create the Beautiful Moment" was intended to explore "shapes and colors for [their] own sake." Brown starred one particular part of the description of this assignment: "When you are neutral, most egoless then you are open to a pure aesthetic, poetic experience (moment of poetry) from this experience, a metaphor for dance." Brown also noted something that Dlugoszewski presumably professed in class: "A woman needs to experience passion right in the truth of herself." Another assignment called "Toss It Off" came back to the metaphor of giving the audience a flower: "a flower to break the shell of indifference / know when to give the next flower / the flower can be there but inadequate performance can conceal it." Dlugoszewski also lectured about the practices of Buddhist monasteries, where monks had a "1-year standard requirement just like armed service for young men." She discussed the practice of walking meditation and potential theatrical uses of walking: "[The meditating monks] don't tell us about walking—they are walking." She also discussed music's basic elements of pitch, dynamics, time, and timbre. On 15 July, Brown took extensive notes on one of Dlugoszewski's favorite topics, namely, the "poetry of juxtaposition," which was closely related to her thoughts on "immediacy," "suchness," and "epiphany." Explaining that the music and dance did not have to express the same ideas at the same time—"that's death," Brown noted—but that their "mysterious relationships" should function like "two little theatres occurring at the same time." Musically, Dlugoszewski cherished the incongruent possibility that "a loud sound can happen when I lift my finger."

Brown continued her studies with Dlugoszewski over the following few summers, taking notes on her teacher's views on things like the "irrational logic of dreams," and "Freud's influence on the music of Schoenberg, esp. *Pierrot Lunaire*." In June 1970, Brown took notes on Dlugoszewski's "Dynamic Scale," a graphic and metaphorical tool for expressing specific states of intensities to the dancers in her class.[64] On another occasion, Dlugoszewski explained the difference between the Romantic ("personal emotions, hopes and fears, in relation to other people") and the Poetic ("a sense of wonder"). She criticized the Cage-Cunningham method of creation via chance operations: "It's like saying to your guests I don't always do it the same / Yesterday it was delicious but today maybe I'll be serving you a mess." On the contrary, Dlugoszewski expressed the view that composition was an old-fashioned craft in which the artist must remain in control—a contradiction to her claim in other contexts that sound should exist for its own sake.[65]

SPACE IS A DIAMOND

In May 1969, *BMI* magazine published an article on Dlugoszewski by dance critic and writer Walter Terry, who was quick to invoke the inevitable comparison to "today's most renowned dance-music team" Cage and Cunningham, and used the (unknowingly apt) metaphor of marriage to describe the creative partnership of Dlugoszewski and Hawkins. Terry commented on the differences between Cage's prepared piano and Dlugoszewski's inside-the-piano techniques, and also described Dlugoszewski's "sunny spirit" and her physical placement on stage in the middle of the action, where "Hawkins threads her presence and even her musical gestures into his dance, and she serves as a sort of incantational figure, not somber but rather gay, involved intimately in a dance ceremony."[66]

Dlugoszewski and Hawkins premiered their new work, *Black Lake*, just a few months later, on 20 October 1969, in New York City. Choreographed for seven dancers, the piece was divided into nine sections meant to offer a "metaphor of the eight [*sic*] different evocations of the sky at night," though "literal imitation is put aside in favor of poetic essence."[67] The dance was accompanied by a piece of Dlugoszewski's titled *The Suchness of Nine Concerts*, scored for clarinet, violin, two percussionists, and a precisely notated timbre piano part. She gave the "eight and one-half different structures" of the music different titles from the dance, using a variety of Chinese and Japanese terms used by calligraphers and haiku poets and evoking the pure matter of "the uncarved block." A program note explained: "The musical construction of *Black Lake* is a specific synthesis of Western and Eastern structural principles—for example, Western formal disciplines of fugue (flight) and chaconne (pool theater) and Eastern formal canons of nondevelopment (nageire) and transparency (muga), radical density of uncarved block (p'o), emptiness of things (sabi), lightness (karumi), and talentless rejoicing (wabin)."[68] An undated notebook entry indicates that Dlugoszewski considered her work on *Black Lake* a culmination of aesthetic—"not emotional"—concerns, the exploration of which started with her work on two earlier dance collaborations with Hawkins: *Lords of Persia* (1965) and *Tightrope* (1968). Another notebook entry drew connections between *Lords of Persia*—scored for B-flat clarinet, B-flat trumpet, bass trombone, violin, and extensive percussion and titled by Dlugoszewski *Balance Naked Flung*—with an earlier solo work, premiered at a Living Theatre concert in 1952:

> Structurally the score of *Lords of Persia* on all levels
> is springtime music in the way Buddhist and any other
> radical empircists [*sic*] would extract aesthetic principles
> from such seasonal preoccupation
> Structurally being springtime,
> the music is a constant nageire.
> The intense excitement of spring
> the incredible alertness of spring
> *The space of March and April and May*
> *has turned the world on its tender side*
> *and we have to turn the same way.*[69]

Except for one major work in the early 1970s and a few other sporadic works thereafter, *Lords of Persia* and *Black Lake* would bring to a close an intense decade of dance-music collaboration between Dlugoszewski and Hawkins. In light of the recent crisis she had endured in her private life with Hawkins, she may have been considering such a professional break for some time. An undated diary entry from around 1970 noted: "This dance co. is too self-centered dance / I never seem to get back anything in return for all I give / They don't separate personal affirmation from pure aesthetic triumphs!"

Perhaps as an initial attempt to branch out on her own, in April 1970, Dlugoszewski composed what would arguably become her best known stand-alone work: the virtuosic solo trumpet piece *Space Is a Diamond*, written for Gerard Schwarz (b. 1947), who would soon come to be an important advocate along with a handful of other musicians and conductors who championed her music during the 1970s and beyond.[70] In her notes about *Space Is a Diamond*, published with the score by Gunther Schuller's Margun Music, Dlugoszewski wrote of the piece: "Sense of hugeness, transparency, delicacy of brilliance, speed and frequency of sudden daring leaps into disparate dynamics and the passionate capacity for expression of a solo instrument with essentially linear possibilities."[71] The ten-minute piece for B-flat trumpet, divided into six sections played without breaks, required a "choreographic unfolding of mute changes" with the player juggling seven different mutes, reading graphical symbols designating each particular mute, with green and red colors indicating the insertion or removal of a particular mute.[72] Extended techniques were also used in order to maximize the variety of timbre over a range of four-and-a-half octaves. She employed half-valve glissandos, "flap whisper" trilling techniques, double-tonguing, "percussive bubbles" ("produced by depressing the appropriate valves and gently hitting the mouthpiece with the palm of the hand"), "flap tongue," and whistle tones.[73] A composition notebook for *Space Is a Diamond* contains sketches showing that Dlugoszewski associated this piece with the concept of *nageire* ("flung into"). In her prefatory notes to the score, she described the virtuosity required by the piece:

> *Space Is a Diamond* involves various "calligraphies" of speed that often brush only the outermost reaches of registers, leaving an unsounded emptiness in between, or spiraling parabolas of melodic variation in calligraphic flights. Finally, like the taut mystery of a straight line, the formal organization distills itself into the sharp transparency of a long set of variations on a single note. The music, then, assumes an entirely different dimension. The line flowers into a variety of oscillations, including quarter-tone trills, until it reaches a new concentration of tautness and finally severs itself so that a fragile hanging bridge spans the silence of the ear.[74]

In 1972, after some thirty years of composing, *Space Is a Diamond* became Dlugoszewski's first work to be released on a professional recording, appearing on the Nonesuch label with a performance by Schwarz. Called *The New Trumpet*, the disc included additional pieces by Peter Maxwell Davies and William Hellermann. Composer William Bolcom, who wrote the liner notes, proclaimed: "With Lucia Dlugoszewski's *Space Is a Diamond*, we enter a new sound world."[75] Virgil Thomson, in his book published in the same year Dlugoszewski composed *Space Is a Diamond*, wrote of his friend's bold work: "Typical of Miss Dlugoszewski's practicality and imagination, *Space Is a Diamond*, 1970, is an eleven-minute trumpet solo unaccompanied that seems virtually to exhaust the technical possibilities of the instrument without becoming didactic."[76] A description of the piece published decades later "paradoxically" acknowledged that "the work for which this instrument inventor is most known was written for the trumpet."[77]

In the years to come, Dlugoszewski would continue to explore the power and potential of brass instruments, as she turned her attention more and more toward stand-alone chamber works for contemporary music ensembles. Only one major Hawkins dance created during the 1970s was set to a new score by Dlugoszewski: *Angels of the Inmost Heaven* (1971), accompanied by her brass quintet score titled *Densities (Nova, Corona, Clear Core)*—one of her most adventurous and captivating works, and most likely the brass quintet she referred to in her private writings during the height of her marital crisis. At the beginning of the new decade, Dlugoszewski was primed for a new chapter in a compositional career increasingly independent from her work with Hawkins, though their private and professional lives would remain intertwined for the rest of their lives.

SIX

Aesthetic Immediacy (1970–80)

> From 1952 to 1972 I wrote all the music for Erick's pieces. Then I began having too many orchestral commissions.[1]

TWO WEEKS AFTER DLUGOSZEWSKI'S fiftieth birthday, Chester Dlugoszewski died at the age of eighty-eight, following a long illness that took Dlugoszewski back to Michigan for several extended visits. In an undated journal entry, Dlugoszewski reflected on the loss of her father, whom she had adored as a child, and to whom she once wrote, "Your ethics stand unflinching":

> Luci Czesio
> he is not at the graveyard
> he is not in heaven
> he is nowhere
> and there is no place
> like nowhere in the human heart
> so we invent places for him
> but truly truly
> he is Luci Czesio[2]

Chester's death and Dlugoszewski's subsequent grief—which triggered bouts of insomnia—came in the middle of a fertile period of compositional activity that included a number of commissions, performances, and recordings by various individuals and groups interested in her music, including Pierre Boulez and the New York Philharmonic. During this decade she was also recognized with awards: granted a Guggenheim Fellowship in 1977, she then became the first woman to win the Koussevitzky International Recording Award in 1980.

Whereas during the 1960s Dlugoszewski had been active through her collaborations and touring with Erick Hawkins, during the 1970s she proved herself as an independent composer of stand-alone concert works: *Fire Fragile Flight* (1974; chamber orchestra); *Abyss and Caress* (1975; trumpet solo and chamber orchestra); *Amor Now Tilting Night* (1978; chamber orchestra); *Tender Theatre Flight Nageire* (1978; brass sextet and percussion); *Amor Elusive Empty August* (1979; woodwind quintet); and *Pierce Sever* (1979; timbre piano). These compositions, some of them premiered by renowned conductors and ensembles, brought wider attention to Dlugoszewski's compositional abilities. Due to the shift in her professional focus, she wrote only one piece for Hawkins during this period—the brass quintet she called *Densities* (1971)—though she continued to tour with the Company and to provide musical accompaniment in revivals of older works. The positive publicity she would receive during this decade was foreshadowed by a supportive assessment of her work in the *New York Times* as early as 1971, in a Sunday article by Allen Hughes: "Miss Dlugoszewski has had a remarkable, though little publicized, career of creation and performance that has linked her at one point or another with avant-garde manifestations in poetry, painting, and motion pictures as well as dance. And in an age when experimental music has seemed to grow noisier and more haphazardly organized with every passing year, her scores have been characterized generally by refined, often delicate sonorities, and scrupulous attention to structure and form."[3] The article included a photograph of an elegantly dressed Dlugoszewski playing some of her hand-held percussion instruments.

Around the same time as Hughes's article, a feature article in *Vogue* magazine written by cultural critic John Gruen described Dlugoszewski as "a pretty, Detroit-born woman of Polish extraction, whose makeup-less face, quick smile, and friendly eyes seem to belie the fierce independence of her spirit and dedication to a profession notorious for its disdain of women." While asserting that Dlugoszewski had "produced a body of work on par with that of her far more celebrated contemporary John Cage," Gruen also predicted that "after twenty years underground, her emergence is overdue and imminent." Gruen concluded that "the fact that she is a woman—and a shy one, at that," had made acceptance of her work difficult.[4] Two years later, Dlugoszewski would tell a *Detroit News* reporter: "A few years ago, when women's lib was breaking on the American scene, *Vogue* magazine trotted me out as a rarity—a woman composer." Claiming "whenever the media wanted to show exceptional women, they threw me into the story," Dlugoszewski admitted: "It was nice to be in after being out so long."[5]

DENSITIES (ANGELS OF THE INMOST HEAVEN): NEW CONCEPTS IN PHRASING

During the early 1970s, Dlugoszewski and the Erick Hawkins Dance Company continued to tour and perform around the country, including engagements at small schools in Louisiana, Maryland, and Arkansas.[6] But they mainly focused on preparing their new collaboration for its first performance. On 11 October 1971, Hawkins's dance *Angels of the Inmost Heaven* premiered in Washington, D.C., accompanied by Dlugoszewski's new brass quintet, *Densities*. Her score was dedicated to Ralph and Mary (Norton) Dorazio. The title of the choreography referenced a piece of writing by Swedish theologian and philosopher Emanuel Swedenborg called *Heaven and Hell* (1758). Here Swedenborg discussed the concept of different degrees of heaven, in which "the angels of the inmost heaven are not clothed": Hawkins's choreography called for nearly naked dancers. "Wearing nothing but G-strings and their dignity," *New York Times* dance critic Anna Kisselgoff wrote after a Joyce Theater revival of the piece in 1984, "these dancers danced marvelously."[7]

Densities, subtitled *Nova, Corona, Clear Core*, focused on extremes of range, texture, and timbre between the instruments, and is perhaps Dlugoszewski's work most clearly inspired by Varèse. In the score's manuscript, which was made available in facsimile form by Gunther Schuller's Margun Music in 1975, Dlugoszewski described *nova* as a "mobile explosion" burst of energy, *corona* as "decay" (also: "delicate like rain"), and *clear core* as a "static high density wall" (or: "static solid flickering wall of extreme density"). For some of the glissandi, she indicated that they should make an "angelic sound"; at times, the brass players are asked to sing and play simultaneously. In *AllMusic Review*, pianist and writer "Blue" Gene Tyranny noted that the piece's "extraordinary variations of glissandos, fast lip and finger trills, [and] constant shifting of mutes are the ingredient techniques of a very unique style that flows with high energy and also the eloquence of a Debussy orchestral brass section."[8] Dean Suzuki, reviewing the recording for *OP* several years later, wrote: "[Dlugoszewski's] *Angels of the Inmost Heaven* explores three major structural levels: timbre, density, and phrase permutations."[9] "The result is a work of great intensity and power," he concluded.

Scored for a brass quintet—two B-flat trumpets, French horn, tenor trombone, and bass trombone—the eight-minute *Densities* was divided into eight large structural phrases of fifty-five seconds each (with the final section being slightly longer). Six pages of charts and prose explanations of her theoretical ideas preceded the fifty-page manuscript. These explanations included: a "dynamics/density map" (phrasing); a "pitch range/density phrasing map"; a list of "timbre permutations"; "definitions involving new density-phrasing concepts"; a prose explanation of "new concepts in phrasing"; and a numerical chart of "density ratios." Similar to the demands placed on the trumpet in *Space Is a Diamond* of the previous year, Dlugoszewski drew on a variety of extended techniques for brass instruments, including many expressions of glissandos, flutter tonguing, lip and finger trills, and the constant shifting of mutes. In her writing on "new concepts in phrasing," she offered further explanations regarding metrical divisions, phrase lengths, and "epiphanies of densities." Reminiscent of Varèse's frequent use of scientific vocabulary, like his metaphor of "crystallization," Dlugoszewski's focus on the intensity of isolated sound masses described in astronomical terms placed texture at the forefront of her composition.[10] The result is heterophony, full of gestural bursts, nervous motion, sharply articulated discrete pitches, static repeated tones, and glissandi. Sounding like random explosions of sound, the score is precisely and meticulously notated. Hawkins scholar Julia Keefer observed that "the high dynamics and extreme dissonance of the trumpets" in *Densities* contrasted starkly with the "serene, poised fluid arabesques of the dancers."[11]

Dlugoszewski completed her score for *Densities* in September 1971, just shy of the October premiere in Washington. In early May 1972, the American Brass Quintet performed the work again in Philadelphia at the Walnut Street Theatre. *Village Voice* critic Leighton Kerner, a loyal fan of Dlugoszewski's, took this opportunity to hear the new work. Writing that her music "breathes a kind of super-oxygen that would burn up the product of most other contemporary composers," he described how "the more hair-raising eruptions of music accompany the most quiet sections of dance movement," resulting in both tension and "uncommon power" between "what the ear hears and what the eye sees."[12] Other pieces on the program included *Cantilever*, the "phenomenal" *Black Lake*, and two piano solos from *Here and Now with Watchers*—all of which, Kerner concluded, "are dazzling examples of American music here and now."[13]

MOVES TOWARD ARTISTIC INDEPENDENCE

In August of 1971, Hawkins had written to Virgil Thomson, telling him how grateful they were that Thomson had written so supportively of

Dlugoszewski's work in his recently published book *American Music Since 1910*: "Naturally she has taken such a beating for working with me so extensively, instead of having her music taken with the deep seriousness she has put into it, not just as an adjunct to the dance."[14] A few months later, Hawkins expressed his gratitude again (apparently having forgotten the almost identical content of his earlier letter): "She has been so selfless in working with me that she hasn't of course pushed her work in the music field, and I am sorry for that for her sake."[15] Dlugoszewski remained close to Thomson during this period of intense compositional activity. In an undated letter written in the mid-1970s, she informed Thomson of her father's illness: "You know I've been in Detroit for 2 months because my father has been seriously ill and we almost lost him and being an only child and loving him so very much made it a very upsetting experience for me. Thank goodness, he's pulled through and is finally out of the hospital and so I'll be back in two weeks.... I've missed you very much and I love you the way I do my father."[16]

Though Dlugoszewski had not collaborated on any film scores since her work with Jonas Mekas on his film *Guns of the Trees* ten years prior, in 1971 she served as a sound consultant and composed and performed music for the credits of poet/writer/filmmaker Ruth Stephan's film *A Zen for Ryoko-in*. The film meant to allow "insight into true Japanese living and otherwise unspoken Japanese philosophy."[17] In a letter to the Arizona Poetry Center, Stephan described the importance of Zen as an influence on poets, including an increasing number of poets from the West: "It is important for these poets, young and old (if poets ever grow old), to begin to see Zen as it really is."[18] As a poet herself, a student of Zen Buddhism, and an admirer of Japanese aesthetics, it is not surprising that this emphasis on Eastern poetry and philosophy would have appealed to Dlugoszewski's own spiritual and philosophical interests.

During the early 1970s Dlugoszewski also began exploring the possibilities of text setting, albeit only briefly; she had mostly avoided composing vocal music up to this point in her career—and would largely continue to do so.[19] In 1971 she seems to have been working on an opera called *The Heidi Songs*, based on poetry by John Ashbery: the work appears to have never been completed.[20] Another occasion around this time caused Dlugoszewski to try her hand at text setting again. In April 1972, New York's Whitney Museum hosted an event in honor of poet Frank O'Hara, who had died in an accident in 1966. The museum invited seven composers to have works performed: Lester Trimble, Virgil Thomson, Ned Rorem, Lukas Foss, Charles Mingus,

Jimmy Giuffre, and Dlugoszewski. Dlugoszewski's contribution was a rare vocal setting, namely of O'Hara's poem "In Memory of My Feelings," first published in 1967. In the *New York Times*, Allen Hughes reported that out of all the pieces on the Whitney concert, Dlugoszewski's *In Memory of My Feelings*, sung and spoken by tenor Paul Sperry against a "subdued but inventive accompaniment" played by seven instruments, "was the longest and most far out of all." Pointing out that up to now Dlugoszewski had been almost exclusively a composer of instrumental music, Hughes added that he "had the feeling that [she] may occasionally have become impatient at having to deal with all those words."[21] Mingus biographer Gene Santoro described this occasion as more of a contest than an invitational event, for which Mingus set an O'Hara poem for voice and string quartet; Jimmy Giuffre, Santoro claimed, "led a jam session, and won first prize."[22]

Dlugoszewski's "tenor concerto" (as she subtitled *In Memory of My Feelings* on the cover of a pencil draft) featured a combination of spoken, whispered, and sung text. The sung pitches include frequent sliding tones; otherwise the vocal part is mostly syllabic, making the text easy to understand. Though the instrumental parts have not been located, a pencil draft of the vocal score shows that Dlugoszewski gave special attention to the syllabic settings of O'Hara's poetry, with specific emotional qualities assigned to many of the fourteen parts: "warm playful sensuous / whisper very clear and fast / very mysterious and passionate / as poignant and tender as possible / erotic emotion (as fast as is good for singer) / playful fragile delicate erotic-mysterious / erotic as well as awesome transparent." *In Memory of My Feelings*, performed once at the 1972 Whitney Museum event and evidently never again, would remain Dlugoszewski's largest and most ambitious vocal work.

"WHAT IS SOUND TO MUSIC?"

Dlugoszewski's 1973 article titled "What Is Sound to Music?" is important to an understanding of her aesthetic positions during this period. The article was published in *Main Currents in Modern Thought*, the journal of The Center for Integrative Education, which described itself as "a cooperative journal to promote the free association of those working toward the integration of all knowledge through the study of the whole of things, Nature, Man, and Society, assuming the universe to be one, dependable, intelligible, harmonious."[23] The issue's cover featured a photograph of an artfully arranged array of

Dlugoszewski's percussion instruments. F. S. C. Northrop served on the journal's editorial board, and was likely responsible not only for her inclusion in the journal, but also for her article's placement as the lead piece in this special issue on philosophical investigations of music, and the color photograph of her instruments on the cover.

Dlugoszewski had published a number of shorter writings in the past, but "What Is Sound to Music?" represented a significant codification of her ideas as they had been developing since the early 1950s. The inclusion of her writing in *Main Currents in Modern Thought* also placed her ideas in conversation with an intellectual milieu of philosophically minded thinkers: a group of which she would have been thrilled to be considered a member. In one passage, Dlugoszewski explained some of her core ideas:

> I have always been troubled by the degraded role of sensuous immediacy in the relative values ascribed to music. Was music even considered sound at all? If not, some of the most beautiful music is clearly unjustifiable: Bartók, Varèse, Ruth Crawford, Debussy, the "klangfarbenmelodie" factor of Webern. The existence of this musical beauty degenerated into an uneasy defiance, and sometimes disappeared with the poignancy of infertile seeds. For the same reasons, some of the loveliest of the arts were also marginal, inexplicable: the nature writing of Nabokov, verbal metaphor in general, Japanese poetry. Those seriously concerned with verbal poetry recognize the absurd talking-in-circles that the attempted justifications of the metaphor bring about: Japanese poetry itself is dismissed as merely an instrumentality (17 syllables) of a vaguely Romantic nature content—whereas Nabokov criticism sinks in a fog of psychology. The antagonism between Logos and Eros, the theoretic and the aesthetic, is still part of our cultural life, as Northrop has pointed out—with the theoretic in the ascendency.... What was evident in all the arts has also been true of the last three decades of musical history: ever more ruthless upheavals and ferocious contradictions (what someone wittily described as composers calling each other liars); severe antagonisms between Logos and Eros, Classicism versus Romanticism, boredom, violence; total rigidity, total license—artificiality, ennui, chaos and a general unliving quality about it all. Everything was a feverish epidemic of the "new."[24]

Further, she mused: "There is something about listening which reaches beyond all concerns with pattern, information, symbol, language, communication—something about sheer listening so extraordinary that it causes people to dedicate their lives as composers, musicians, listeners."[25]

Her essay asked questions like "What Is the Place of Logos in Music?" and "Is Music Sound?" and discussed recurrent topics such as "What You Think Is

Beautiful May Not Be What I Think is Beautiful," "The Fallacy of Misplaced Concreteness," "The Thinking-Feeling Diseases of Imperfect Man," and "Musical Feeling That Is Not Emotion." The last part of the article explained her compositional development up to that point as having occurred in three stages: First Development (1954–63), "Pure Radical Empirical Immediacy"; Second Development (1966–72), "The Uncarved Block"; and Third Development (1972–73), "New Roles for Logos."

The publication of "What Is Sound to Music" roughly coincided with a number of other significant events. For one, she gained the confidence to begin applying for major grants. Virgil Thomson agreed to serve as a confidential referee for her first Guggenheim application, and he did so in unequivocally enthusiastic terms: "Lucia Dlugoszewski is a remarkably skilled and original composer," he declared. Thomson continued:

> Being a woman, she has seldom till recently received her needed and just share of the prizes, awards and commissions. Now it begins a little bit. May it continue! I admire her work highly and respect it profoundly. Her project for a large dance-vocal and orchestral work is one for which she is admirably prepared by a long experience in writing for the dance and by much reflection and study of the aesthetics involved in all theatre work. Her composition, long known favorably to a small musical group, has in the last few years matured strikingly and in doing so has attracted the attention of a larger public as well as of the more knowing musicians. She merits help and she needs it at this time, which would be, in her whole growth and career, just the right time.[26]

Dlugoszewski would not be awarded a Guggenheim Fellowship until five years later.

Around this time Dlugoszewski met the composer-conductor Joel Thome, and she wrote to Thomson about this "most wonderful conductor."[27] (Thome recalled first meeting Dlugoszewski at a concert of Eleanor Hovda's in New York, while Dlugoszewski reported meeting him while on tour in Philadelphia.[28]) Like Dlugoszewski, Thome had grown up in southeastern Michigan, and he felt that they were bound together in a variety of ways: "musically, poetically, personally, and philosophically."[29] Thome reflected on shared characteristics of their Michigan upbringings, and their early interest in composing, which helped bond them as adults:

> We were both from the same area, that Michigan kind of affinity for each other, same way of speaking, the love of the night sky in Michigan.... And Lucy loved the sky, she always spoke about how inspired she was by the sky

in Michigan and by the lakes, by the nature, she was a nature person, and we shared that.... So we had that love of the Michigan sky, as a child, I used to spend hours upon hours looking at the night sky, and she did the same.[30]

Thome's father, a podiatrist, had known Dlugoszewski's parents, and the families interacted over a period of many years. Thome would come to have a significant impact on the success of her larger-form works of the 1970s and 1980s.

FIRE FRAGILE FLIGHT

On 11 March 1973, conductor Dennis Russell Davies and The Ensemble premiered a seventeen-minute new work by Dlugoszewski called *Fire Fragile Flight*, which had been commissioned by the Lincoln Center Chamber Music Society. This performance took place in Alice Tully Hall as part of a series called "New and Newer Music." In an interview conducted on WNYC some ten years later, Dlugoszewski explained what she was trying to express in that work:

> Flight was the nageire idea; fire was the passion idea I was trying to put in; fragile was the idea of early spring in the lake country, the Great Lakes country where I'm from, where you still have the deciduous trees that have their delicate, delicate branches showing. And remember I said that's where the season was, very, very early spring, and so I was trying to bring in that long line, so I wouldn't have Romantic destructiveness, and yet that sense of total aliveness of constant surprise ... in fact, in this piece—I never managed it since—I was trying to have something new happen in every second, just new material, new material, new material, constantly.[31]

In a program note, Dlugoszewski called *Fire Fragile Flight* a "17-layer concerto" and again explained the title's concepts as "a sense of architecture based on the delicacies of speed."

> *Flight* is essentially sudden leaping, elusive open-ended, huge, narrowing distances. Flight is actually the English word for "fugue" and even in its Classical essence one sees a characteristic elusive, swift open-endedness and width of dimension.
> *Fragile* embodies quick falls into tenderness, transparency.
> *Fire* metaphorically brackets all the 25 climbing intensity-arrivals expressed through rapid dynamic, density and wide-narrow register shifts, pitch interval bracketing, rates of speeds and a wide spectrum of timbre.

The timbre piano part for *Fire Fragile Flight* included detailed instructions for the employment of wire brushes, yarn mallet bows, glass bows, knife bows, rasps, hairpin steel mutes, and comb mutes inside the piano. Other materials included thimbles, ladder harps, water, glass jars, wood tangents, moving finger mutes, and other sonorous things. Dlugoszewski sought unusual playing from her musicians, including that the bassoon start "without reed," and that the oboe play a high "whistle" note in the dynamic marking (added in red) *pppppppp*. The full complement of instruments included five string players, four woodwind players (with flute doubling on piccolo and clarinet doubling on bass clarinet), four brass players, harp, and several percussionists (playing slide whistles, along with more traditional percussion).

In a letter to Isamu Noguchi, Hawkins described the April 1974 premiere of *Fire Fragile Flight*, which occurred during a break from touring. He wrote of Dlugoszewski's "nerve-wracking" work on the piece during the tour: "It was almost touch and go as to whether she would get it done in time for them to rehearse it," Hawkins disclosed. The performance was a success, however, with the audience applauding and calling out for an encore. According to Hawkins, conductor Davies turned to the audience and said: "I don't think we could get through that again!" Further, as Hawkins reported to Noguchi, Louise Varèse (Edgard's wife) called the performance a "historic premiere," and conductor Joel Thome hoped to record the work "if Dennis [Russell Davies] will release it."[32] Thome indeed recorded the piece on the Candide label with his Philadelphia-based ensemble Orchestra of Our Time. Released in 1979, the recording won the Koussevitszky International Recording Award in 1980—the first time the award was ever given to a woman composer since the establishment of the prize in 1963. (The first recipient of the award was none other than Edgard Varèse, who won it for a recording of his 1927 work *Arcana*.)

In 1976, Thome conducted *Fire Fragile Flight* at the Seventh Inter-American Music Festival in Washington, D.C. A *Washington Post* reviewer wrote: "These sounds... were obviously at the command of a superb intelligence who sought, by these means, to suggest the 'sudden leaping' of flight, the 'quick falls' of 'fragile,' the 'climbing intensity-arrivals' of fire."[33] "It is a bravura piece," the reviewer concluded. Similarly, critic and soon-to-be-friend and champion Jamake Highwater singled out Dlugoszewski's piece as a highlight of the festival:

> The music which brought cheers and a very long ovation was composed by a U.S. delegate named Lucia Dlugoszewski. *Fire Fragile Flight* is an absolutely

astonishing piece of music which, like so much of Dlugoszewski's composition, extends the sonic potential of the chamber orchestra quite beyond imagination. Yet this vast palette of sound remains utterly transparent and, though lacking the rhythmic narrowness of much contemporary percussion music, *Fire Fragile Flight* possessed a refined center of energy which moved clearly and dramatically towards a superb climatic resolution. All the paraphernalia which taxes the musicians, all the curious sources of tone, all the novelties of sonic atmosphere do not in the slightest detract from the purely musical shape of Dlugoszewski's work. When all the sounds and clusters of tone ended the audience seemed to agree that it had been taken from one place to another. *Fire Fragile Flight* was a marvelous musical experience: like a dream we felt for certain that we had been emotionally affected by[,] an experience we did not quite comprehend. That, for me, is the ultimate nature of musical response.[34]

Reviewing the recording of *Fire Fragile Flight*, *San Francisco Chronicle* critic Heuwell Tircuit called the piece a "winning, quite exceptional fantasy," and gave it his highest recommendation: "There is intelligence and originality in her work, as evocative as [George] Crumb's music, and astoundingly balanced in form as [Pierre] Boulez, as rich as most [Luciano] Berio." He concluded in no uncertain terms: "Clearly, this is one of America's most commanding composers, one you should know."[35]

ABYSS AND CARESS

On the advice of composer and conductor Stanley Silverman, the New York Philharmonic and the National Endowment for the Arts commissioned an orchestral work from Dlugoszewski in 1975.[36] *Abyss and Caress* received its first performance on 5 December 1975 with Pierre Boulez conducting. Gerard Schwarz played the solo trumpet part (doubling on flugelhorn); the rest of the orchestra included winds, brass, violins, cellos, and piano. Other pieces on the program of the premiere included Donald Martino's Pulitzer Prize–winning chamber work *Notturno* (1974) and Harrison Birtwistle's *Verses for Ensembles* (1969). Dedicated to Boulez, Gerard Schwarz, and Dlugoszewski's father, the piece's manuscript was dated from September 1973 to 22 February 1975. Sketches indicate that she originally called the piece "Sabishisa Abyss and Caress," using the Japanese word for loneliness: "Most interesting to me now is the possibility of exploring music for chamber orchestra where each player is intensely alone and himself on the knife's edge of radical empiricism," Dlugoszewski had written just a few years earlier in "What Is Sound to Music."[37]

The inside cover of the 207-page bound score included a note after the instrumentation: "When orchestras divide into accelerating and metric orchestra, the metric orchestra plays as usual. The accelerating orchestra plays discontinuous bursts at ever increasing shorter duration of entrance inspired and cued by the conductor. The accelerating orchestra is realizing the ideogram." The "ideogram" following this note consisted of a simple drawing with X's and lines indicating the increasingly rapid entrances of the "accelerating" orchestra. Dlugoszewski's division of the orchestra into a metrically regular one and an accelerating one evoked Charles Ives's *Central Park in the Dark* (ca. 1906) and other Ives works from early in the twentieth century. Dlugoszewski might also have been thinking of Ives and his experimentation with the spatial separation of parts of the orchestra—as in his *The Unanswered Question*, a companion piece to *Central Park in the Dark*—in her placement of the trumpet player, who was instructed to start the piece at the back of the orchestra. At measure 97, the trumpeter is instructed to take "tiny step[s] forward" until arriving, via "faster and larger steps," in front of the orchestra.

A lengthy program note written by the composer for the premiere explained the piece in poetic images of "both the reckless energy intensity of the 'abyss' principle and the equally reckless erotic tenderness intensity of the 'caress' principle," claiming that this idea led her to structure sound in choreographic terms of "leaping movement into strange juxtapositions, exciting off balances." Her program note also mentioned the birth of Schwarz's baby daughter, and the physical demise of her father: "Finally," she wrote, "there seems to be no leap so dangerous as the precipice cut off of human dying." These intense life events caused her to use visceral language: "a kind of peeled raw explosion of hearing" was akin to living totally in the unexpected, "the surprise like freshly broken glass." The program note went on to describe the structure of *Abyss and Caress* as "a fierce-fragile curve of leaping intensities expanding 15 times" into what she called "15 movement arrivals." She continued: "Structurally *Abyss and Caress* concerns itself with distance—dangerous, elusive flashes of speed, explosions of energy flashing through the erotic delicacy and power of 17 instruments, leaping for the flexibility of the mind, for the strange risk of hearing whose moment in time is always daybreak."[38]

Though her compositional interests were clearly moving in the direction of larger ensembles, Dlugoszewski's process of composing *Abyss and Caress* was not easy. In early 1975, Hawkins confided in Virgil Thomson that once she had finished the piece, Boulez decided he had overcommitted his rehearsal time and postponed the performance until December. "Lucie nearly killed herself getting it done," Hawkins revealed, while also telling Thomson how anxious she was to hear the work performed.³⁹ In a memoir published in 2017, Gerard Schwarz also recalled the circumstances of Dlugoszewski's experience with Boulez:

> When Boulez looked at the score, he called me into his study. I knew this was not the style of music he generally liked: it was long, with extensive use of scales and gestures, and quite a thick score. Boulez asked if I was a friend of Lucia's. I said I was. He said, "Would you please ask her to cut two pounds from this piece?" We had a laugh, but when I asked Lucia, she was not happy. Because of her tremendous respect for Boulez, she did make some cuts.... Gunther Schuller... programmed *Abyss and Caress* [in 1976], minus the Boulez cuts, at Tanglewood. Gunther was happy to show the Philharmonic how the piece should have been done in its entirety.⁴⁰

A manuscript of the work held by the New York Philharmonic includes notes on the title page that indicate eighty-seven measures of cuts for the premiere performance given by Boulez.

Despite occasional behind-the-scenes challenges like this, Dlugoszewski continued to receive praise and attention. In June 1975, the month of her father's death and her fiftieth birthday, *High Fidelity/Musical America* named her "Musician of the Month" and placed her portrait on the issue's cover alongside the phrase: "focus on women composers, musicians—a not-so-silent minority." Tom Johnson contributed an in-depth article pointing to Dlugoszewski's ongoing obscurity, despite the admiration she enjoyed among musicians. "This may be partly due to the simple fact that she is a woman," he concluded, adding: "It probably has much to do with the difficulty she has always had in meeting deadlines and working under pressure, and with the fact that she has never promoted her music as avidly as many composers do."⁴¹ Calling her compositional process "purely intuitive," Johnson imposed a problematic concept onto an intentional compositional agenda, given the fastidious way she notated her scores and the articulate—if opaque—manner in which she discussed her goals and processes in recent pieces like *Densities, Fire Fragile Flight*, and *Abyss and Caress*.⁴²

In August 1976, Dlugoszewski shared a concert called "Fellows of the Berkshire Music Center" with Gunther Schuller, Milton Babbitt, and others at the Tanglewood Festival of Contemporary Music—the occasion on which Schuller conducted *Abyss and Caress* in its entirety as originally intended.⁴³ Replacing dedicatee Schwarz, Charles Berginc played the trumpet solo. A review of the festival appearing in a local paper a few weeks later referred to Dlugoszewski as a "lesser-known composer," and stated that *Abyss and Caress* "managed an entire composition where instruments never uttered a single sound they were actually designed to produce."[44] (It is unclear whether this comment was meant as a compliment or a criticism.)

A few months later, Virgil Thomson wrote a glowing letter on Dlugoszewski's behalf to the National Endowment for the Arts, in which he explained that his admiration for her music had continued to grow. He endorsed her proposal to write a new orchestral piece, a plan he approved with "all vigor." Calling her "an artist of great originality, of very high musical and intellectual powers," he made the extraordinary claim that "there are very few composers of her quality anywhere in the world," while also admitting, more pragmatically, that "she does need money badly and she has so little of it."[45] A few months later, on the occasion of Boulez's final concert as music director of the New York Philharmonic, Dlugoszewski was photographed in Avery Fischer Hall alongside Milton Babbitt, Earle Brown, John Cage, Elliott Carter, Aaron Copland, Mario Davidovsky, David Del Tredici, and Boulez himself; of the roughly two-dozen composers included in the photo shoot, Dlugoszewski was the only woman.[46]

AMOR NOW TILTING NIGHT AND THE AESTHETIC NOTEBOOKS

Dlugoszewski called her next independent concert piece, *Amor Now Tilting Night*, a "triad," drawing on the triptych idea she had explored in *Fire Fragile Flight*. Describing "three simultaneous lines of thought from which the music derives," she explained: "*Amor* is the mythic 'imprint' of the inner mind, the feeling ambience of the music, in honor of a long fragile love"; "*Now Tilting* is a formal and structural kinesthetic inspired system of dangerous and delicate balances (it also refers to the Joycean concept of aesthetic arrest, what oriental artists call *kireji*)"; and "*Night* is the long night of the two autumns and winters during which the music was composed in 1976–7 and 1977–8 and the nature meditations involved."[47] Drawing on what she called Wittgenstein's and Northrop's definition of the mystical, she reasserted her belief that radical empirical immediacy "was the source of all poetic experience." As a composer, she went on, "the challenge of musical composition was the search for the efficacious ritual in the world of sound that would bring this about."[48]

Dlugoszewski kept dozens of notebooks full of sketches for various pieces-in-progress, and at least one such notebook was devoted to *Amor Now Tilting Night*. These store-bought standard composition books usually were adorned with elaborate composite titles on their front cover like the one for this piece (capitalizations hers): "star thrower's summer diary principles II aug 1978 Feb 7, 1980 NOW TILTING NAKED BOOK IB." Other notebook titles gave ranges of dates and subject matter, freely stringing together words similar to ones featured in her other poetic rants and rambles, including: *amor, terrible freedom, quidditas, now tilting balance, pierce sever, wigilia, epiphany, passion*, and so on. These notebooks are difficult to decipher, as they contain compositional notes, personal observations, diary entries, and what appear to be long passages copied out from an eclectic array of sources: Japanese poetry (including much Basho), Willa Cather, Joan Didion, Isak Dinesan, Goethe, Joyce, John Keats, Doris Lessing, Thoreau, and many others. She also included page-long musings on her favorite words, in Polish, Japanese, English, and Spanish. Other fragmentary writings focused on sexuality—in particular, Erick's (one notebook is titled "Amor Eros Diary"); others quoted extensively from Annie Dillard's 1974 book *Pilgrim at Tinker Creek*. A startling amount of free writing displayed extensive repetitions of constellations of other words that seemed to haunt her thoughts: *empty, suddenly, carefully, elusive, radiant, danger, total, absolute danger, distance danger, reckless, leaping,* and *absolute freedom*. Some of the notebooks' contents seem to indicate that Dlugoszewski and Hawkins had another relationship crisis from early 1978 until early 1979. During this time Dlugoszewski had considerable trouble sleeping, and frequently made notes about her struggles in the middle of the night. One notebook included an entry labeled "Lucia healing Feb. 18, 1979," and contained a contemplation on technology: "We know in our hearts / that we are not / machines / and grow lonesome / in a universe where we / are little aware of / anything else / which is not."

In the middle of this tumultuous period, *Village Voice* critic Tom Johnson brought Dlugoszewski's name into a review of a concert by composer Nigel Rollings, who made extensive use of radio sounds, a toy piano, homemade wind chimes, and found objects. Johnson wrote that Rollings's "general openness to all sounds clearly have roots in the kind of explorations that John Cage, Lucia Dlugoszewski, and others began making years ago.... And of course, Cage and Dlugoszewski continue to find new objects that make new sounds."[49] Johnson had been following Dlugoszewski's career for nearly a decade, having written about her on at least two occasions prior to the

1975 *High Fidelity* "Musician of the Month" piece, the first of which being a short article about Dlugoszewski and cellist/performance artist Charlotte Moorman, published in the *Village Voice* on 6 July 1972. In 1974, Johnson had placed Dlugoszewski on a par with better-known composers associated with "phenomenological points of view," including Morton Feldman and Chou Wen-chung: "Individually they are as different from each other as they are from Varèse, but that is because they are interested in different types of sounds," Johnson wrote. "All three are more concerned with sounds themselves than with any intellectualized relationships between the sounds."[50] Despite this occasional attention from an influential critic in the downtown arts scene as represented by the *Village Voice*, many of Dlugoszewski's contemporaries would continue to perceive her as an established "uptown" composer, ensconced in and supported by official institutions of high-class culture.

TENDER THEATRE FLIGHT NAGEIRE

On the occasion of Lukas Foss's premiere of Dlugoszewski's next large-scale piece *Tender Theatre Flight Nageire* at the Brooklyn Academy of Music, Jamake Highwater published an in-depth article in the *Soho Weekly News* in the spring of 1978. Highwater's portrait of Dlugoszewski was notable for its complete lack of mention of Erick Hawkins or Dlugoszewski's history of work with dance. Highwater reinforced a constructed reputation for Dlugoszewski as an "unconditionally individual [and] determined loner," "lack[ing] the applause of powerful music clans," "ignored by the conservative music community," and "carefully avoided by avant-garde music circles." The recent commission from Boulez and the New York Philharmonic, Highwater claimed, brought her "a measure of respectability ... even in this era of an avant-garde for the masses."[51]

Close on the heels of Highwater's lavish endorsement, American composer and serial memoirist Ned Rorem (b. 1923) wrote in a *Vogue* magazine article that if he were "forced to name the six best living American composers, three of them would be women: Barbara Kolb, Lucia Dlugoszewski, and Louise Talma."[52] In an earlier memoir called *An Absolute Gift* (1978), Rorem had praised Dlugoszewski's originality, calling her "The Queen of Dance," and claiming that she was only one of two American composers—Leonard Bernstein being the other—to have "come up with memorable ballet scores in thirty years." That is, he added, "since the happy postwar collaborations of Martha Graham with Copland, Schuman, Barber, Dello Joio." Further, Rorem was impressed by the fact that Dlugoszewski performed "on instruments by her own strange construction," thus, he added, "replacing the late irreplaceable Harry Partch."[53]

In May of 1978, one month after its premiere by Lukas Foss and members of the Brooklyn Philharmonia, the composer-supervised company Composers Recordings Inc. (CRI) recorded the twenty-minute-long *Tender Theatre Flight Nageire*, performed by a brass ensemble that included Gerard Schwarz, Edward Carroll, and Norman Smith on trumpets; Robert Routch on horn; David Langlitz on tenor trombone, David Taylor on bass trombone; and Dlugoszewski playing percussion. On the typescript cover to the manuscript, she listed the following "small orchestra of percussion instruments newly invented": "ladder harps of wood, metal, glass, and paper; tangent rattles of skin, wood, metal, and brass; closed rattles of skin, wood, and paper; unsheltered rattles of plastic and paper; square drums of skin and wood." She dedicated the piece to her mother, Jennie, and her stepfather, Floran Orvis, whom Jennie had married in February 1976, less than a year after Chester's passing. Many of Dlugoszewski's aesthetic concerns of the 1970s can be observed in her descriptions of *Tender Theatre Flight Nageire*. She originally conceived of the piece for an April 1971 production of a Hawkins dance called *Of Love*; after putting it aside for several years, she revised and completed it in 1978, renaming it *Tender Theatre Flight Nageire* when Lukas Foss premiered it as a stand-alone instrumental work.[54]

As with the conception of *Densities* and *Abyss and Caress*, Dlugoszewski felt compelled to explain a number of aesthetic, theoretical, and structural ideas of this partly theatrical piece, which also called for an unusual placement and movement of the trumpet player, lighting and blowing out of matches during a metrically strict percussion cadenza (alternating bars of 6/4, 7/4, 4/4, and 5/4), and other dramatic effects. A list included at the beginning of the bound manuscript titled "Structural Descriptive—19 minutes 39 seconds," included cryptic information on the five main sections. Additional notes diagrammed "spatial placement and choreographic instructions for instruments," including a raised back portion of the stage for the percussion orchestra, a ground-level placement of four of the brass instruments, "new invented percussion notation," and the "choreographic path of antiphonal trumpet" from stage "front left" to "back." *Tender Theatre Flight Nageire* included a number of interesting features, including brass players required to sing and play at the same time, and completely notated percussion cadenzas, which the composer played herself. The cadenzas included gongs, "delicate paper rattles," wire brushes and rasps, and the hitting of a paper sheet, in addition to the lighting and blowing out of matches.

Other charts were labeled "Dynamic Timbre Structure Map" and "Ratios of Phrasing." Subsections of the structural map indicated metaphoric images for certain sections: "very long pure flight"; "nageire within nageire: extreme speeds changing timbre every note"; "pseudo flights through tonguing gradually acquiring higher densities"; "pure flight very long"; and "grand nageire transparency (nageire almost invisible transparent densities gain dominance)." Another page of explanation, titled "General Information and Definitions," included descriptions of the words in the piece's title:

NAGEIRE: Generic Oriental principle of nondevelopmental or "leap" progression. The "nageire" principle is used here for quick variations and sudden leaps in and out of very high densities

FLIGHT: Generic translation of fugue

THEATRE: Immediacy of happening in time and space

TENDER: Expressive sound through devices of vulnerability or delicacy into performance

Further explanations elaborated on these core ideas, especially in terms of phrasing dependent on mathematical ratios, extreme speeds, and high densities. Describing Dlugoszewski's performance on the 1978 recording of *Tender Theater Flight Nageire*, Hal Rammel wrote: "Soft rattles, louder wooden ladders, frame drums, rotating drums, delicate glass chimes, flexatone, wobble boards, and larger tubular chimes burst forth like startled birds throughout the entire performance."[55] In October 1978, a reviewer of the recording of *Tender Theatre Flight Nageire* wrote derisively about Dlugoszewski's insistence on explaining her ideas in cryptic terms, while Andrew Stiller, a music critic for the *Buffalo Evening News*, gave the piece three stars out of four—"consistently interesting and entertaining"—praising the piece for its "startlingly fresh and virtuosic, but totally idiomatic brass writing."[56]

JAMAKE HIGHWATER AND *PIERCE SEVER*

Dlugoszewski's agitated and sometimes angry state of mind increasingly disturbed her sleep. In January and February of 1979 she kept a notebook labeled "Pierce Sever [...] 1979 epiphany diary" in which she made a number of entries about being awake and looking out of her window in the middle of the night. On the morning of 7 February, she wrote of "interrupted sleep—that anxiety before music rehearsal / the anxiety of the eruption of the prosaic world." Another undated diary page read: "worried fruitless day / worried about Erick's performance... Lucia *lost* / woke at 3 AM in terrible state / did chores till 5 AM / to see the star." Other entries made in the loneliest hours of the night expressed how "troubled" and "disturbed" she felt. Her "aesthetic diary" entries at this time also expressed irritation and frustration with sociopolitical and cultural trends of the time. One early February morning at 4:30 a.m., she ranted to herself about the implications of Frederic Rzewski's recent piece *The People United Will Never Be Defeated*.[57] "New song Revolutionism / Latin American passion / mixed with Marxist materialism / That's the Rzewski Romanticism / take poignant Latin American sense of humor tragic sense of life which is in all folk music / the minor 6ths—the tragic sense of life! / Then taking all the flashes of human musical insight / Bach Schumann Webern Boulez Cage Jazz Rock and transform this... 'we don't do theatre anymore that was the 60s.'"[58] Her early morning thoughts also turned to the treatment of women in contemporary society, arguing that "the feminine sense of nurture" was one of the most "civilized attributes / that elusively evolutionarily / welled up in the human!" She concluded that "all feminine attributes / except those that cater / to masculine narcissism are / spat on!!!"[59]

At this time Dlugoszewski and Hawkins lived on the same floor of a building on East 11th Street, with each of them maintaining separate apartments for their own work. Hawkins scholar Julia Keefer described Dlugoszewski's private space:

> The bed is strewn with pages of unfinished work, and the atmosphere of the place reveals an artist whose work comes first. However, she loves nature and her plants are almost as important as her piano. She collects exotic flowers, and has pasted leaves to the windows so that the sun heightens the gold, red and green colors of the leaves when it shines through in the morning. She has an Eastern view and loves to watch the sun rising, the moon, and the stars. For composing, she cherishes the early morning hours when the sun shines brightly through the window. Although New York City is not the best place for nature-lovers, she makes the best of it and "knows every tree in Washington Square Park."[60]

Keefer added that Hawkins and Dlugoszewski enjoyed eating Armenian food several times a week at a locale on University Place called Dardanelles, Hawkins's favorite restaurant.[61]

In April 1979, Dlugoszewski wrote several times to Aaron Copland, whom she might have felt could help advance her career. Effusive with flattery, and insisting that she had felt too "shy" to write him in the past, she went so far as to claim him as her "wonderful secret teacher." Considering that she had told her parents an anecdote about meeting him in May of 1950, and also that she had attended his fiftieth birthday party at the Museum of Modern Art in November of that year, it is odd that she claimed here to have now "finally met" him at a *Dance Magazine* awards event and again at a concert at the Whitney Museum:

> When I first came to New York as a teenager to study composition with Edgard Varèse and piano with Grete Sultan on recommendation from [my] teacher in my native Detroit, as you can imagine, contemporary music as a heard experience was totally unknown for me. And my first concert was to hear *The Piano Fantasy* of yours played by Billy Masselos and it was the great inspiring beginning piece of music for me and I still think it's the great piano work of the 20th century along with your Sonata and Variations.... I have always treasured it as the ultimate creative model for myself. I know no other piece that has such an exquisite structure and sensuous beauty and, for me, more wondrous still, that moment by moment creative surprise that electrifies the ear.[62]

The next day, she wrote to Copland again, announcing that she was sending him her recent CRI record of *Tender Theatre Flight Nageire*, as well as a packet of reviews and biographical materials "that you might like to look at in terms of my recent developments." She reiterated that his music had been "so important to my own creative growth even though, of course, we are quite different."[63] It would seem that through adulation, she was aggressively trying to ingratiate herself to a man widely dubbed the "Dean" of American music, and thus, presumably, capable of influence. In a third (undated) letter to Copland, she told him she hoped he would be able to hear her new woodwind quintet—most likely her *Amor Elusive Empty August*, written in 1979. Again, she appealed to him through flattery: "Your music has been one of my earliest inspirations—especially the piano sonata which I think is one of the most beautiful pieces of contemporary music ever written."

Dlugoszewski's woodwind quintet *Amor Elusive Empty August* (1979), commissioned by the Boehm Quintette, inspired a five-page, single-spaced typescript of the same name, which mused on many of the themes presented in Dlugoszewski's other writings. The essay included section titles such as "Energy, Mystery, and Stillness," "Joycean Quidditas: Alternatives to

Classicism-Romanticism," "Elusive Throat: An Alternative Energy," "Architecture of Speed," "The Beauty and Terror of Our Existence," "In Search of the Non-Logical Elegant," "Empty: Elegant and Naked," and "The Long Line." Dated 1 August–24 December 1979, the essay ended with the claim that during the writing of *Amor Elusive Empty August*, she told herself every day:

> to listen!
> to live an infinitely long elegant, recklessly, multi-sever line of experience as often as I had courage to make it happen!
> I was to fly with Eiseley's beautiful migrating monarch butterfly!
> to dangerously awaken the dangerous mind without fixing it!
> to perform that strange risk of hearing whose moment in time is always daybreak:
> "so that the universe might find itself living."

The over-100-page full score of *Amor Elusive Empty August* reveals traits common to this period of her compositional development: extended techniques, including a heavy reliance on mutes, glissandi, and sliding tones; theatricality in the form of lighting effects; and the lighting and blowing out of matches.

Diary entries from mid-1979 described Dlugoszewski's planting of flowers, her attending a "tedious avant-garde concert," and her feelings of deep sadness on the night of her fifty-fourth birthday. On 28 June, she made further references to her age-related woes: "after terrible middle age dislocation . . . the artist eternally getting young or younger." On 21 August, however, following a medical exam, she wrote in elated terms of her own good health, adding: "then walked 1st Ave. to 17 2nd Ave park still simple and lovely / remembered little 21 yr. Lucia on 17th street so grown up brash and scared and passionate and ardent and unknowing!" A few days later, her good-health-inspired enthusiasm waned: "Aug 28 1979 / Hopeless / Filthy hot day / and not feeling well." (Now in her mid-fifties, perimenopausal symptoms might have been responsible for her occasional feelings of ill health.) Around this time she also began reading Emily Dickinson: in a notebook entry dated 2 October 1979, she wrote "For E.D.: writing poetry = act of courage / meant to affirm her fragile life / create away a measure of her terror / by facing it squarely / transform human frailty fear and anxiety / into the highest levels of art." Dlugoszewski might have been talking about herself.

By the mid-1970s Dlugoszewski had established a friendship with the writer Jamake Highwater (1931–2001). In an interview conducted later, she recalled first meeting him when she performed *Here and Now with Watchers* in 1958 at a theater "he was running" in San Francisco: "Then we lost track of each other until he became music critic of the *Soho News*, and he came when Boulez did *Abyss and Caress*."⁶⁴ In 1979, Dlugoszewski wrote a new solo timbre piano piece that she dedicated to her new friend. Born Jackie Marks into a Jewish family in Los Angeles, Highwater later created a false identity as a Native American, writing books and receiving grants from the Public Broadcasting Company for television documentaries under that guise; muckraker-columnist Jack Anderson exposed Highwater's fraudulent persona in a *Washington Post* article published on 16 February 1984. That same year, Highwater founded an institution called Native Land Foundation, the Board of which included several of Dlugoszewski's oldest friends: Joseph Campbell, Erick Hawkins, Lillian Kiesler, Ned Rorem, and Virgil Thomson.⁶⁵

Perhaps through his work in dance with the San Francisco Contemporary Dancers between 1954 and 1967, or perhaps through Dlugoszewski's having been drawn to Highwater's writings on spiritual topics, the two became close friends and correspondents, and he became an unwavering champion of her music. One of the earliest known letters in their written exchange dates from May 1977, when Dlugoszewski thanked Highwater for coming to Washington, D.C., to hear a performance of her music.⁶⁶ When Highwater's book titled *Dance: Rituals of Experience* was published in 1978, its epigraph consisted of a quotation from F. S. C. Northrop's 1946 book *The Meeting of East and West*, which had had a profound influence on Dlugoszewski and Hawkins. Highwater's book included a dramatic photograph of Dlugoszewski and Hawkins performing together in *Geography of Noon*. In a section called "Notes on Ten Contemporary Rites," he praised her music for their 1969 work *Black Lake*: "Behind and ahead of these ageless processions of human animals is the music of Lucia Dlugoszewski, rising out of the uniqueness of the human ear just as Erick Hawkins' movement arises from the singularity of our animal bodies."⁶⁷

Dlugoszewski's new piece, *Pierce Sever*, was premiered along with works by Joel Thome, John Cage, and William Hellermann at the Drawing Center in New York City on 23 January 1980, in conjunction with an exhibition titled *Musical Manuscripts* and performances by the Orchestra of Our Time. For this occasion Dlugoszewski wrote a long, two-part program note/essay labeled *Pierce Sever I* and *Pierce Sever II*.⁶⁸ She described the beauty of her nocturnal wanderings through the streets of New York in search of the January morning star, calling on her trusty muses to help express her ideas: Aquinas, Blyth, Dillard, Eckhardt, Joyce, Lawrence, Northrop, Stein,

Webern, Wittgenstein, late Schubert sonatas, and "some Japanese poets and Taoist painters." Always striving for something seemingly unattainable, she described missing in music "a kind of energy release we call generosity, a kind of challenge to a more reckless level of sensitivity in our consciousness.... What I wanted was a kind of total giving of the spirit both in energy and feeling—ultimately the great energy of tenderness." She quoted Basho, as translated by Blyth: "Nothing intimates / In the voice of the cicada / How soon it will die."[69] She claimed to be looking for "a new kind of elegance that did not jeopardize immediacy."

"Pierce Sever," like "aesthetic immediacy" or "terrible freedom," seems to have been a concept representing a key notion of visceral juxtaposition for Dlugoszewski, one that she continually tried to express through her use of metaphors, nature imagery, and borrowings from other writers and artistic attitudes, concluding that "the skill of a composer is to put the whole beautiful process in a ritual of sound that we can hear":

> PIERCE SEVER indicates disciplines of strangeness, great dislocations of constant surprise and kinesthetic recklessness, to keep both the logical mind and the emoting ego from interfering in this arrest-aesthetic experience of intense aliveness that Joyce calls ground of being Quidditas. It is Einstein's definition of energy, "in cosmic terms," an effect that continually eludes our grasp. It is Whitehead's fallacy of misplaced concreteness, correctional seizure, this necessary strangeness to make the universe real.... It is a series of juxtapositional techniques to generate dislocations in order to pierce-protective, linear, naive-realistic callousness of our ears so that we could achieve what Blyth, Basho and Dillard wanted: "to hear for the first time." It is the impossible reckless leaps in dynamic, pitch, timbral shifts, for that swift and sudden quality of recognition found in some Japanese poets. It is Cocteau's "Orpheus" being told to "astonish us," in order to make the universe real. It is Eiseley "trembling before the unexpected." It is Stein knowing that "you have to put some strangeness in a sentence before the noun comes alive."

Dlugoszewski concluded this long essay, and thus her productive yet troubled decade, with a reference to her youth in Michigan, invoking a Japanese poem that "reverberates fear into my childhood": "Detroit," she wrote, "where I lived as a little girl, is full of viaducts and sweeping road-bridges over railroads and highways and the river itself, and I remember when I was about 10 years old having this first experience of PIERCE SEVER with which the Japanese poet touches our hearts: I walk over it alone / In the cold moonlight / The sound of the bridge."

SEVEN

Rage (1980–87)

I am a desert talking to myself.[1]

During the 1980s, Dlugoszewski's life continued to be professionally eventful and privately fraught. Filled with concerts and commissions from venerable institutions like the Library of Congress, The Kitchen, and the Chamber Music Society of Lincoln Center, Dlugoszewski struggled to balance these high-pressure opportunities with her obligations to the needs of her mother in Michigan, whose failing health repeatedly brought her only child back home for long, emotional visits until Jennie/Jolas's death in early 1988. During this decade both old and new friendships thrived—with Jamake Highwater, Lillian Kiesler, Katherine Duke, and John Ransom Phillips, among others—and her letters and poetry written for these friends, along with her extensive diary writings and other spontaneously scribbled "rants" allow some insight into the composer's volcanic state of mind and the creative storms through which she raged, alternately frenzied or exhausted. Some undated handwritten weekly calendars listed mundane details like meal plans ("chow mein," for one), but also labeled entire days as "pure Lucia," perhaps reserving blocks of time when she could think and work without interruption. She continued to align herself with the haiku poets: "For Basho and Lucia life was never deep enough intense enough," she wrote repeatedly.[2] She also indulged her stargazing hobby, clipping "Sky Watch" star charts from the *New York Times* and pasting them into her composition notebooks and "aesthetic diaries" for several years starting around 1984.[3]

AESTHETIC DIARIES: "THE RAGE NECESSARY"

Dlugoszewski's private writings during the 1980s became increasingly manic. Filling page after page with large cursive words scrawled in blue crayon or wax pencil, then circled, underlined, colored over, and further annotated, she recycled words that seemed to obsess her, with "rage" (and "outrage") being at the center of many of these writings: "Rage necessary to ignite passion"; "utter rage other"; "rapt rage stairs that don't fit"; "find the rage necessary"; "your outrage other"; "total rage toward everything and everyone"; "rage pierce waiting to be born"; "your commitment which is rage"; "rage of being"; "shout of rage centering"; and "rage necessary to utterly surpass yourself." She also filled notebook after notebook with messages to herself, existential creative pep talks of a sort: "Lucia you alone / have the responsibility / to fight for your talent / as if no one were listening," she wrote on many occasions. She also spoke of her own genius as an exceptional rarity: "Lucia your genius / your unspeakable matchless unique poetic genius / ... Lucia you: hanging by the sudden intense ears / where the outrageous tear of being / throbs and growls and sings." She assured herself: "Your unspeakable genius has never happened before and will never happen again," though she often amended such sentiments with the bleak lines: "with unflinching sincerity"—and again: "as though no one / was listening."[4]

These agitated sessions of composing and writing were documented in cryptic ways (e.g., "Dec 30, 1980 beautiful sleep worked foggy one candle private secluded 4 AM morning").[5] They appeared alongside descriptions of day-to-day events like cooking dinner for Erick ("sliced up my left index finger cutting bread"), worrying about coop tenants' meetings (thankfully, she reported, "Erick went to the meeting"), and fretting over her work ("anxiety about deadlines").[6] "Fling yourself, Lucia, out of yourself!" she commanded on other occasions, as if frustrated by her own nervous navel-gazing.[7]

Around 1981, Dlugoszewski became obsessed with a particular literary image—"hurler of stars"—from a story by Loren C. Eiseley called "The Star Thrower," which had been included in a collection of autobiographical essays first published in 1969 as *The Unexpected Universe*. The story included the phrase "walks always in desolation, but not in defeat," which Dlugoszewski also adopted as a private mantra during this period. The "star thrower" was a fisherman who threw live starfishes back to sea—thus the "hurler of stars."[8] According to literary scholar Susan Balée, Eiseley was an insomniac who would wake up early and look out into the dark.[9] Dlugoszewski, seemingly an occasional insomniac herself, began to imagine herself as this figure: "The hurler of stars / she walks because she chooses / always in desolation always alone / but never in defeat," as she wrote in her diaries and notebooks dozens of times, while also documenting her own restless wandering through the neighborhoods of Greenwich Village and along the Hudson River.[10]

Thoughts about sleeping, trying to sleep, trying to stay awake, or of being unwillingly awake in the middle of the night permeated her writing during this period. Sometimes her efforts at sleep were frustrating ("trying to sleep after 3 AM"), while at other times her work seems to have flourished after dark. An undated note to Hawkins announced: "Darling—I'm pushing through a very difficult part so I'm going [to] work through the night." Indeed, Dlugoszewski would often work all night long, frequently calling friends at three or four in the morning when she ran into blocks in her composing: "So we would talk her through it, which would take three or four hours, we would spend hours and hours while she was writing *Abyss and Caress*, it was nonstop," conductor Joel Thome recalled.[11] Another eccentricity developed during the early 1980s involved a kind of alternative dating system: A number of entries in October 1981 were dated "October 32" or "October 33," as if she was not ready for the month to end. Similarly, she also often referred in her writings to "extended" days (e.g., "extended Monday 3 AM before dawn").

Dlugoszewski's diaries included a number of writings labeled "credo," featuring unrelated words randomly splattered around a single page of paper: "outrageous / spiritual / refinement / elegance / spiritual knife-edge purity of discipline / swift / sudden / ontological / deep—mystery deep / dark deep / enormous deep / sabi deep / duende deep + vulnerable / emotional / beauty," is just one of many such examples.[12] Another "credo" dated 26 November 1983 described seeing herself from the outside, as "elegant aloof sheer / vulnerable tragic intimate / Lucia standing on a hill looking down." She also frequently characterized herself as a tightrope artist, one who was at once "reckless dangerous [and] elegant."[13]

Starting around May 1984 Dlugoszewski's writings became even more extreme, capitalizing and underlining emphatic phrases like "outrageously startling," "unspeakably extravagant," "wildly sensitive," "utterly poetic," "utterly alive," and "terrible freedom." She often focused on a command: "Show me the face / before you were born." The elusive image of a "cutting wheel" also occupied her imagination with sharp focus, as did the key words she returned to like old friends: duende, quidditas, nageire. In September, she allowed her "intense rage" to begin a relentless "reconquest of self," fixating repeatedly on her desperate query: "Why don't you fight your way out?" Privately tormented, Dlugoszewski struggled to keep her professional life on track.

AMOR ELUSIVE EMPTY AUGUST AND OTHER WORKS

Much of the latter half of 1979 had been consumed by the composition of a large woodwind piece for the Boehm Quintette, which commissioned and premiered the work. Dlugoszewski gave a copy of the completed one-hundred-plus-page score to Jamake Highwater with a handwritten inscription on the title page: "To my dearest, most beloved brother in poetry, with total love and Buzi."[14] Titled *Amor Elusive Empty August*, the quintet was premiered on 11 January 1980 at the Library of Congress.[15] A review published the following day in the *Washington Post* referred to the concert as a "joy" and a "breath of fresh air," and offered praise for Dlugoszewski's "amusing and touching, always arresting" work, and no less than "the centerpiece of the evening": "Her surprising juxtapositions require a certain surrender from the listener but the reward is a journey to realms that offer revelations beyond logic," wrote the *Post* critic.[16]

One of the musicians involved in the premiere of *Amor Elusive Empty August* had a less positive recollection of both the piece and his interactions with Dlugoszewski, recalling that the score seemed unfinished at the time of final rehearsals, even suggesting that she did not seem to understand the instruments for which she was writing.[17] The musicians might have been perplexed by Dlugoszewski's increasingly bizarre ways of describing her compositional intentions. On page 111 of the massive score, for example, she wrote, with an arrow pointing toward one of the piece's final measures, "fresh leap into new territory." Soon after, the clarinetist was instructed to light three matches. The concert hall lights were then to go out, and the piece ended in darkness, with the matches burning out in an ashtray. At the end of the score she wrote two cryptic structural annotations: "sixth curve energy intense arrest transparent" (m. 199) and "seventh curve arrest transparent sever 6" (m. 204). The Boehm Quintette performed *Amor Elusive Empty August* again at the Cooper Union in New York on 1 February 1980.

On 27 and 28 March 1980, Dlugoszewski premiered a piece called *Swift and Naked* at The Kitchen on Broome Street, with soloists David Taylor, Donald Palma, Linda Quan, Chris Finckel, and Lewis Paer, among other musicians.[18] A publicity release included laudatory press excerpts: "One of the most original composers before the public today" (Leighton Kerner, *Village Voice*); "arresting originality, poetical vibrancy, compositional energy, and visceral impact" (Peter G. Davis, *New York Times*); "some of the most unusual and arresting music of our time" (Speight Jenkins, *New York Post*). John Ashbery was quoted as well: "Lucia Dlugoszewski's marvelous music made from and embodying wood, straw, wax, gravel, pebbles and air." Jamake Highwater referred to her "the composer of music too eloquent to be called 'difficult,' too fragile to be called 'bold,' and too significant to be called 'experimental.'"[19]

Dlugoszewski's star was on the rise, but fame remained elusive. After the Koussevitzky prize had been announced in 1980, a critic writing for *High Fidelity* commented on the state of music prizes: "For the first time we gave the Koussevitzky prize to a woman composer, Detroit-born Lucia Dlugoszewski, whom none of us had previously known."[20] The phrase "whom none of us had previously known" must have stung the composer who had been active in public concert life in New York City and elsewhere now for thirty years. Dlugoszewski documented her own reaction to the prize in a letter written years later to Isamu Noguchi: "I seem to be the first woman to have won such an award and I guess this makes me a [sic] 'official art' but you have always loved me when I was a rebel and reckless adventurer and I haven't changed and your sculpture has always been an inspiration to my own composing."[21] The summer after the award was announced, Hawkins wrote to his friend Sallie Wagner of Dlugoszewski's activities:

> She has been working for several months now on a piece for our eight musicians for which Robert Motherwell will do the set. She has had the lovely privilege of working without a deadline, and I think she has been quite happy being able to dig as deeply as she can into new areas. Then, from a bad tooth, she started taking lots of aspirin, and got aspirin gastritis, and poor girl, has been eating boiled chicken and mashed potatoes and apple sauce for two weeks! But she is better, thank heaven.[22]

A few months later, he wrote to Wagner again, seemingly full of compassion for Dlugoszewski's struggles with her work on the Motherwell piece, which had her "in the doldrums." Chalking her mood up to "just existential sadness, I guess," Hawkins speculated that "maybe getting older is just hitting her a little harder right now."[23] Hawkins was now in his early seventies. Dlugoszewski was fifty-six, but most people thought she was just fifty, since she usually listed her birth year as 1931 instead of 1925. It is unclear whether Hawkins knew her true age. An undated diary entry from around this time reveals that she felt troubled, lonely, and alienated, and that she worried "about age + its humiliations."

AN UNREALIZED "BREAKTHROUGH":
WILDERNESS ELEGANT TILT

In an eight-page handwritten letter to Jamake Highwater in the early 1980s, Dlugoszewski praised his new book *The Primal Mind*, and mused on the state of culture and criticism, in particular, "the devastating and destructive attitudes" of dance critics, whom she referred to in no uncertain terms as "fascists." Her scoffing included the recent popularity of minimalism in both composition and choreography. From the safety of a private letter, she allowed herself to rant, not only about the politics of President Ronald Reagan, whom she saw as destroying a robust infrastructure for support of the arts, but also what she perceived as the "vulgarity" of recent trends in music and dance—indeed "one of the frightening illnesses of our time"—specifically, the work of composers Philip Glass and Steve Reich, and choreographers Trisha Brown and Laura Dean, whose work she considered to be "watered down Merce," and who she collectively referred to as "the Soho sophists."[24]

In late 1981 Dlugoszewski wrote to Highwater about her and Hawkins's financial troubles, which she called "the worst financial setbacks in our history."[25] Blaming "the Reagan cutbacks to the arts" and the money they lost on the recent premiere of Hawkins's piece *Heyoka* (with a score by Ross Lee Finney), despite the fact that the event sold out, she admitted feeling utterly defeated.[26] Aside from practical problems, like the threat of her electricity being shut off except for an emergency loan from a friend, Dlugoszewski revealed to Highwater that she had put her own work on hold for several months while supporting the preparations for Hawkins's performance. Affected by his dark mood—"a terrible but understandable anger"—she struggled with the fact that "such anger doesn't make it easy to live with him and certainly not the best climate for creativity." (A friend who knew the couple well during this period described their relationship as intense, codependent, and volatile, with Dlugoszewski constantly embattled and embittered by Hawkins's self-involved irritability.) For three weeks that September, she confessed to Highwater, "I just fell apart but you will be proud of me to know that somehow I did pull myself together and kept on working on the piece and this is the first time I didn't give up at such a time on my own things." She credited Highwater with "understanding and support," which gave her much needed "courage and confidence" she could not get from Hawkins.

Dlugoszewski considered the piece she struggled to write during this time, titled *Wilderness Elegant Tilt*, to be a "breakthrough" piece: "The one I've been looking for for *ten years*," she wrote. But the time she lost in September due to Hawkins's depression cost her the performance, as the Lincoln Center schedule decided to push the premiere out to the following year—after she had delivered the score on 15 November. "The day they told me about the postponement," she wrote to Highwater,

> I was so blue I just came home alone and lay down and began to read *The Primal Mind* because my struggle with my breakthrough and my piece is all that you are so eloquently talking about in *The Primal Mind* and, you know, after reading in it a couple hours I was healed and I just love my piece and how I did it this way. You know and I know that I could have delivered *a* piece to them, but not *the* piece and at this time in my life, just a performance no longer means so much. It needs to be a performance of course, but a performance that's the fulfillment of a courageous and amazing search and I'm happy to say *Wilderness Elegant Tilt* is finally just that.[27]

A brief article titled "Chamber Music Society Postpones *Wilderness*," published in the *New York Times* three days after this letter was written, announced: "The premiere of Lucia Dlugoszewski's *Wilderness Elegant Tilt*, scheduled for the next trio of concerts by the Chamber Music Society of Lincoln Center, has been postponed to next season because the score is unfinished."[28] *Wilderness Elegant Tilt* was replaced on the program by a piece by Benjamin Britten. There is no evidence that Dlugoszewski's "breakthrough" piece was ever performed—or, perhaps, even completed.

Dlugoszewski soon turned her attention to a new piece. *Cicada Terrible Freedom*, for two violins, flute, bass trombone, cello, and contrabass, which received an incomplete performance at Merkin Concert Hall before it was premiered in full at Carnegie Recital Hall in the spring of 1982. The program for the latter concert, held on 31 May 1982 and conducted by Braxton Blake, listed the sections of the piece as "hearings" to be heard without pause:

Hearing I
    ending with swift and naked transparency
    first violin solo
Hearing II
    ending with seizure of unfixed cello solo
    expanding into contrabass quidditas solo
Hearing III
    ending with whisper bass trombone solo
    expanding into total whisper

> Hearing IV
> ending grace reckless second violin solo
> followed by passionate seizure of unfixed bass trombone solo
> Hearing V
> ending in passionate grace reckless flute solo, followed by dark transparency cello and bass trombone duo, followed by pure silence expanding to second pure silence

During the Carnegie Hall performance, the piece was repeated after the intermission. Reviewing the concert for the *Village Voice* some months later, Leighton Kerner wrote of the atonal lyricism and structural cohesion of Dlugoszewski's music, despite a "spontaneous sounding" quality: "The combination of free-form appearance and firm compositional plan is especially striking in this big, substantial (more than half-hour) piece," which, he explained, was "built on a succession of gradual intensifications followed by sudden drops in dynamics, instrumental densities, and pitches, [with] a wider structure that dramatically varies the five movements."[29]

Perhaps frustrated by the unpredictable demands and non-lucrative results of composition as a vocation, in 1982, Dlugoszewski wrote a proposal for a class she tentatively titled "Intensive Aesthetic Seminar in Music and Dance—Goals for Composers and Choreographers." For those people familiar with Dlugoszewski's influences, inspirations, and aims, this proposal would have read like an oddly consistent affirmation of her beliefs, albeit one rife with run-on sentences:

> In terms of content the absolute goal is aliveness—a death-throwing, death shedding, pierce-waiting-to-be-born ritual of immediacy. It is passionate commitment to the aesthetic dimension. James Joyce's "Quidditas," Loren Eiseley's "Unexpected Universe" or the Buddhists' "Suchness." It presupposes courage acceptance of necessary new composing and performing disciplines of kinesthetic recklessness and great disclosures of constant surprise (leaping for the flexibility of the soul) in terms of energy, mystery, and stillness (the aesthetic dimension is most deeply ritualized from a kinesthetic base).
>
> In terms of psychology the inspiration is from an Apache-friend—a new development that added to the poetic immediacy of my given feminine sensibility that recklessness of spirit and masculine energy and courage that gave my musical consciousness an androgynous totality that every artist hungers for in terms of the largest possible vision.... This is not the safe meditation-chanting of withdrawal from the painful joy of the world, but at the very center of the dangerous and tragic universe—the pierce-sever, clear, defiant shout into the very core of the beauty and terror of reality. What I want is

both the singing of my own courage and the sublime singing of the ground of being at the same time.

In terms of structure and form the goal is an alternative elegance, a new non-logical elegance which is neither predictable continuity nor chaotic discontinuity. It has two points of reference: I. Einstein's definition of energy ("in cosmic terms an effect whose cause eludes us completely"); and II. the almost severed, inexplicably continuous long line of the late Schubert Sonatas—a kind of elusive courage for the delicacies of daring constructions.[30]

As she neared age sixty, Dlugoszewski's eccentricity and self-consciousness swelled—both in her private writings and in her descriptions of her compositions and her creative process. Following the uninhibited ramblings of her essay on *Pierce Sever*, her writing now gained a sense of exhausting urgency, and she seemed obsessively driven to explain her ideas.

In August 1983, she wrote an extensive program note for a new duo—bass trombone and timbre piano—called *Duende Newfallen*.[31] After expounding on her interest in the Spanish word *duende*—which she quoted poet Miguel de Unamuno as having defined as "the tragic sense of life," though the term is more frequently associated with Federico García Lorca and his 1933 Buenos Aires lecture titled *"Juego y teoría del duende"* ("Theory and Play of the Duende")—she went on to list "the 4 Immediacies deeply concerning me now":

Quidditas: the aesthetic decision;
Newfallen: the elegant decision;
Amor: the ethical decision (the preparation for immediacy through the nakedness, stillness, and radiance of feminine sexuality);
Duende: the courage decision (the shouting, tragic, fragile, momentary, energy-creative leap out of the bleak, permanently asleep, inanimate universe)

Ever concerned with her music's expression of "the here-and-now," or "being in the moment," she insisted on avoiding both "nostalgia" and "future paradises." She explained her rejection of a common music-historical dichotomy: "In terms of 'duende' and aesthetic immediacy the goal was to present two alternatives to general developments of form and content: an alternative to the Classical, essentially, logical canon of form and elegance and the alternative to the Romantic, emotional, past-future, ego-oriented quality of feeling." She further expanded her descriptions of the "4 Immediacies," somewhat redundantly, in a long manifesto-cum-program note that reiterated implications of the piece title's key words and their connections to Basho, Blyth, Eiseley, Joyce, Northrop, Wittgenstein, the Polish Christmas Eve ritual of Wigilia ("the pierce-waiting-to-be-born"), and other usual suspects. The note ended with a list of "What I want now." The fifth and last item on the list desired "delicacy of feminine sexuality." A few months after she wrote this *Duende Newfallen* manifesto, André Bernard interviewed her on the radio station WNYC, during which, feisty and opinionated, she talked about Cage's "dedication to discontinuity." She disapproved of it, claiming, "Right now, what I'm most interested in, is vulnerability, on the one hand, and elegance on the other."[32]

Dlugoszewski wrote *Duende Newfallen* for trombonist David Taylor, whom she first met in the late 1960s through their mutual friendship with Gerard Schwarz. In 1983 she wrote another duo for David Taylor and herself, for bass trombone and timbre piano, which she called *Duende Quidditas*. In notes for a recording made in 1996, she wrote: "Shattering the clichés of the instrument and the clichés of notation—the remaining hugeness strangely understood—if it is dark enough, can be called *duende*." In his own liner notes for the recording, Taylor wrote that when he first encountered the score of *Duende Quidditas*, he was frightened of the notation's "incredible intensity, density, and velocity." The composer also described the piece in dynamic yet cryptic terms: "leaping for the flexibility of the soul—dangerous but alive." Further, she wrote that the piece presupposed "a wild extravagant Universe of swift time, swift dynamics, and even swifter change with simultaneously another very different imperative—the depth lived—as if no one were listening—suchness, *Quidditas*, of each unique, careful sound being heard, for the first time including even the *Quidditas* of a match being struck and blown out and another struck again and burning itself to the end."[33]

EXILE IN MICHIGAN (1985–87)

In March 1985 Dlugoszewski spent time at her mother's house at 425 Morningside Drive in Pontiac, Michigan, as she did over the next few years due to her mother's declining health. Several undated notes include personal details about Dlugoszewski's daily schedule—including when to sleep, put on makeup, cook, shop, make her bed, exercise, brush her teeth, bathe, and so on—as well as frequent mentions of the "west private room" where she would try to work, and her hopes that her mother (Jolas) and stepfather (Floran) would go to bed early so she could compose without being disturbed. In her many letters to Hawkins, she meticulously described the weather, her domestic errands, and her efforts to keep up the spirits of Floran and her mother by watching television and listening to music: "That clapping together to the music is one of the most healing things people can do for the darkness of the soul," she concluded, while also admitting to her own despair and sleepless nights. (Two days later she would write: "At a terrible moment yesterday when both Floran and my mother were in a terrible mood, I desperately began to sing songs from World War I when they both were young and suddenly they both joined me singing and everything got a little better. *I see now what song is*!!!")[34] Thanking Hawkins for a star chart he had sent, she asked him to also send some stamps: "It's so awkward to get anything here," she complained, due to the suburban location of her mother's house.[35]

Dlugoszewski also wrote about the physical beauty of where she was, something she felt no one around her noticed: "The stars, the weather, the trees, the birds, the lake, the swamp water, the returning flying geese, this is what I wanted so much in my childhood but we lived in Detroit slums and this kind of nature only came to my parents after I left for New York."[36] At the time, Jolas's eyesight was failing, and Dlugoszewski was deeply saddened by the ways this restricted her mother's aesthetic experience of nature. Sounding like any grown woman stuck at home with her parents instead of at home with her partner—the "banished and exiled composer," as she started calling herself—she admitted to Hawkins: "I miss my life with you!"[37] (Around the same time, she wrote to her "dearest poetic blood brother" Jamake Highwater that she felt "like those exiled Soviet dissidents in Siberia.") Two days later she described "a nightmare day psychologically," but also proclaimed that she was determined to "take every experience in one's life, no matter how disastrous and convert it into a creative act," as inspired by her "meditating" on Sartre.[38] Spending as much time outdoors as the late winter weather would allow, she described her joy at finding pussy willows in the snow in the woods while walking the family dog.[39] A few days later she described to Hawkins her four-mile "hike" to the supermarket, and her avian observances along the way, including a bare tree full of brightly colored cedar waxwings. The sight inspired her: "It gives energy to fight the despair and to remember that something exists so beautiful and [that if] I can love the beauty of their existence I must still be a composer!"[40]

In letters to Highwater, Dlugoszewski also lamented the "sadness and frustration" of her exile, and complained about her "mother's husband's family and the rest of the populace around here," which she characterized as "cultural devastation": "They seem to me the very worst of Anglo-Saxon Protestant America," she wrote.[41] Sneering at the industry her father had worked in, and simultaneously apologizing for her sarcasm, she described the men and women of her environment:

> I have never seen more arrogantly confident machoism than in automobile mechanics. I think it's because their engineering and mechanical minds are so secure in the solution they command when they get their head under the hood. For the engineer, the world is so beautifully confidently made up of utterly solvable problems. No ambiguities, no paradoxes, no confusions, no dangerous subtleties. So their walk reads very clear body language. In their coveralls they smugly swagger forward leading with the cock. And the girls have shelves and shelves of curlers, hair dye, dryers, shampoo, conditioners, etc. at the shopping malls and when they aren't working they are busy with their hair hours a day. The result is that they all look like "Barbie Dolls" listening to Jimmy Swaggart. After all, they have to catch and marry one of these oafs, . . . and these obtuse males truly have a "Barbie doll" for a brain.

She described being viewed as an oddity by the locals because of her insistence on walking the four miles to the grocery store—"of course physically hard because there is lots of deep snow and ice and vicious traffic on the highway"—rather than "beg a ride from my mother's husband's family or pick up a ride from weird looking men in cars on the road." "Naturally, both unacceptable options," she added: "This, a country where nobody walks—and here is this communist walking!" Still, she found deep beauty and wonder in her environs in the midst of her emotional upheaval:

> Somehow in Michigan, because it is wetland country, there still remains a kind of nature aesthetic closest to my heart. The wetlands maintain a kind of mysterious rawness that make an ambience of wilderness and Quidditas and suchness which is aesthetically closest to my heart. My father chose the site for their house so that the big living room window faces a swamp forest. This was considered very foolish by contractors but he thought it was beautiful. Such subversive communist thought! Now that swamp woods *still* remains although realtors have built all around it because swamps still defy our technology. The swamp is still home for all birds, pheasants badgers, woodchucks raccoons rabbits snakes and even deer and these wasps around here don't even shoot them here anymore because there are houses and children all around. This swamp woods is my private medicine. When my mother and her husband go to bed at 6 p.m. and before they wake up at 7 a.m., when I deal with all their traumas, I keep my private daily and nightly aesthetic meditations

for health and sanity. I not only feel terrible sadness for my mother and utter repulsion for the culture around me but I have such a rage inside that I am not composing and these three negative emotions make a wild stew of explosive feeling inside me.

She also complained about constant disturbances to her work: "My mother even wakes up several times a night to 'check if I'm still here,' so, with all my good intentions of trying to compose at night, I'm always interrupted."[42]

In February 1986, Dlugoszewski was back in Michigan, writing again to Hawkins of the wilderness and swampy wetlands, the fog, snow, mud, and, of course, the night sky.[43] She again described herself as "the exiled composer in outer Siberia Michigan," adding as an afterthought in parentheses: "aesthetically geographically Siberia is also probably breathtaking."[44] The clipping of star charts continued; in mid-March 1986 she carefully followed the path of Halley's comet.

Back in New York in late winter 1986, between 6:30 p.m. on March 24 at Washington Square Park and midnight on March 25 at the Morton Pier, Dlugoszewski wrote a series of at least eight poems and/or birthday notes for her "sweetest," "adorable," "dearest" friend Lillian Kiesler (b. 26 March 1911), many of which were accompanied by graphic realizations of the poems themselves, and whose poetic imagery centered around the "dog star" Sirius.[45] The poems for Kiesler display a fiery ecstasy typical of Dlugoszewski's nocturnal writing at this time.

For several weeks late in 1986, including the Thanksgiving and Christmas holidays, the now sixty-one-year-old Dlugoszewski again lived in Michigan, sequestered at home with her mother ("my fragile troubling Jolas") and stepfather Floran ("the house vibrates with my father," she mourned for Czesio). She sought out the sanctity of her "west room fortress" where she would light candles, display flowers (zinnias, carnations, chrysanthemums, white roses), watch the morning birds (cardinals, chickadees), contemplate the winter sky and stars outside her window, and write of her loneliness and despair: "the anxieties of aging / + the terror of memory loss / in this strange / open / anxious night," she fretted. Embracing the disruption of her insomnia, she marveled at the movement of specific stars, and often wandered outside for a better look:

> suddenly deliciously secretly
> went out to the backyard
> barefoot on the cold dew grass

> and saw an incredible crystal sky
> orion + the winter triangle
> utterly glittering
> in the east south
> sirius like the wildest
> most recklessly
> vulnerable
> drop of utter
> water
> and the big dipper in the north
> + Jupiter setting west
> and a wild scatter of stars
> that I don't quite know

She wrote of daily events, like shopping at the supermarket, watching the sunsets, the stress of being around her mother and stepfather, and the comforting refuge of her private room. At 1 a.m. on 8 December 1986, her despair reached a peak: "In all this emotional isolation / + trauma anguish / + even crying inconsolably / I have tried to do everything right / all my life never to hurt anyone / why is God punishing me!"

On 21 December, Hawkins joined her in Michigan; Dlugoszewski continued her nightly wanderings while he slept. Early in the morning on 23 December, she wrote in her notebook of a "terrible traumatic night" spent with her mother, apparently talking about "wrenching memories" from her childhood: "I am in limbo between Jolas-Lucia childhood / + Lucia artist autonomous / + who I am this / strange troubled / night morning?!," she wrote in the family's living room at 4:00 a.m., sitting in front of the Christmas tree while Hawkins slept in her room. On Christmas Eve (*Wigilia*) she woke before the rest of the household, writing at 7:45 a.m. of her mother's diagnosis of deteriorating retinas and her need for an "old fashioned cataract operation," a situation Dlugoszewski found devastating. A half hour later, with Hawkins, Jolas, and Floran still sleeping through the austere winter gloom, she made another diary entry, this time allowing her mind to drift back to her own work: "1st insight into motherwell orchestra," she wrote. A few days later, she would write of a "troubled identity crisis," despairingly wondering "who am I + where is the composer?"[46]

Back in New York soon after Christmas, Dlugoszewski and Hawkins went to see a movie called *The Mission* (1986), starring Robert de Niro and Jeremy Irons, which she described as a "wrenching exquisite deep portrayal of human universal culture hell" peopled by "beautiful aesthetic Indians / idealists

Jesuit / + colonialism + commercialism."⁴⁷ On the last day of the year 1986, she described "walking home after buying white roses and / expensive Moet champagne / for greeting New Year with / my beloved Erick"; the following morning, she met the new year with an affirmation: "Lucia you alone are reckless + dangerous / enough to confer being on some measure of existence [. . .] Lucia you alone / have the terrible courage / to know what beauty is."

By the end of January 1987, Dlugoszewski was back at her mother's house, where she wrote of the "clouded desolate Michigan dawn" while musing on Motherwell ("huge") and de Kooning ("rage + terrible freedom") as metaphors for different manifestations of her own creativity.⁴⁸ Struggling to maintain a sense of self, she came up with a "new plan for morning work / daily and nightly schedule / for Lucia somehow re conquest of self": healthy food (herbal tea, bananas, oatmeal, vitamin B), personal hygiene, shopping, cooking, tidying her west room, and time for her own work were listed in a kind of schedule intended to give her life-in-exile a semblance of intentional structure. Struggling to find undisturbed work time, she attempted to wake herself up at 3 or 4 a.m. for several hours of "deep pristine poetics." She stayed busy keeping the household well supplied and fixing up minor things. But "career anxieties" bothered her: at 3:00 a.m. on the morning of 31 January, she wrote an ambitious list of people she intended to reach out to, including "Virgil, Thome, Schuller, Kerner, Hanahan [Henahan], Hughes, Davis, Porter, B. Holland, Rockwell, Carter, Foss, Schuman, Babbitt, Solberger [Sollberger], Ashbery, Carlton, J. Smith." Dlugoszewski also began writing to herself "in sudden fierce search of self."⁴⁹ Often these comments began with some variation of "Lucia you alone," as in the frequently appearing statement: "Lucia only you have the responsibility to fight for your talent."⁵⁰ As she traveled from Michigan to New York and back again, she pined for her short visits in her own home in the West Village. Back at her mother's house in June of 1987, she made lists of things to buy (bowls, colander, aprons, bedspread, curtains) and things to fix (stove, floor, washing machine, locks on front door). At the end of September, Dlugoszewski sat desolately in an airplane at Newark airport, waiting for the weather to clear in Detroit so she could fly back to Michigan yet again.⁵¹

In December 1987, Hawkins went to Florida, and Dlugoszewski stayed in New York alone. In a notebook labeled "Radical Quidditas Dewtear Duende heartstopping rage harsh," she wrote extensively of her activities during his absence: taking "relaxing pills," eating soup, watching the stars, and staying up too late. Her handwriting became erratic, as she wandered between different parts of their apartments: "east house," "south house," and "south kitchen." Her "aesthetic diary" notebooks of December 1987 were full of "creative rage of being," "disparate stairway unsupported," "heart-stopping rage hush most ferocious," and "bone austere immediacy of dawn." She even "dated" individual sheets of paper, covered with the scrawling word cycles and bundled collections of writings, compulsively revolving around particular words, as "20th rage dawn" or "3rd rage" or "10th rage," and so on. Dlugoszewski's financial difficulties at the time might have contributed to her general state of rage and anxiety. Her work as a composer brought in almost no money at all. In December 1987, she received a royalty statement from Margun, Gunther Schuller's publishing company: For the trumpet solo *Space Is a Diamond*, she earned a total royalty of $7.20 (nine copies sold) and for *Angels of the Inmost Heaven* she earned royalties of $3.00 (one copy sold). Her household expenses at the time, outlined on budget lists, included rent, telephone, doctors, professional expenses, makeup and drugstore items, dry cleaning, publicity, and music equipment. Considerable resources must also have been spent on the constant trips back and forth to Michigan.

In an interview conducted in the early 1990s, Dlugoszewski reflected on how her ongoing family situation in Michigan had interrupted her thriving career in the 1970s and 1980s:

> I have a feeling that if both my parents hadn't fallen apart then with mortal illness, it would have been a wonderful period for me. I would have just gone on and on and on. But it was a very hard, tragic hiatus. I wasn't going to lock them away somewhere. I was the only child, and my father died in '75 and my mother in '88. That whole interval was very hard, especially from '81 to '88. I was just taking care of her because I loved her, I loved the poetry she gave me. When I was a baby, she went out in a snowstorm with a dish to show me the fun of snow. She was my haiku poet friend. I think a man might have just walked away from a responsibility like that, probably, because his career would be first, but I couldn't turn my back on my haiku friend of years.[52]

A diary entry Dlugoszewski made in a 1979 composition book included a passage that similarly revealed her ongoing inner struggle between personal ties and professional ambition: "Lucia / torn apart agony. . . . This torn apart / between / equivalent / loving + compassionate / + self realizing needs." Caught between the obligations of her relationships and the relentless call of her creativity, the composer continued to struggle with feelings of isolation in the decades to come: "I am a desert talking to myself," she admitted in one of her most anguished, private expressions of loneliness.

EIGHT

Losses (1988–2000)

No artist should be afraid to die alone.[1]

JENNIE (JOLAS) DLUGOSZEWSKI ORVIS, Dlugoszewski's mother, died at the age of eighty-four in the Pontiac Osteopathic Hospital on 1 March 1988. Handwritten notes by Dlugoszewski in preparation for the memorial service, held four days later, featured a familiar hymn, perhaps one of her mother's favorites, and perhaps one that Dlugoszewski sang at the memorial ("Jesus loves me / This I know / For the Bible tells me so").[2] Perhaps it was also a hymn Dlugoszewski used to sing with her mother as a girl; it is one of the few instances of Christian religious views to be found in all of Dlugoszewski's papers, though there are indications in some of Dlugoszewski's writings that her mother was a churchgoer, and the family may have attended St. Hyacinth Roman Catholic church in East Detroit's "Poletown" when she was a child.

At 4:00 a.m. on the morning of Jennie's memorial service, Dlugoszewski wrote a note to herself by hand: "morningside west wide room / of Jolas's emptyness / oh Jolas / oh Jolas / can you realize how much . . . I miss you." Months later, she wrote of "trying to heal Jolas' terrible degradation of dying," adding: "+ in search of myself again."[3] Dlugoszewski also wrote about her father, drawing again on her favorite imagery from Eiseley: "Czesio Hurler of stars / He walked because / he alone chose / always in desolation / never in defeat."[4] On the one-year anniversary of her mother's death, the emotionally exhausted daughter wrote: "I never stop mourning." Dlugoszewski's mother's will, which had been signed in 1975, designated "Lucille Ruth Dlugoszewski Hawkins" as her sole heir. She designated her son-in-law, Erick Hawkins, as a second sole heir if Lucille pre-deceased him, even though Jennie was still married at the time to her second husband, Floran Orvis. At the time of her death, Jennie owned the house at 425 Morningside Drive in Pontiac.[5]

Several months after Dlugoszewski's mother's death, a feature article published in the *New York Times* spotlighted "The Composer Who Energizes the Erick Hawkins Dancers."[6] Dance critic Jennifer Dunning described Dlugoszewski as "small, round and breathlessly voluble, given equally to laughter and tears as she talks of Mr. Hawkins's work and of her own music, which has gained her distinction as a highly original avant-garde composer." The article also quoted Dlugoszewski as saying that from 1952 until 1972, most of her compositional work had been for Hawkins's choreography, before she started to enjoy more support through orchestral commissions.

In the early 1990s, Dlugoszewski began trying to put her career back on track. *Radical Quidditas for an Unborn Baby*, a forty-minute solo percussion work written for percussionist William Trigg (and in honor of Hawkins Company dancer Katherine Duke, who was pregnant at the time), was premiered on 26 June 1991 at a New Music Consort concert at Symphony Space.[7] Reviewing the performance for the *New York Times*, music critic James R. Oestreich complained that Dlugoszewski's piece "got the concert off to a slow, agonizing start." Her cryptic title and ornate program notes did not help Oestreich from feeling that the piece was like "a charmless Young Unperson's Guide to the Percussion Section," while Trigg's virtuosic performance of flogging, scraping, bowing, and shaking "a stageful of instruments," amounted to "precious little musical purpose." Oestreich added: "It was left to the other composers to show how real music could be made with so formidable an arsenal."[8]

Three months later, The University of the Arts and The Native Land Foundation presented "Festival Mythos" featuring "Suchness Concert Otherness Concert," billed as "World Premieres of Three Works by Lucia Dlugoszewski Dedicated to Jamake Highwater." The concert consisted of three pieces: *Otherness Narrow Concert (Radical Narrowness Concert Other)*; *Suchness Concert (8 Clear Places)*; and *Radical Otherness Concert*.[9] During this period Dlugoszewski also appears to have devoted significant energy to a piece called *Radical, Strange, Quidditas, Dew Tear, Duende*, which does not appear to have ever been completed or performed.[10] In 1993, Dlugoszewski referred to *Radical Quidditas for an Unborn Baby* as "the first big premiere" she had had in some ten years.[11]

Though she increasingly sought out undisturbed time close to nature—a diary entry indicates that she spent her sixty-third birthday at artist John Ransom Phillips's country home in upstate New York, a place she would visit frequently in the years to come—an article written for *Ballet Review* in 1993 shows that Dlugoszewski also cherished her experiences in her urban neighborhood, which continued to be a source of inspiration:

> I live on the top tenth floor in a studio with two east windows flung open to dawn where at 5 A.M. in late August the high wild throb of Sirius tosses an unknown horizon. My studio is on Eleventh Street and I keep walking the seven blocks to the Hudson River when it ends, where the evening star and the passionate mortal voices of the cicadas dominate the season in which this music is composed. This high wild throb of the evening star, vulnerable as an unclosed wound and recklessly, exquisitely unshed—! And I used to walk home with tear-stabbed feet. On the most west Eleventh Street edge of the river in that intense crystal lense [sic] of twilight, a composer can easily and uneasily ask: what is so perilously real, hanging by the sudden intense ears where the outrageous tear of being throbs and growls and sings.[12]

That year, Dlugoszewski and Hawkins completed what would be their last collaboration, a piece for eleven dancers titled *Each Time You Carry Me This Way*, accompanied by Dlugoszewski's chamber ensemble score titled *Radical Narrowness Concert* (flute/piccolo; clarinet/bass clarinet; trumpet; trombone; violin; bass; percussion).[13] The printed score displays polyphonic melodic writing, extended techniques (string players using thimbles on the strings, a technique she used in several pieces), and some graphic notation, indicating wide-ranging tremolos and glissandi. A program note for the piece, which premiered at the Joyce Theater on 23 February 1993, acknowledged several sponsors, including Meet the Composer/Choreographer Project, a national program funded by the Ford Foundation and the Pew Charitable Trusts, while also giving "special thanks to John R. Phillips for his unending support on every level. The aesthetic of this music, begun in his barn in Columbia County, New York, became the basis of his one-man show of new paintings, which opened February 16 at the Paulina Rieloff Gallery." (Special thanks was also given to Renate Ponsold Motherwell, Robert Motherwell's wife.) Artist and writer John Ransom Phillips met Dlugoszewski and Hawkins in the mid-to-late 1980s; they became friends, and eventually he served on the Board of the Erick Hawkins Dance Company, and provided financial support to the production of *Each Time You Carry Me This Way*.

In October of 1994, Dlugoszewski traveled with Hawkins by train to Washington, D.C., where he received the National Medal of Honor, a National Endowment for the Arts award, from President Bill Clinton during a ceremony on the South Lawn of the White House. According to Phillips,

Mikhail Baryshnikov had nominated Hawkins for the award.[14] (Hawkins had been honored occasionally with other awards, such as an honorary degree of Doctor of Fine Arts from Western Michigan University, conferred on 23 April 1983; in June 1988 Hawkins won the Scripps American Dance Festival Award, which came with a check for $25,000.)[15] Other recipients of the National Medal of Honor that year included Harry Belafonte, Dave Brubeck, Julie Harris, Pete Seeger, Celia Cruz, and another accomplished dancer: Gene Kelly. A photograph published in *Ballet Review* in the fall of 1996 showed an obviously delighted Dlugoszewski meeting President Clinton, with a smiling Hawkins looking on in the background. She would later convey happy memories of "dancing the two-step in the White House ballroom along with Bill and Hillary Clinton."[16] Returning from Washington to New York via Penn Station, the pair walked home with their luggage to their building at 15 East 11th Street in order to save money on a cab: their poverty at the time was dire.[17] During Hawkins's memorial service just a few weeks later, Dlugoszewski would speak about the choreographer's fear that the National Medal of Honor would be taken back if it was discovered that he owed income tax. "You see, that's the artist's life," Dlugoszewski conceded.[18]

Erick Hawkins's health had been poor for several years—following a stroke in 1988 he had undergone a series of CT scans and X-rays for various medical conditions between that time and 1993. A little over a month after the Washington trip, Hawkins died at Lenox Hill Hospital, on 23 November 1994, at the age of eighty-five.[19] A few weeks later, Dlugoszewski wrote a draft of a letter to Anna Kisselgoff, dance writer for the *New York Times*, explaining the circumstances of Hawkins's death, and its effect on her own emotional state. "I'm the one that somehow died with him and the pain of it seems to be destroying me day after day," she wrote:

> On Nov. 21 he miraculously survived his heart attack with complete recovery.... They moved him out of cardiac emergency into an ordinary hospital room with everybody being optimistic about his recovery and on Nov. 22 he made me bring your [Hannukah gift book] to the hospital... and the very next day he died at 1:45 p.m. No one expected this because the prostate cancer causing his death was of a rapid undiagnosable kind in his right [kidney?] that no CAT scan or blood test could detect, only the autopsy revealed this.[20]

A few weeks after Hawkins's death, on 5 December 1994, Dlugoszewski's community celebrated "The Life and Career of Erick Hawkins, 1909–1994," at a memorial event held at the place they had performed most frequently in recent years, the Joyce Theater. A small army of devoted friends and collaborators spoke, including (in this order) Dlugoszewski, Ralph Dorazio, Cora Cahan, Francis Mason, Charles Reinhart, Nancy Meehan, Lillian Kiesler, Jean Erdman, Randy Howard, David Briskin, John Ransom Phillips, Katherine Duke, Mariko Tanabe, Catherine Tharin, Kathy Ortiz, Michael Moses, Ralph Lee, and Robert Engstrom. Dlugoszewski also offered "final remarks." A documentary film by Phyllis Oyama called "Erick Hawkins: Poet of Modern Dance" was shown. Dlugoszewski's remarks offered the startling revelation that the two had been married, a fact unknown to many people closest to them. Her comments characterized Hawkins as "genuinely a strange man, this quintessential American." Professing that this was "the first time I have publicly faced the world as his wife," she claimed that "he was the most beautiful man I ever knew / He was the sexiest man I ever knew / He was the most gloriously reckless man I ever knew, in his work, in his beautiful mind, in his heart / And I loved him more than my own life." *Ballet Review* magazine later published two features that included transcriptions of many of the eulogies offered during the memorial.[21] Though unable to attend Hawkins's memorial service, Helen and Elliott Carter sent written condolences to Dlugoszewski, in which they acknowledged her place in Hawkins's life and work: "This must have been such a severe blow to you who were so important to him artistically with all your remarkable scores for his works and for your great personal devotion to him especially during his last difficult years."[22]

Dlugoszewski spent her first Christmas without Hawkins at John Ransom Phillips's Columbia County country home.[23] Dlugoszewski and Hawkins had been visiting Phillips's upstate New York property in Old Chatham since at least 1991, when she first came to use his large, empty, rat-and-bat-infested barn as a makeshift studio. They also spent some of Hawkins's periods of illness there. In response to watching Dlugoszewski work in his dilapidated outbuilding, Phillips created a series of watercolors that responded to her creative process. Working in the barn, "she placed tree branches here, bales of hay there, and tacked poems and fragments all over the walls. . . . Lucy kept alternating her surroundings and came back and wrote the music. Rats gnawed at the papers plastering the walls," described art historian Barbara MacAdam, who wrote the catalog essay for Phillip's series called "Lucy in the Barn."[24] Phillips similarly described Dlugoszewski's activities in the barn in a letter to friends: "She began by creating an environment in the barn:

branches of trees, flowers, stones, rearranged hay—making it a sort of magic place."²⁵

In the months and years to come, Dlugoszewski continued writing graphic poetry, and scribbling obsessively in the middle of the night, always noting the time of her writing: "after 11 p.m."; "3 a.m."; or "6:30 a.m." She seems to have kept track of when she slept—mostly short naps and then long periods of work—and these pages, often labeled "pure Lucia," were letters to herself, similar to her letters to her parents when she was young, referring to herself in the third person. Now, in Hawkins's absence, she wrote to herself about her own grief, and about her own self-confirmed power: "Lucia your fierce reckless genius / your unspeakable unique poetic genius / your gigantic frightened poetic genius / your outrage other that throbs and growls," she wrote in a notebook on 16 April 1995. Less than a month later, Dlugoszewski's lifelong friend Mary Norton Dorazio died, on 12 May 1995.

Despite these private rants, Dlugoszewski managed to function competently in more public ways. In a glowing letter of recommendation for Joel Thome—"an artist, very impressive in both insight and originality"—she allowed her professionalism to shine. Written by hand in careful and elegant cursive, the clarity of this letter contrasted starkly with the uninhibited private scribblings of late-night "pure Lucia":

> What makes Joel Thome such an unusual artist is the uniqueness and immediacy of his interpretations. Perhaps it is because he is a composer as well as a conductor that he has this capacity to bring to his performances a special insight into the creative process at that exciting point when the music first came into being, be it 200 years ago or yesterday. As a result, his performances are unmatched in a particular vitality of creativity which is probably what is most important about any music whether it be Bach or Boulez or Beethoven or Strawinsky [sic].²⁶

Thome was appointed conductor of the Erick Hawkins Theater Orchestra six months later.

After forty-three years of life with Hawkins, Dlugoszewski now had to find her way through the world completely on her own: "For the first time in my reckless aesthetically adventurous life I'm as helpless and weak and totally vulnerable as a baby," she wrote to Kisselgoff.²⁷ Dlugoszewski found her way in part by embracing the stewardship of the Erick Hawkins Dance Company, which consumed much of her energy until the end of her own life, just over five years later.

Fairly quickly after Hawkins's death, Dlugoszewski became even more involved in managing the Erick Hawkins Dance Company, with the devoted assistance of former dancers Gloria McClean and Cynthia Reynolds. Eleanor Hovda recalled that "[Dlugoszewski] became more and more involved in the choreography, and she was even more involved with the company than she had been before, because now she was doing all of it."[28] During the summer of 1995, just after her seventieth birthday, Dlugoszewski was entrenched in "composing mode," according to David Guion of the Company, who wrote to Baryshnikov of her progress on the score for *Journey of a Poet*, a piece choreographed by Hawkins that would be danced in its premiere by Baryshnikov himself.[29] Years later, Dlugoszewski would write to Baryshnikov and Christina Sterner, the managing director of the Baryshnikov Arts Center and the White Oak Dance Project: "Finally I am sending you both this magnificent appreciation of Misha's exquisite dancing in Erick's *Journey of a Poet*. I still get shivers remembering that beautiful performance of his."[30]

For *Journey of a Poet* Dlugoszewski composed an explosive string quartet, which she titled *Disparate Stairway Radical Other*.[31] In an interview, she explained the variation on her enduring metaphor of a "disparate element," namely, what "disparate stairway" meant to her: a kind of immediacy and aliveness. "I remember seeing a Japanese architecture where, for no reason, there was off to the side a stairway," she said in an interview. "It was just there. And I always call it the disparate stairway."[32] The piece was dedicated to Baryshnikov, Hawkins, and Mary Norton Dorazio, and was commissioned by the White Oak Dance Project. Sketches include a multicolored, hand-drawn, exhibition-worthy, six-page "scroll" that mapped out the sequence of events in the music, and, presumably, the dance as well. Notes on manuscript sketches made in 1995 show Dlugoszewski's struggles with the score: "I guess at the moment I can do no better than this," she admitted to herself on one page. "I think this is finally it," she triumphed—at 2:15 a.m.—on another.

In a document titled "Composer's notes on *Journey of a Poet*," Dlugoszewski evoked again and again the idea of "the disparate element," and preached about the virtues of live (acoustic) musicians rather than electronic media, a mantra she and Hawkins had repeated since the 1950s in an attempt to set themselves apart from Cage (who had died two years before Hawkins, in 1992) and Cunningham's use of electronic music: "For many people the perception of the arts in the '90s is synonymous with a deadened defeated and strangely unreal society.... We are in a time of claustrophobic technological take-overs of our lives when the belief in the authenticity of personal experience is increasingly called into question, where experience itself and spiritual connections with the real world are often lost, jettisoned or forgotten. What is increasingly at stake is our capacity to feel alive."[33]

Disparate Stairway Radical Other, one of Dlugoszewski's last pieces, is a formidable stand-alone string quartet. Recorded in 1999 by the White Oak Ensemble (Conrad Harris, Margaret Jones, violins; David J. Bursack, viola; Dorothy Lawson, cello), the twenty-two-minute piece is divided into seven cryptically titled sections varying from about two to six minutes, and it tapped into Dlugoszewski's career-long fixation on timbral diversity. Drawing on her Varèse-inspired attention to density (and intensity), she maximized the variety of materials she used to draw sound from otherwise conventional instruments. In his liner notes for the CD release of *Disparate Stairway Radical Other*, Hal Rammel explained the formal design of the piece, which was divided into "Phrases," some of them labeled "Disparate." He also described the materials, methods, and sonic impact of the piece:

> She favored a particular style of Swiss comb and had used it in earlier works such as *Fire Fragile Flight*. Glass slides produce the delicate koto-like tones, percussive taps, and gentle glissandos at the end of this Disparate passage. These various strategies alternate throughout the balance of this performance, creating an atmosphere of agitated movement. Sounds collide and cascade, sigh and shout, leap into space, land at the same point for a second of rest and repose (the delicate "sea gull glissandos" that conclude Disparate 16), then float away as the bows of the four string players lightly richochet [sic] into distant space (at the end of Disparate 22).[34]

Soon after the completion of *Disparate Stairway Radical Other*, Dlugoszewski composed a "Symphony for Seven Instruments" titled *Depth Duende Scarecrow Other* (score dated 27 January 1996). The piece included sections that were "structured in fields of feeling" (i.e., "Field I is subliminal"), and required the conductor to begin the piece by lighting and blowing out matches while the curtain rose on a stage set in complete darkness.[35] The piece made use of the same instrumentation as *Radical Narrowness Concert*, namely, seven players playing nine instruments; Joel Thome conducted the premiere. As in many of her pieces, instruments playing wide glissandi were pitted against other instruments playing fast lines of melodic sixteenth-notes. At some point in the piece all the instrumentalists were asked to play "violent shakes" on "bean closed rattles"; later they would play "paper closed rattles" as loudly as possible.

STEERING THE DANCE COMPANY: DLUGOSZEWSKI AS CHOREOGRAPHER

In November 1997 Dlugoszewski sent her friend Lillian Kiesler a poster for the Erick Hawkins School for Dance, which was now located at Chelsea Piers. Dlugoszewski served as artistic director, as she had since almost immediately after Hawkins's death. On the poster she wrote a personal note: "We are so excited about our Winter Intensive this year and I, in particular am such an aesthetic 'freak' that I intend to take the most intense far out aesthetic journey with my choreography and I'm totally loving to take anyone with me who's reckless enough to come on this journey."[36] The poster featured a quotation by Michael Silverton from *Fanfare Magazine*: "Lucia Dlugoszewski's genius is at once iron-clad and endlessly poetic." The poster copy announced: "Ms. Dlugoszewski's classes are training grounds for future Company apprentices and continue to inspire many successful choreographers." Students would also receive private choreography sessions with Ms. Dlugoszewski, the ad announced. (The course cost $350 and was to take place from 29 December 1997 to 9 January 1998.) The Erick Hawkins School faculty at the time included rehearsal director Kathy Ortiz, and dancers Julia Baumgarten, Pascal Benichou, Lara Bujold, Georgia Corner, Katherine Duke, Louis McEwen, Gloria McLean, Michael Moses, Cynthia Reynolds, Todd Rosenlieb, and Catherine Tharin.

A document titled "Adventures of the Hawkins Year" listed achievements for the Company since their "very successful critically acclaimed season at the Silvia and Danny Kaye Playhouse in February, 1997," including the establishment of their new home base at Chelsea Piers, company classes there, and choreography classes taught by Dlugoszewski once a week.[37] For the 1997–98 Winter Intensive, Dlugoszewski offered a whimsical "Statement of Belief" for her choreography classes, challenging the dance establishment with the question: "Who can actually teach choreography?"[38] Other "Statements of Belief" written by Company instructors offer insight into what qualities of Hawkins's technique Dlugoszewski must have foregrounded in her own move toward choreography: "living kinetic architecture of the human body" (Louis Kavouras); "listening to the pelvis as the center of our weight" (Reynolds);

"free flow—the careful balance of action and effortlessness" (McLean); "new dimension[s] of sensuous subtlety and delicacy" (Benichou); "technical demands and... effortlessness" (Duke).[39] In a letter to Lillian Kiesler written in late November 1997, Dlugoszewski further informed her friend of her activities with the Company. Noting the one-year anniversary of Hawkins's death, she admitted to "falling apart" while also exalting in "the beautiful friendship" she had with one of the company dancers, Pascal Benichou, which she claimed went "a long way toward making me more sane"; she admitted to "creating some very special choreography on his body."[40] (This might have been a piece called *A Fountain in the Middle of the Room*, which Katherine Duke recalled Dlugoszewski creating for Benichou, and which remained unfinished at the time of her death.)[41]

On 2 January 1998, the Company held a Hawkins New Year's Celebration Loft Concert at the Broome Corner Loft in Soho.[42] In addition to a number of newer and revived dances, Dlugoszewski performed the premiere of a new timbre piano piece commissioned by Composer Recordings Inc. (CRI) for their upcoming spring release of an all-Dlugoszewski CD—her first ever. The recording included the new commission, which she called *Exacerbated Subtlety Concert (Why Does a Woman Love a Man?)* Hal Rammel wrote of this piece in his liner notes for the CRI release: "'Exacerbated' signals *otherness, strangeness*, and *intensity*, here coupled with *subtlety*." He went on to list materials she applied to the strings of the piano: "All varieties of paper, hairpins, rubber wedges, thimbles, Gerbers' baby food jars, tuning forks, flexatones, and various combs are among the implements of this transformation of the familiar."[43]

Nearly five years after Hawkins's death, Dlugoszewski stepped out as a choreographer at Playhouse 91, then under the direction of Joan Finkelstein of the 92nd Street Y Harkness Dance Project. The *Village Voice* announced the upcoming performance: "Lucia Dlugoszewski, Hawkins's longtime collaborator, makes her choreographic debut at the Playhouse March 23."[44] Dlugoszewski's dance, called *Taking Time to be Vulnerable* (1999), was reviewed—not entirely favorably—in the *New York Times* by Anna Kisselgoff, who noted that "the music continued whether the dancer was onstage or not": "As a one-woman orchestra playing her specially prepared timbre piano, Ms. Dlugoszewski went back to the ideas one heard from her in the 1960's." Kisselgoff added: "There was paper tearing and meowing sounds but also a sharp way with percussion that fit the outbursts onstage."[45] Deborah Jowitt reviewed the performance for the *Village Voice*, paying closer attention to Dlugoszewski's way of musically framing the dance—"she might let a burst of motion fall into silence, or create a thunderstorm on the piano while a dancer delicately picked his way across the stage"—while also assessing the composer's choreography in another piece called *Radical Ardent* (1999), a fifty-minute work accompanied by *Exacerbated Subtlety Concert (Why Does a Woman Love a Man?)*: "The core of [*Radical Ardent*], a series of male-female duets, is sound as a nut, and the music caresses them, deliciously undercutting sweetness with a slightly raucous or abrasive touch. In the small theater, your eye travels from the complicit bodies to a musician shaking a sheet of paper or tinkling little glass chimes.... A composer makes a successful beginning as a choreographer. Amazing!"[46]

As a choreographer, Dlugoszewski created several other works, including *Why Does a Man Dance* and *Last Love Duet*. Katherine Duke recalled *Last Love Duet* as being related to the earlier Dlugoszewski-Hawkins collaboration *Each Time You Carry Me This Way*, drawing attention to Dlugoszewski's influence in general on the creation of several earlier dances of Hawkins, including *Cantilever Two, Intensities of Space and Wind, Each Time You Carry Me This Way, New Moon,* and *Killer of Enemies: The Divine Hero*, pieces all created after Hawkins's health started to fail. As the choreographer's ability to function at full capacity waned, Dlugoszewski, alongside his company's dancers, provided ideas, perspective, and creative inspiration.

Dlugoszewski's increasingly depleted creative psyche might have been strained further by the new pressures of both choreography and composition. Though a Detroit newspaper article published when she was fourteen years old claimed that "[Dlugoszewski] never leaves a tune unfinished once she begins work on it," people who knew her during the final years of her life observed that she had trouble completing her work early enough to allow for adequate rehearsal time.[47] (This may explain the problem with her "breakthrough piece" *Wilderness Elegant Tilt* of 1981, which was commissioned by the Lincoln Center Chamber Music Society, but never performed.) Gerard Schwarz recalled: "She was frequently late completing the scores, often making the music available to us at the first performance."[48] He also recalled occasions when musicians would frantically copy out parts backstage while the start time to a concert was delayed, as happened at the premiere of *Black Lake* at Riverside Church, for which the parts were not ready in time for the performance; on another occasion he said the musicians had to improvise a score, because Dlugoszewski's was not finished in time.[49] Eleanor Hovda remembered similar situations: "She had a lot of trouble finishing things.... This was one of the things that she always wished wasn't true of herself.... I guess the reality of it was that, she often wouldn't finish the pieces until the dress rehearsal, and so the dancers didn't have a clue of what they were going to be hearing... and it was a kind of stressful situation."[50] Percussionist William Trigg likewise recalled: "She always scrambled to barely meet the deadline of the first rehearsal.... Dancers were constantly cutting and pasting from a copy of the score to create instrumental parts."[51] The continual stress of choreography, composition, and running a dance company might have contributed to the deterioration of Dlugoszewski's own health. Six years before her own death (and just a few months before Hawkins's), she seemed to take stock of her own life, drawing on many of the words that had captured her imagination for so long:

> *I loved*
> I lived
> I suddened the disparate stairway
> I carefulled the shatter of form
> I was urgent
> breathless
> lifted
> "muddied"
>
> I loved receding newfallen
> pierce waiting to be born
> exacerbated subtlety without respite
>
> I dared daily grave intense alien other
>
> For the millionth time, I lived
> scarecrow tear growl
> scorn intense arrogant insurgent
> to wrest being from non-being
>
> I was the person who jumps
> the strange resumption of world as freedom
> I never failed to try with Hue Neng
> to put the pitcher on its side
>
> I thrilled with the tragic lightness
> of being alive.[52]

DLUGOSZEWSKI'S DEATH

Lucia Dlugoszewski died alone in her Greenwich Village apartment on 9 April 2000, just shy of her seventy-fifth birthday. According to Ellen

Borakove, spokeswoman for the New York City Medical Examiner, the death was due to natural causes.[53] Nevertheless, some friends questioned the state of her health—both physical and mental—and wondered whether her death might have been a suicide, or perhaps an overdose; others directly connected the stress of an upcoming premiere to a fatal breakdown of some sort, maybe related to a congestive heart condition. The night Dlugoszewski died she was awaited at the dress rehearsal for her new choreographic work titled *Motherwell Amor*—"a two-part homage to the Abstract Expressionist painter Robert Motherwell, a friend and colleague"—scheduled to receive its premiere the following evening.[54] When the composer-choreographer did not appear at the rehearsal Joan Finklestein called the police, who reportedly broke down the door and found Dlugoszewski dead in her bathtub. The Company premiered *Motherwell Amor* as planned the following evening, but as a stunned and spontaneous memorial. The dancers asked that there be no applause, and they took no bows; William Trigg explained to the audience that Dlugoszewski had not quite completed *Motherwell Amor*'s musical score for timbre piano, percussion, and six other instruments.[55]

In addition to the *New York Times* obituary written by Anna Kisselgoff, in which the sometimes glib dance critic described the "poetic, gutsy" composer's "hectic, usually disheveled exterior," the 92nd Street Y ran a more reverent announcement and remembrance in the *New York Times* on the same day:

> The 92nd Street Y mourns the loss of composer and choreographer Lucia Dlugoszewski, who, with her husband, Erick Hawkins, created an entirely new vocabulary of music and movement that stretched the boundaries of modern dance performance. After Hawkins's death in 1994, Dlugoszewski took the reins of The Erick Hawkins Dance Company, making her choreographic debut at the 92nd Street Y in 1999, as her husband had done in 1942. She died just as the company was beginning its second season at the Y under her direction, premiering the stunning *Motherwell Amor*. After the company performed last year, the *New York Times* called Dlugoszewski a modern dance choreographer of exceptional promise, while *Dance Magazine* proclaimed that the Hawkins legacy was in good hands. The 92nd Street Y is honored to have provided a platform for her unique art. She will be missed.[56]

On the same day that these obituaries and tributes were printed, the *New York Times* also printed a review of the premiere of *Motherwell Amor*. Noting that Dlugoszewski had only started presenting her choreographic work in public one year prior, Jennifer Dunning observed "several interesting solos"—"chief among them an eerily lolloping, charging dance in the second part that exploits Louis Kavouras's distinctive blend of sharp focus and lumbering looseness"—while also noting that "her choreography... in *Motherwell Amor* has been weakest in its infrequent attempts to have the dancers travel across the stage." Finally, Dunning noted Dlugoszewski's lifelong celebration of the sensual:

> What she brought to this promising new career was long experience as an independent composer and a collaborator with Hawkins, an unashamed delight in the bawdy side of life and an avid interest in poetry. The score for *Motherwell Amor II* chuckles and sighs comically at times. The men and women performing the choreography gently kiss, nuzzle and trace the lines of the inner leg and other parts of the body with a frank eroticism that is seldom seen in dance.[57]

On Friday, 8 December 2000, a memorial service, open to the public, was held at the John Jay College Theater. The *New York Times* ran an announcement for the memorial two days prior, stating that the event would "feature performances of her music by the Graham Ashton Brass Ensemble, conducted by Joel Thome, a film by Jonas Mekas, and reminiscences by Leighton Kerner, the music critic, and others."[58]

· · · · ·

Throughout Dlugoszewski's music-filled life, poetry remained a constant source of comfort and inspiration. As she grew older, it might have helped her confront her own mortality. In the late 1970s, Dlugoszewski began inviting Emily Dickinson's nineteenth-century poetry into her constellation of favored verse. Noting Dickinson's psychological profile as that of "a gifted woman," Dlugoszewski copied out many of Dickinson's poems into her notebooks, including one of Dickinson's most well-known works, written around 1862. Dlugoszewski might have been drawn to Dickinson's contemplation on the nature of death:

> It was not Death, for I stood up,
> *And all the Dead, lie down*—
> It was not Night, for all the Bells
> Put out their Tongues, for Noon.
>
> It was not Frost, for on my Flesh
> I felt Siroccos—crawl—

Nor Fire—for just my Marble feet
Could keep a Chancel, cool—

And yet, it tasted, like them all,
The Figures I have seen
Set orderly, for Burial,
Reminded me, of mine—

As if my life were shaven,
And fitted to a frame,
And could not breathe without a key,
An 'twas like Midnight, some—

When everything that ticked—has stopped—
And Space stares all around—
Or Grisly frosts—first Autumn morns,
Repeal the Beating Ground—

But, most, like Chaos—Stopless—cool—
Without a Chance, or Spar—
Or even a Report of Land—
To justify—Despair.[59]

In the same (undated) notebook, Dlugoszewski described her own impression of the poet: "psychological calamities / decades of frustration / isolation + loneliness all created a void / that Emily Dickinson's talent / rushed in to fill / Without this void / There might well have been no poet / (the facing / the courageous facing of the cutting wheel / Wild Reality / Terrible Freedom) / Abyss Naked Empty." Perhaps Dlugoszewski found a kindred spirit in Dickinson, one who would have appreciated her lifelong quest "to dangerously awaken the dangerous mind without fixing it."[60] Terrible freedom, indeed.

Out from the Shadows

A CONCLUSION

> people simply don't realize how much they can risk without danger if they knew they would go mad from regret at not having been more daring[1]

THOUGH I STATED IN THE INTRODUCTION to this book that Lucia Dlugoszewski is no longer a difficult subject to research, she remains a challenging subject to understand, as do her erratic aesthetic positions and far-reaching philosophies. Characterized by friends contradictorily as affectionate, bitter, demonstrative, ebullient, eccentric, exasperating, gregarious, intense, paranoid, passionate, self-absorbed, sensitive, and underappreciated, the force of her personality seems to have overwhelmed many of those around her. A woman who reportedly loved chocolate ice cream and wore flowers in her hair, Dlugoszewski's charm was genuine and disarming, according to those who knew her well. If she were under psychological care today, she might be diagnosed as having a bipolar or schizoaffective disorder, as she seems to have endured episodes of hypomania, leading to disordered sleeping, expansive thinking, uncontrollable elation, delusions of grandiosity, despairing melancholy, and unfocused rage.[2] Despite the challenges presented by such mood fluctuations, and for a woman many experienced as a chronic procrastinator, Dlugoszewski created an impressive body of work, both in quantity and complexity. That work still needs to be analyzed, performed, and recorded to be fully appreciated.

Dlugoszewski's name still seems to appear most frequently in connection with Edgard Varèse, who was once her teacher—albeit briefly and just at the start of her career. Scholars have taken differing views on this legacy. As mentioned in the introduction, Kyle Gann dismissed her as dying in obscurity, "having achieved little more than a shadowy reputation," despite his claim that she was "possibly the leading direct inheritor of Varèse's aesthetic."[3]

Austin Clarkson, on the other hand, put a positive spin on this inheritance: "She realized the Varèsian aesthetic with extraordinary invention, skill, and bravura in compositions and performances that spanned five decades."[4] Hal Rammel, arguably one of Dlugoszewski's most outspoken champions in her later life, insisted she be included in a pantheon of better-known composers: "Dlugoszewski is one of the most inventive and forceful voices of the late twentieth century, deserving her place alongside such visionary composers as Harry Partch, Ornette Coleman, and John Cage," he wrote in no uncertain terms.[5] Others have merely lamented the "unfortunate neglect" of "one of the most interesting people" as a minor aside, a footnote to the history of twentieth-century American music.[6]

Like Dlugoszewski's lack of place in music histories, Erick Hawkins has been somewhat marginalized within the American modern dance canon. In the revised edition of Walter Terry's *The Dance in America*, for example, which traces various lineages of twentieth-century dance from Isadora Duncan and Ruth St. Denis through Balanchine, Graham, the Denishawn School and beyond, Hawkins is mentioned only once, in passing, embedded in a list of choreographers of a completely different generation, including Yvonne Rainer (b. 1934), Twyla Tharp (b. 1941), Meredith Monk (b. 1942), and others. (Meredith Monk was just two years old when Hawkins was dancing in the premiere of *Appalachian Spring*.) Terry also erroneously placed Hawkins in the performance spaces of postmodernism and happenings: corridors, galleries, museums, beaches, and lobbies, with occasional audience participation. Due to his affinity for the traditional dance recital hall and his refusal to incorporate any kind of electronic music into his performances, Hawkins seems to have been viewed as a choreographer from a bygone era, one whose conservative aesthetics aligned more with the beginning of the twentieth century than the end. Nonetheless, Yvonne Rainer, a cofounder of the radically experimental Judson Dance Theater, claimed, in recalling the beginnings of her career: "I saw *Here and Now with Watchers* and decided to become a dancer."[7]

Following her Detroit upbringing, Dlugoszewski's career followed a path similar to the professional trajectory of many other composers who came to New York from somewhere else, drawn first to the private lofts of lower Manhattan in the 1950s and later to commercial spaces like Lincoln Center in the 1980s and 1990s. For better or worse, she experienced American culture's dramatic changes just like everyone else. Yet she remains an outsider, partly due to her own characterization of herself as such in her interviews and writings—and even in private correspondence. In this sense, she may have sabotaged her own reputation by insisting on portraying herself as a neglected, excluded figure. Though her isolation might have been a self-perpetuating myth, her presence can be easily found in the programs and publications of her era. Nevertheless, she is almost completely absent from retrospective accounts of this historical period.

Dlugoszewski's reception also seems to have been complicated by historians' and critics' tendency to put composers into groups. In her case, it seems that the uptown contemporary music establishment considered her too bohemian for black-tie concert culture, while the downtown experimentalists considered her too dressed up for their shoestring Do-It-Yourself aesthetic. In the words of composer Lois V Vierk (b. 1951): "The two main NYC new music camps were extreme and well-defined [by the 1980s] and perhaps Dlugoszewski was not really in either camp."[8] Dlugoszewski herself drew battle lines between "the official uptown school" and "the more avant-garde composers," neither of which accepted her—to the contrary, she claimed, "the serious concert world was shut for me."[9] Citing almost exclusively the support she received early on from Erick Hawkins, Virgil Thomson, and F. S. C. Northrop, she overcame a situation in which she "just wasn't given a chance anywhere else."[10] As we have seen, this exaggeration is far from the truth. Yet she distorted her own past again and again, freely blending her claims of exclusion with her impenetrable theories, as if the two went hand in hand: "In 1957 I was a rebellious, independent and lonely youngster ignored by the whole official music community because I was committed to pursue the search for the aesthetic dimension in music as purely as I could manage—that sheer radical empirical immediacy of Joyce's 'Quidditas' and Northrop's thesis: 'poetry and mysticism are pure fact.'"[11] In her quest for intense and immediate sonic experiences, Dlugoszewski invented new instruments, explored new playing techniques, and created textured walls of sound—"Curtains of Timbre"—she hoped would inspire the "sheer wonder of making and hearing a sound with no logical or emotional inference."[12] Perhaps this is the clearest statement of her life's work, her compositional intent.

Because of the discrepancies mentioned above, writing about Dlugoszewski has turned out to be a more difficult task than I had first imagined. The chasm between her own eccentric writings and the glowing professional assessment of her reputation by someone as well-known as Mikhail Baryshnikov—who called her work "startling, fresh, and uncompromising" just months before her death—presents particular conundrums for a biographer.[13] How to characterize someone who seems to have functioned—and been received—so differently in distinct spheres of her life? Even after years of studying nearly every currently knowable shred of evidence she left behind, it is still unclear to me how this obsessive, manic, self-involved yet self-aware creative force was able to balance her private struggles against her public competence for so long. In the end, she might have burned out just due to the sheer exhaustion of this lifelong effort.

A few years ago, I became intrigued by a letter published in *The New Yorker* magazine regarding the reputation of Italian composer Antonio Salieri (1750–1825), whose compositional life has been historically overshadowed by his better-known contemporary, Wolfgang Amadeus Mozart: "The process of canonization is often considered to be akin to evolution, whereby the fittest survive, and the cream rises to the top. The truth is more complex, as [Alex] Ross's piece illustrates, and circumstances having little to do with artistry are often decisive in establishing an artist's place in history. Do we like Mozart the most because his music is superlative? Or because his portrayal as a towering genius is so pervasive in our culture that we listen to him with reflexive deference? It may be impossible to know."[14]

"Circumstances having little to do with artistry" might help to explain Dlugoszewski's lingering, up until now, in the margins, shadows, and footnotes of history, though I do *not* believe it is "impossible to know" whether or not a historically neglected figure deserves a place in the history books. Through a deeper understanding of Dlugoszewski's life, relationships, inspirations, struggles, and creative work, we can now begin to reevaluate the historical placement of this "disparate element": a woman and artist who doesn't fit neatly into any of our well-established historical "camps" but who deserves to be considered on her own terms. "Precarious" is a word that could be applied to any life's chance of being remembered, and Dlugoszewski celebrated that very quality in her own work: "That is [music's] great treasure of essence," she declared, "that exacerbated elusively dangerous exquisite precariousness."[15] Still, there are empty spaces on the shelves of music libraries where her scores should be.

APPENDIX 1

Selected Works List

Notes: The following list of works is compiled from

- lists of Dlugoszewski's works included in a variety of sources, including *Soundpieces 2* (1993);
- Dlugoszewski's own resumes and works lists;
- the LC Erick Hawkins Papers Finding Aid (as accessed in 2015);
- Kevin Lewis's thesis (2011); and
- other published biographical dictionary sources.

Some juvenilia are mentioned in Dlugoszewski's scrapbook, including youthful works like *Song of Young Writers* (1939), *Halloween Symphony, Bells of Christmas*, and others. I cannot verify the existence of all of the pieces listed here. Works mentioned in the main text are pieces I have been able to study through extant manuscripts, recordings, program notes, and/or other written material.

1946	*Construction for Orchestra*
1947	*Construction for String Quartet*
1948	*For the Time Being: A Christmas Oratorio* [based on poem by W. H. Auden]
1949	Piano Sonata No. 1 [or 1948?]
1949	*Melody Piano Sonata (No. 2)*
1949	*Moving Space Theater Piece for Everyday Sounds*
1950	*Melodic Sonata* for piano
1950	Piano Sonata No. 2
1950	Piano Sonata No. 3 and Piano Sonata No. 4
1950	Flute Sonata

1951	*Transparencies for Everyday Sounds 1–50*
1952	*Transparencies* for string quartet
1952	*Orchestra Structure for the Poetry of Everyday Sounds*
1952	*Transparencies for Harp*
1952	*Transparencies for Flute*
1952	*Transparencies for Harp and Violin*
1952	*Everyday Sounds for [bright?] e.e. cummings with Transparencies* [or 1951?]
1952	*The space of March, April, and May has turned the world on its tender side, and we have to turn the same way* (timbre piano)
1952	*Apple Sonata*
1952	*Desire Trapped by the Tail* theater score for upright timbre piano and voice
1952	*Ubu the King* theater score (*Structure for the Poetry of Every Day Sounds*), for "orchestra of everyday sounds"
1952–53	*openings of the (eye)* for flute, timbre piano, and percussion (dance by Erick Hawkins)
1953	Music for Marie Menken's film *Variations on Noguchi*
1953–70	*Silent Paper Spring and Summer Friend Songs*
1953	*Tiny Opera* for four poets, moving voice, dancers, and piano
1953	*the black house and the living water* (dance) [later retitled *Sudden Snake-Bird*]
1953	*Two Songs for Everyday Sounds*
1953	*Moving theatre piece for many players*
1953	*Gong and Snowball Piano Sonatas*
1954	*Arithmetic Progressions* for orchestra [or: 1955: *Arithmetic Points for Orchestra*?]
1954	*More Songs for Everyday Sounds*
1954–57	*Archaic Timbre Piano Music* [or 1953–56] [*Here and Now with Watchers*] (timbre piano solo)
1955	*Orchestral Radiant Ground* for orchestra
1955	*Arithmetic Points* (orchestra)
1956	*Naked Wabin* for flute, clarinet, timbre piano, violin, bass, and percussion
1956	*Flower Music for Left Ear in a Small Room* for eight players
1956	*Visual Variations of Noguchi* film score of everyday sounds [*The Poetry of Natural Sound*]

1957	*Instants in Form and Movement*
1957	*Chamber Orchestra and Timbre Piano*
1958	*Music for Small Centers* for piano
1958	*Separated Music* (from *Suchness Concert*)
1958	*Music for Left Ear* for piano
1958	*Flower Music for Left Ear in a Small Room* (flute, clarinet, trumpet, tb. 2 perc., violin, double bass)
1958–60	*Suchness Concert* [for *8 Clear Places*, dance by Erick Hawkins] ["for invented percussion orchestra of 100 instruments, including wood, metal, paper, glass, skin plastic, ladder harps, tangent rattles, closed rattles, unsheltered rattles, wave rattles, square drums, and quarter tone gongs"]
1959	*Rates of Speed in Space* for ladder harp and chamber quintet
1959	*Flower Music* for string quartet
1959	*Delicate Accidents in Space* for five unsheltered rattles
1959–60	*Music for Left Ear in a Small Room Nos. 1–20* (timbre piano)
1960	*Concert of Many Rooms and Moving Space* for flute, clarinet, timbre piano and four unsheltered rattles (theater score for *Women of Trachis* ["Non-stop evening structure of music for flute and clarinet moving in space; timbre piano, unsheltered rattles with four percussionists variously positioned in space"]
1960	*Orchestral Radiant Ground* (orchestra)
1961	*Five Radiant Grounds* for timbre piano (*Early Floating* dance by Erick Hawkins)
1961	*Archaic Aggregates* for timbre piano and percussion
1961	*White Interval Music* for timbre piano
1961	*Guns of the Trees* film score for Jonas Mekas and Cinematique, for chamber ensemble
1961	*Sudden Snake-Bird* (dance)
1963	*Spring Azure* (dance)
1963	*Untitled* (for 2 flutes and violin)
1964	*Four Attention Spans* (timbre piano) (*Cantilever* dance by Erick Hawkins)
1964	*Skylark Cicada* (violin and timbre piano)
1964	*To Everybody Out There* for chamber orchestra (dance by Erick Hawkins)
1964	*Geography of Noon* for 100 invented percussion instruments (dance by Erick Hawkins)

1965	*Beauty Music* for clarinet, percussion, and timbre piano
1965	*Beauty Music 2* for percussion and chamber orchestra
1965	*Beauty Music 3* for timbre piano and chamber orchestra
1965	*Violin Music for Left Ear in a Small Room*
1965	*Clarinet Music for Left Ear in a Small Room*
1965	*Percussion Airplane Hetero* for 100 invented percussion instruments
1965	*Percussion Flowers* for 100 invented percussion instruments
1965	*Percussion Kitetails* for 100 invented percussion instruments
1965	*Quick Dichotomies* (clarinet, 2 trumpets, percussion)
1965	*Suchness with Radiant Ground* for clarinet and percussion
1965	*Swift Music* for two timbre pianos
1966	*Balance Naked Flung* for clarinet, trumpet, bass trombone, violin, and percussion (*Lords of Persia* dance by Erick Hawkins)
1966	*Dazzle on a Knife's Edge* for timbre piano and orchestra [dance]
1966	*Naked Flight Nageire* (chamber orchestra)
1966	*Sayatasha Shape* (3 timbre pianos, winds, violin, percussion)
1967	*Naked Quintet* (brass quintet)
1968	*Hanging Bridges* (string quartet [or: *for Orchestra?*)
1968	*Agathlon Algebra* [dance]
1968	*Kitetail Beauty Music* (violin, timbre piano, and percussion)
1968	*Naked Swift Music* for violin, timbre piano, and percussion
1968	*Leap and Fall, Quick Structures* (clarinet, 2 trumpets, percussion, 2 violin)
1968	*Lords of Persia No. 2* [dance]
1969	*Theatre Flight Nageire* (timbre piano, clarinet, percussion)
1969	*Cicada Skylark Ten* (for ten instruments)
1969	*Skylark Concert: An Evening of Music* (chamber orchestra)
1969	*Tight Rope* for chamber orchestra [clarinet, percussion, violin] (dance by Erick Hawkins)
1969–70	*The Suchness of Nine Concerts* for clarinet, violin, two percussion, and timbre piano (*Black Lake* dance by Erick Hawkins)
1970	*Space Is a Diamond* (trumpet)
1970	*John Ashbury Poetry* (voice, chamber orchestra)
1970	*Parker Tyler Language* (voice, chamber orchestra)
1970	*Swift Diamond* (timbre piano, trumpet, and percussion)
1970	*Velocity Shells* (timbre piano, trumpet, and percussion)

1970	*Pure Flight [Air]* (string quartet)
1970	*Sabi Music* (violin) [from *The Suchness of Nine Concerts*]
1971;78	*Tender Theatre Flight Nageire* for brass sextet and percussion (*Of Love* dance by Erick Hawkins)
1971	*A Zen in Ryoko-In* (film score of everyday sound, for film by Ruth Stephan)
1971	*Lords of Persia No. 3* (dance)
1971	*A New Year's Song for V.T.*
1972	*In Memory of My Feelings* (tenor and chamber orchestra)
1972	*Densities: Nova, Corona, Clear Core* for brass quintet (*Angels of the Inmost Heaven* dance by Erick Hawkins)
1972	*Kireji: Spring and Tender Speed* (chamber orchestra)
1972	*The Heidi Songs* (chamber orchestra/opera) (work-in-progress)
1972	*Naked Point Abyss* for timbre piano (work-in-progress)
1973	*Theatre Flight Nageire* (timbre piano, clarinet, invented percussion)
1974	*Fire Fragile Flight* for 17 instruments [or 1973?]
1975	*Abyss and Caress* (trumpet and chamber orchestra)
1977	*Strange Tenderness of Naked Leaping* for string orchestra, two trumpets, and two flutes/piccolos (work-in-progress)
1977	*Do Not Go Gentle into That Good Night*
1978	*Tender Theatre Flight Nageire* for brass sextet and percussion
1978	*Amor Now Tilting Night* (chamber orchestra) (work-in-progress)
1979	*Amor Elusive Empty August* (woodwind quintet)
1979–80	*Swift and Naked* (string quintet, timbre piano, bass trombone)
1979–80	*Pierce Sever* (timbre piano)
1979–80	*Now Tilting Naked* (string quintet, timbre piano, bass trombone)
1980	*Amor Elusive April Pierce* for chamber orchestra (work-in-progress)
1980–81	*Cicada Terrible Freedom* (flute, string quintet, and bass trombone)
1981	*Startle Transparent Terrible Freedom* (orchestra) (work-in-progress)
1981	*Wilderness Elegant Tilt* (eleven players) (work-in-progress)
1982–83	*Duende Newfallen* (bass trombone and timbre piano)
1983	*Avanti* for seven instruments (dance by Erick Hawkins)
1983	*Quidditas Sorrow Terrible Freedom* (orchestra) (work-in-progress)
1983	*Duende Quidditas* (timbre piano, percussion, bass trombone)
1983	*Song Sparrow Lifted Snow* (orchestra) (work-in-progress)
1984	*Quidditas* (string quartet)

1985	*The Woman Duende Amor* (dance)
1985	*God's Angry Man* (dance) [per Lewis: Music by Charles Mills for the original dance *John Brown* (1945); orchestration and additional music for *God's Angry Man* by LD]
1987	*Radical, Strange, Quidditas, Dew Tear, Duende* for orchestra (work-in-progress)
1988	*Four Attention Spans* for piano and full orchestra (solo piano and flute, clarinet, trumpet, French horn, bassoon, trombone, violin, bass, and percussion) [per Lewis: same score as *Cantilever*] (*Cantilever Two* dance by Erick Hawkins)
1991	*Radical Quidditas for an Unborn Baby* (100 invented percussion instruments)
1991	*Radical Otherness Concert* (flute, clarinet, trumpet, trombone, violin, and bass)
1991	*Radical Suchness Concert* for flute, clarinet, trumpet, trombone, violin, and bass
1992	*Radical Narrowness Concert* (flute, clarinet, trumpet, trombone, violin, bass, percussion) [for *Each Time You Carry Me This Way*; 1993?]
1994	*Last Love Duet* (dance)
1994	*Journey of a Poet* (dance)
1994	*Why Does a Man Dance?* (timbre piano/dance)
1995	*Disparate Stairway Radical Other* (string quartet/for dance *Journey of a Poet*)
1996	*Depth Duende Scarecrow Other*: "Symphony for Seven Instruments"
1997/2000	*Exacerbated Subtlety Concert (Why Does a Woman Love a Man?)* (timbre piano)
1999	*Taking Time to Be Vulnerable* (timbre piano, percussion/dance)
2000	*Duende Wilderness Radical Elegant Tilt* (chamber orchestra)
2000	*Motherwell Amor* (timbre piano, chamber orchestra/dance)

APPENDIX 2

Lucia Dlugoszewski–Erick Hawkins Collaborations

Dlugoszewski often gave her scores different titles than the dances they accompanied. Those titles are included here in brackets.[1]

1952: *openings of the (eye)*; *Black House*
1957: *Here and Now with Watchers* [*Archaic Timbre Piano Music*]
1960: *8 Clear Places* [*Suchness Concert*]; *Sudden Snake-Bird* (also called *the black house and the living water*)
1961: *Early Floating* [*Five Radiant Grounds*]
1963: *Spring Azure*
1963–64: *Cantilever* [*Four Attention Spans*]
1964: *To Everybody Out There*; *Geography of Noon*
1965: *Lords of Persia* [*Balance Naked Flung*]
1966: *Dazzle on a Knife's Edge*
1968: *Tightrope*
1969: *Black Lake* [*The Suchness of Nine Concerts*]
1971: *Of Love* [rev. 1978; *Tender Theatre Flight Nageire*]; *Angels of the Inmost Heaven* [*Densities: Nova, Corona, Clear Core*]
1980: *Avanti*
1988: *Cantilever II* [*Four Attention Spans*]
1993: *Each Time You Carry Me This Way* [*Radical Narrowness Concert*]
1994: *Many Thanks*; *Journey of a Poet* [*Disparate Stairway Radical Other*]

APPENDIX 3

Discography

As of this writing, only eight of Dlugoszewski's works have been released on commercial recordings. They are listed here in chronological order of recording release date.

[1] *Space Is a Diamond* [solo trumpet; 1970]. Nonesuch H-71275, 1972
   Gerard Schwarz, trumpet

[2] *Angels of the Inmost Heaven/Densities* [brass quintet; 1972]. New American Music Vol. 2; Smithsonian Folkways FTS 33902, 1975
   Mark Gould, trumpet
   Louis Ranger, trumpet
   Per Brevig, trombone
   David Taylor, trombone
   Martin Smith, French horn
   Gerard Schwarz, conductor

[3] *Tender Theater Flight Nageire* [brass sextet and percussion; 1971; rev. 1978]. *Sonorous Explorations*, CRI 388, 1978.
   Gerard Schwarz, trumpet
   Edward Carroll, trumpet
   Norman Smith, trumpet
   Robert Routch, French horn
   David Langlitz, trombone
   David Taylor, bass trombone
   Lucia Dlugoszewski, percussion

[4] *Fire Fragile Flight* [17-piece orchestra; 1974]. Candide Label CE 31113, 1979.
   Orchestra of our Time (conductor, Joel Thome)

[5] *Duende Quidditas* [bass trombone, percussion and timbre piano; 1983], New World Records 80494, 1996.

    David Taylor, bass trombone

    Lucia Dlugoszewski, percussion and timbre piano

[6] *Disparate Stairway Radical Other* [string quartet; 1995]. New World Records/ CRI, NWCR 859, 2007. This disk also includes rereleases of *Tender Theater Flight Nageire* and *Space Is a Diamond*

    White Oak Ensemble:

        Conrad Harris violin

        Margaret Jones, violin

        David J. Bursack, viola

        Dorothy Lawson, cello

[7] *Exacerbated Subtlety Concert (Why Does a Woman Love a Man?)* [solo timbre piano; 1997/2000], included on *Disparate Stairway Radical Other* [6].

    Lucia Dlugoszewski, timbre piano

[8] *openings of the (eye)* [piano, flute, percussion; 1952]. Bandcamp, 2019.

    # Ensemble [Hashtag Ensemble]:

        Ania Karpowicz, flute

        Piotr Salajczyk, piano

        Hubert Zemler, percussion

Exacerbated Subtlety Concert (Why Does a Woman Love a Man?) [solo timbre piano; 1997/2000] Neuma Records, 2021.

    Agnese Toniutti, timbre piano

NOTES

ABBREVIATIONS

AAA	Archive of American Art, Smithsonian Institution
EH	Erick Hawkins
GRI	Getty Research Institute
LC	Library of Congress, Special Collections, Music Division [unless otherwise noted, all sources cited from LC are in the Erick Hawkins and Lucia Dlugoszewski Papers]
LD	Lucia Dlugoszewski
NYPL-Dance	Jerome Robbins Dance Division, New York Public Library
NYPL-Manuscripts	Manuscripts and Archives Division, New York Public Library
NYPL-Music	Music Division, New York Public Library
NYPL-Sound	Archive of Recorded Sound, New York Public Library
NYPL-Theatre	Billy Rose Theatre Division, New York Public Library
PSS	Paul Sacher Stiftung
Ransom	Harry Ransom Humanities Research Center, University of Texas, Austin
Stanford	Archive of Recorded Sound, Stanford University, Olivia Mattis Collection
UCSC	Special Collections, McHenry Library, University of California, Santa Cruz
UCSD	Mandeville Special Collections, University of California, San Diego
Yale-Beinecke	Beinecke Rare Book and Manuscript Library, Yale University

Yale-Gilmore   Irving S. Gilmore Music Library, Special Collections, Yale University

MARGINS, SHADOWS, AND FOOTNOTES: AN INTRODUCTION

1. LD, excerpt from essay titled "Amor Elusive Empty August," dated 1 August–24 December 1979.
2. LD, interview with Olivia Mattis, 29 December 1989; Stanford.
3. Julia L. Keefer, "Erick Hawkins, Modern Dancer: History, Theory, Technique, and Performance" (PhD dissertation, New York University, 1979), 275f.
4. Ruth Solie, "Afterword," in Sophie Drinker, *Music and Women: The Story of Women in Their Relation to Music* (1948; repr., New York: Feminist Press at the City University of New York, 1995), 363.
5. Jane Bowers and Judith Tick, "Introduction," *Women Making Music: The Western Art Tradition, 1150–1950* (Champaign: University of Illinois Press, 1987), 10.
6. Judith Tick, promotional blurb for Amy C. Beal, *Johanna Beyer* (Champaign: University of Illinois Press, 2015).
7. "Galleries Uptown," *The New Yorker* (22 May 2017), 16.
8. Steve Smith, "Classical Recording," *The New Yorker* (24 August 2020), 6.
9. Linda Dahl, *Stormy Weather: The Music and Lives of a Century of Jazzwomen* (New York: Pantheon, 1984), x.
10. Kyle Gann, "'Magnificent—in a Mysterious Way': Varèse's Impact on American Music," in *Edgard Varèse: Composer, Sound Sculptor, Visionary* (Basel: Paul Sacher Stiftung, 2006), 427. Preceding the sentence quoted above, Gann wrote more generously: "The rough-edged sonorities of Lucia Dlugoszewski's music, sometimes changing timbres on a single note by the addition and subtraction of instruments, are certainly Varèsian, and she took the love of specific timbres so far as to spend years inventing and building her own percussion instruments."
11. Tillard, as quoted by Marian Wilson Kimber, "The 'Suppression' of Fanny Mendelssohn: Rethinking Feminist Biography," *19th-Century Music*, 26, no. 2 (Fall 2002), 128.
12. See Beal, *Johanna Beyer*, 89–93.
13. LD quoted in Lucille De View, "She Creates Music to Fill the World," *Detroit News* (11 July 1972).
14. De View.
15. De View.
16. *The Diary of Anaïs Nin, 1947–55*, Gunther Stuhlmann, ed. (New York: Harcourt, Brace, Jovanovich, 1974), 61f. See also Suzanne Robinson, *Peggy Glanville-Hicks: Composer and Critic* (Champaign: University of Illinois Press, 2019).
17. Malina, diary entry, 11 October 1952; *The Diaries of Judith Malina, 1947–1957* (New York: Grove Press, Inc., 1984), 248.

18. From Tanglewood in the summer of 1976, LD wrote to Jolas: "Your architectural elegance as well as your beautiful, beautiful ears have a terrific impact on me. Thank you for being in the world!" (LD to Jolas, 21 August 1976; Betsy Jolas Papers, Yale-Gilmore.) In 1977, LD wrote to Gideon: "You know you were always a special inspiration to me when I was beginning as a composer, and I thought you might like to know this after all these years." (Miriam Gideon papers; NYPL-Music.) I am grateful to Anne Shreffler for sharing the Gideon letter with me.

19. Cole Gagne, introduction to interview with Dlugoszewski, *Soundpieces 2: Interviews with American Composers* (Metuchen, NJ: Scarecrow Press, 1993), 56.

20. Gerda Lerner, "Autobiographical Notes, by Way of an Introduction," in *The Majority Finds Its Past: Placing Women in History* (New York: Oxford University Press, 1979), xiv. Emphasis mine.

21. Ellen Bayuk Rosenman, *A Room of One's Own: Women Writers and the Politics of Creativity* (New York: Twayne Publishers, 1995), 39f. Emphasis mine.

22. William Billings, "To All Musical Practitioners," in *The New England Psalm Singer* [Boston, 1770], *The Complete Works of William Billings*, vol 1., ed. Karl Kroeger (Boston: The American Musicological Society and the Colonial Society of Massachusetts, 1981), 32.

23. Dlugoszewski's music was not included in important published score collections and series of her time like *Notations* (1969); *Source: Music of the Avant-Garde* (1967–73); or *Soundings* (1972–90); neither was she included in Michael Nyman's *Experimental Music: Cage and Beyond* (1974), nor in standard histories of twentieth-century music. Her name does not appear in *Music Index* until 1963, even though some of her early performances were reviewed by *Musical America* during the 1950s.

24. Paul Tai, written communication with the author, 22 April 2015. He added: "I think she's a very interesting but rather overlooked figure who wasn't really embraced by the music folks because of her deep involvement in the dance world."

25. The Erick Hawkins collection came to the Library of Congress in 2001; it was processed in 2007; with the acquisition of new Dlugoszewski materials in 2019, the collection has been renamed the Erick Hawkins and Lucia Dlugoszewski Papers.

26. Without attributing specific comments to specific people, I collectively acknowledge those who answered my inquiries about Dlugoszewski, including Charles Amirkhanian, Barbara Monk Feldman, Daniel Goode, Brenda Hutchinson, John Kennedy, Mary Jane Leach, David Mahler, David Nicholls, Eric Richards, Christopher Shultis, "Blue" Gene Tyranny, Lois V Vierk, Christian Wolff, and Alan Zimmermann.

27. James Atlas, *The Shadow in the Garden: A Biographer's Tale* (New York: Pantheon, 2017), 74, 120. Indeed, a musicologist told me that a textbook proposal reviewer had discouraged them from including Dlugoszewski in a chapter about instrument builders, insisting she was too "esoteric": the proposal reviewer recommended including a better-known "meat-and-potatoes" composer like Harry Partch instead.

CHAPTER 1. LUCILLE IN DETROIT (1925–48)

1. LD, "*8 Clear Places*," *Ballet Review* (Winter 1993), 64.
2. Though the year of her birth frequently appears in published sources as 1931 or 1934, the 1930 census correctly recorded her age as four and a half; her college transcripts list her correct birth date, as does the Social Security Death Index. Almost all of the published sources on Dlugoszewski to date include an incorrect birth date, including Christine Ammer's *Unsung: A History of Women in American Music* (Westport, CT: Greenwood Press, 1980), which devotes four full paragraphs to Dlugoszewski, but also perpetuates a number of items of misinformation from other sources.
3. See David Lee Poremba, *Detroit in Its World Setting: A Three-Hundred Year Chronology 1701–2001* (Detroit, MI: Wayne State University Press, 2001), 248–50.
4. Jennie also had two brothers, Edward and Casimer [?]. These notes were located in a folder/file labeled "Detroit Notes"/Detroit Notes 3"; LC. Chene Street runs through a part of Detroit known as Poletown East. Lucille's parents might also have gone dancing at one of the main Polish music venues, Dom Polski Hall, at 3426 Junction Avenue near Otis, where Eddie Hoyt (Nabozny) and his orchestra (or his "Golden Stars Radio Orchestra") played; See Laurie A. Gamulka Palazzolo, *Horn Man: The Polish-American Musician in Twentieth-Century Detroit* (Detroit, MI: The American-Polish Society, 2003), xxviii.
5. LD, letter to EH, 12 March 1985; LC.
6. In the same interview, she said: "Chopin for me is humility before an instrument and courage before a sensuous experience, not sentimental wallowing, which is *non-Polish*." Later in life she would denounce the whole idea of Romanticism.
7. Lucille De View, "She Creates Music to Fill the World," *Detroit News* (11 July 1972).
8. Information in this paragraph comes from Luther Routé and John Kirsch, "Two New York Composers: Interviews with Ben Weber and Lucia Dlugoszewski," *Wagner Literary Magazine* #2 (1960–61), 76.
9. Richard Bak, *Detroitland: A Collection of Movers, Shakers, Lost Souls, and History Makers from Detroit's Past* (Detroit, MI: Painted Turtle, 2011), 115.
10. Bak, 115.
11. Bak, 152.
12. Dennis Badaczewski, *Poles in Michigan* (East Lansing: Michigan State University Press, 2002), 15.
13. Badaczewski, 15.
14. Palazzolo, *Horn Man*, 44, 27.
15. Bak, *Detroitland*, 156.
16. Palazzolo, *Horn Man*, 29.
17. Jennifer Dunning, "The Composer Who Energizes the Erick Hawkins Dancers," *New York Times*, 7 December 1988.
18. LD, letters to father, 12 and 20 September 1933; LC.
19. LD, letter to mother, 19 April 1950; LC.

20. LD, letter to mother, 6 June 1936; LC.
21. LD, letter to father, 11 August 1936; LC.
22. LD, letter to father, 17 August 1936; LC.
23. Bak, *Detroitland*, 125. Bak writes that in "1936 the auto industry produced nearly 4.5 million cars and trucks."
24. G. A. Bedell, *Methods of Pictorial Representation*, Mechanical Drawing 3, Cass Technical High School, Detroit, Michigan, 1931.
25. To date I have located nearly sixty of Dlugoszewski's graphic poems, usually sent to friends as gifts, some with musical notation and some with elaborate, Fluxus-like musical instructions.
26. LD, letter to mother, 2 January 1951; LC.
27. LD, letter to mother, 7 July 1950; LC.
28. Adrienne Fried Block, *Amy Beach, Passionate Victorian: The Life and Work of an American Composer 1867–1944* (New York: Oxford University Press, 1998), vii.
29. LD, interview with André Bernard, WNYC, 14 December 1983; NYPL-Sound.
30. LD quoted in De View, "She Creates Music to Fill the World."
31. Bill Loomis, *On This Day in Detroit History* (Charleston, SC: The History Press, 2016), 23.
32. An undated, typewritten autobiographical sketch lists four piano teachers: Adelgatha Morrison, Detroit Conservatory of Music, 1934–39; Carl Beutel, Detroit, 1939–45; Edward Bredshall, Detroit Institute of Musical Arts, 1945–47; and Grete Sultan, New York, 1947–51. She also lists as composition teachers: Carl Beutel, Detroit, 1939–45; Felix Salzer, Mannes College of Music 1947–49; LC.
33. Dlugoszewski mentioned playing an all-Bach recital as a young girl in her interview with Olivia Mattis, 29 December 1989; Stanford.
34. The author of the profile added: "[Dlugoszewski] belonged to the Polish Falcons and memorized long recitations for holiday festivals." De View, "She Creates Music to Fill the World."
35. Clippings from the *Detroit News*, 22 October 1938 and 15 January 1939.
36. Grinnell Brothers was considered one of the top music studios in Detroit at the time, dubbed "The Musical Center of Detroit," occupying space at 1515–21 Woodward Avenue in the heart of downtown Detroit. "Although most of the Polish-American musicians frequented Hewitt's on a regular basis, Grinnell's was the most frequented, since the store was able to order sheet music arrangements from other cities." Palazzolo, *Horn Man*, 52. A copy of the *Halloween Symphony* record survives in her scrapbook.
37. Aunt Kaye, letter to LD, 11 September 1939; Dlugoszewski scrapbook; LC.
38. Capitalizations are hers.
39. Aunt Kaye, letter to LD, 6 December 1939; LC.
40. Aunt Kaye, letter to LD, 9 January 1941; LC.
41. Newspaper article titled "Composing Brought About by Mother's Challenge," clipping. Later in life she would remark: "The whole point of poetry is to

elude meaning"; LD, interview with André Bernard, WNYC, 14 December 1983; NYPL-Sound.

42. LD, letter to Jamake Highwater, undated; Jamake Highwater Papers, NYPL-Manuscripts.

43. Many of these published poems were included in her scrapbook, but most of the clippings do not include dates of publication or other information.

44. LD, handwritten letter from Cleveland (Ohio) Hotel, dated 29 November 1940, addressed to Mr. and Mrs. C. Dlugoszewski, 5327 Baldwin, Detroit; LC.

45. Clipping, *Detroit Free Press*, 4 May 1941.

46. A typescript of the full essay is available in her papers at LC.

47. *The Review*, 18 December 1941; the article is not attributed but might have been written by Lucille's friend and coeditor, Mary Staltman.

48. *The Review* ("senior issue" yearbook, January 1942), 11.

49. Bak, *Detroitland*, 152. This is a description of a blackout that occurred on 3 May 1942.

50. Bak, 154.

51. See Poremba, *Detroit in Its World Setting*, 272.

52. Only nineteen awards were made in all, distributed across all of the Detroit high schools.

53. Letters from Wayne State Financial Aids Committee and Dean, 17 July 1942 and 13 August 1943.

54. Thanks to Kelli Jurich, Office of Alumni Relations at Wayne State University, for providing me with a copy of Dlugoszewski's college transcripts.

55. LD, interview with André Bernard, WNYC, 14 December 1983; NYPL-Sound; and LD, interview with Cole Gagne, *Soundpieces 2*, 57.

56. In her early-1990s interview with Cole Gagne, Dlugoszewski mentioned Kuhn as the teacher of a poetry group she was involved with: "[Kuhn] teased me that I was his Rimbaud." See Gagne, *Soundpieces 2*, 60f.

57. Letter from LD to EH, August 1958; LC.

58. Announcement in *Detroit Collegian* (Wayne State University's newspaper), 4 May 1945; letter from Howard F. Shout, Shattuck awards committee chairman, 31 January 1946; letter from Helen J. Hanlon, Supervisor, Language Education Department Detroit Public Schools, 11 February 1946; LC. (Lucille also received $10 for this award; on another occasion she won the Shattuck prize again, this time winning $25.)

59. Undated letter from the National Poetry Association's Los Angeles office. Unfortunately, this prize-winning poem has not been located.

60. *Detroit Free Press*, 23 August 1946.

61. Keefer, "Erick Hawkins, Modern Dancer," 56f. Emphases mine.

62. Jamake Highwater, "Discovering Dlugoszewski," *Soho Weekly News* (11 May 1978). Emphasis mine. Another writer claimed that Dlugoszewski "ran away to New York"; De View, "She Creates Music to Fill the World."

63. LD, interview with Cole Gagne, *Soundpieces 2*, 55. Emphasis mine. In fact, Dlugoszewski started studying with Sultan several years before 1952.

64. Dlugoszewski distorted her own chronology here: she was sixteen in 1942 when she graduated from high school and entered Wayne State; it would have been several years before she was eligible to apply to medical school. LD, interview with Cole Gagne, *Soundpieces 2*, 57.

65. LD, interview with André Bernard, WNYC, 14 December 1983; NYPL-Sound.

66. Bredshall had been the pianist for the New York premiere of Ruth Crawford's *Rat Riddles* in a Pan American Association of Composers concert on 22 April 1930. The concert included works by Carlos Chavez, Henry Cowell, Charles Ives, Vivian Fine, Alejandro Garcia Caturla, Dane Rudhyar, Gerald Strang, and George Antheil. ("Pan-Americans Heard," *New York Times* [22 April 1930], 24; "League of Composers," *New York Times* [26 January 1930], 112.) We can only speculate about whether Bredshall shared some of this ultramodernist repertoire with his young composer-pianist; Dlugoszewski later claimed that she had not encountered Ruth Crawford's music until her studies with Edgard Varèse in New York during the early 1950s (LD, interview with Olivia Mattis, 29 December 1989; Stanford).

67. In 1948, Katja Andy also recommended the young pianist Christian Wolff (b. 1934) to Sultan. Moritz von Bredow, *Rebellische Pianistin: Das Leben der Grete Sultan zwischen Berlin und New York* (Mainz: Schott Verlag, 2014), 315. Wolff's family knew Andy through mutual friends—Richard and Editha Sterba—who also lived in Detroit but summered in Vermont, where Wolff's family would visit. Thanks to Christian Wolff for clarifying this connection. See also *Soundpieces 2*, 57–58.

68. The letter was signed by "N. Lovisco," and dated 16 August 1948. I have not been able to locate any information about this business or its possible connection to present-day Berkshire-related agencies.

69. LD, letter to mother, 8 July 1949; LC.

CHAPTER 2. LETTERS FROM NEW YORK (1949–51)

1. LD, letter to mother, 2 May 1950; LC.
2. De View, "She Creates Music to Fill the World."
3. See Steven Johnson, ed. *The New York School of Music and Visual Arts* (New York: Routledge, 2002).
4. LD, letter to mother, 30 June 1950; LC.
5. LD, letter to mother, 9 February 1950; LC. Before this, auto industry workers, including Dlugoszewski's father, had to work on Saturdays.
6. LD, letter to mother, 19 February 1950; LC.
7. LD, letter to mother, 14 February 1950; LC.
8. LD, letter to father, 9 February 1950; LC.
9. Christian Wolff, "Remembering Grete Sultan (2005)," in *Occasional Pieces: Writings and Interviews, 1952–2013* (New York: Oxford University Press, 2017): 250.

In this brief essay, Wolff adds: "Another of [Sultan's] students was Lucia Dlugoszewski, who also later became a composer," 249.

10. LD, letter to father, 23 April 1950; LC.

11. LD, letter to mother, 28 February 1950; LC.

12. LD, letter to mother, 24 February 1950; and LD, letter to mother, 2 April 1950; LC.

13. LD, letter to mother, 8 March 1950; LC. See also Robert Sabin, "Recitals: Maro Ajemian, Pianist—Carnegie Recital Hall, March 7," *Musical America* (15 March 1950): 34.

14. LD, letter to mother, 28 February 1950; LC.

15. LD, letter to father, 11 April 1950; LC.

16. LD, letter to mother, 9 May 1950; LC.

17. LD, letter to mother, 28 June 1950; LC.

18. LD, letter to mother, 5 June 1950; LC.

19. LD, letter to father, 30 May 1950; LC.

20. LD, letter to mother, 11 February 1950; LC. She added: "I think my new dress will best fit the occasion since Mr. Varèse is French and likes his feminine companions modishly dressed—and pearls and brown shoes so the brown coat will match-ha!"

21. Judith Tick, *Ruth Crawford Seeger: A Composer's Search for American Music* (New York: Oxford, 1997), 313f; see also "ISCM, McMillin Theatre, April 11," *Musical America* (April 1950), 32.

22. LD, letter to father, 11 April 1950; LC.

23. LD, 11 April 1950.

24. Routé and Kirsch, "Two New York Composers," 72.

25. LD, letter to father, 7 April 1950; LC.

26. LD, letter to mother, 10 April 1950; LC.

27. LD, letter to father, 15 May 1950; LC.

28. LD, letter to mother, 24 April 1950; LC.

29. LD, letter to mother, 7 February 1950; LC.

30. Several works lists created by Dlugoszewski at various points in her life indicate that she wrote several numbered piano sonatas around 1950; she also mentions several sonatas in her letters describing her work with Cage; these may have been modeled on Cage's recent *Sonatas and Interludes* for prepared piano (1946–48), which used the pre-Classical, single-movement, binary sonata form typical of Domenico Scarlatti's keyboard sonatas. In March 1950 she described how Cage was helping her make a professional recording of one of her new sonatas; LD, letter to mother, 30 March 1950; LC.

31. LD, letter to mother, 2 May 1950; LC. In a letter written to her mother on 30 June 1950, Dlugoszewski referred to a photograph of herself that captured "the beautiful sculptural bone structure of my Slavic face," revealing "the mood of my character as a very talented composer"; her vanity seems to have increased over the course of the year.

32. LD, letter to mother, 16 May 1950; LC.

33. She wrote: "It was so well received that I was offered a job teaching there but I don't think I would want to go so far south right away next year." LD, letter to father, 27 June 1950; LC. On 2 July 1950, Cage wrote to Pierre Boulez: "I have just got back from New Orleans." *The Boulez-Cage Correspondence*, J. J. Nattiez, ed. (New York: Cambridge University Press, 1993), 68.

34. LD, letter to father, 25 April 1950; LC. Sultan's biographer claims that she had an artistic crisis between the years 1948 to 1951 (overlapping with the years Dlugoszewski studied and socialized with her), and ceased performing during that time. See von Bredow, *Rebellische Pianistin*, 364.

35. LD, letter to mother, 18 May 1950; LC.

36. LD, letter to mother, 19 May 1950; LC.

37. LD, letter to mother, 29 May 1950; LC.

38. LD, letter to father, 20 July 1950; LC.

39. Apparently, she enjoyed *City Lights* very much: she and Sultan would go to see it again in August. LD, letter to father, 9 August 1950; LC.

40. LD, letter to father, 19 June 1950; LC.

41. LD, letter to parents, 24 June 1950; LC.

42. LD, letter to father, 27 June 1950; LC.

43. LD, letter to father, 27 June 1950; LC.

44. LD, letter to parents, 23 October 1950; LC.

45. LD, letter to father, 1 July 1950; LC.

46. On 15 June 1950, Jennie Dlugoszewski had some sort of surgery.

47. LD, letter to mother, 2 July 1950; LC.

48. LD, letter to father, 31 July 1950; LC.

49. LD, letter to father, 10 July 1950; LC.

50. LD, letter to father, 11 July 1950; LC. The *New York Times* front page headline for the late edition that same day declared "Army Calls for Draft of 20,000; U.S. Tanks Enter Korean Battle."

51. LD, letter to mother, 2 August 1950; LC.

52. LD, letter to father, 3 August 1950; LC.

53. LD, letter to mother, 7 July 1950; LD, letter to mother, 19 July 1950; LC.

54. The registry can be viewed on ancestry.com: accessed by the author on 4 June 2019.

55. In her interview with Philip Blackburn, Eleanor Hovda states that Dlugoszewski and Dorazio had been married (Philip Blackburn, "Eleanor Remembers Lucia Dlugoszewski," interview with Eleanor Hovda, *American Mavericks*, May 2003 [St. Paul, MN: American Public Media, 2018]). Other friends and acquaintances offered contradictory accounts of Dlugoszewski and Dorazio's relationship in the early 1950s.

56. According to Hawkins scholar Julia Keefer, who interviewed Dlugoszewski in 1977, "Dorazio was also from Detroit, where he met Dlugoszewski at Wayne State University.... When Dlugoszewski came to New York, Dorazio decided to follow her and pursue an artistic career." Keefer, "Erick Hawkins, Modern Dancer,"

59. Others told me that Mary Norton had also been a friend of Dlugoszewski's at Wayne State.

57. Near the end stages of finalizing this manuscript, previously unavailable correspondence between LD and Ralph Dorazio from the early 1950s surfaced in the Library of Congress collection; I was unable to consult these sixteen letters and other short writings, which may help future scholars understand their relationship more fully.

58. LD, letter to mother, 8 August 1950; LC.

59. LD, letter to parents, 6 September 1950; LC.

60. LD, letter to father, 11 September 1950; LC.

61. LD, letter to father, 15 September 1950; LC. "Way deep in Brooklyn" probably referred to her first address when she moved to New York, which, according to her Wayne State University transcripts, appears to have been at 134 Brooklyn Avenue, in the Crown Heights neighborhood.

62. LD, letter to father, 19 September 1950; LC.

63. LD, letter to father, 21 September 1950; LC.

64. LD, letter to father, 13 October 1950; LC.

65. LD, letter to mother, 5 December 1950; LC.

66. LD, letter to mother, 21 September 1950; LC. Emphasis Dlugoszewski's.

67. LD, letter to mother, 31 October 1950; LC.

68. LD, letter to father, 2 November 1950; LC.

69. LD, letter to mother, 22 September 1950; LC.

70. LD, letter to parents, 23 October 1950; LC.

71. LD, letter to father, 28 October 1950; LC.

72. LD, letter to mother, 3 November 1950; LC.

73. LD, letter to mother, 6 November 1950; LC. See also *Musical America* (1 December 1950), 18.

74. LD, letter to father, 9 November 1950; and letter to mother, 11 November 1950; LC.

75. LD, letter to mother, 13 November 1950; LC.

76. LD, letter to mother, 22 November 1950; LC.

77. LD, letter to mother, 2 January 1951; and letter to father, 3 January 1951; LC

78. LD, letter to mother, 16 January 1951; LC.

79. LD, letter to father, 11 January 1951; LC.

80. LD, letter to mother, 11 January 1951; LC. Schuman's piece was *Judith* (1949).

81. Erick Hawkins, Harvard University application, dated 26 April 1926; Harvard University Archives.

82. See Mark Franko, *Martha Graham in Love and War* (New York: Oxford University Press, 2012); and Victoria Thoms, *Martha Graham: Gender and the Haunting of a Dance Pioneer* (Bristol, UK: Intellect, 2013).

83. EH, "Machine versus Tool," *Ballet Review* (winter 1993), 53.

84. See Francis Mason, "A Conversation with Erick Hawkins and Lucia Dlugoszewski," *Ballet Review* 21/4 (Winter 1993), 50, 52. According to Hawkins, Sultan lived "two doors away from my studio on 17th Street."

85. Mason, 56.
86. LD, letter to mother, 31 January 1951; LC.
87. LD, letter to father, 19 February 1951; LC.
88. LD, letter to father, 29 January 1951; LC.
89. LD, letter to mother, 28 February 1951; LC.
90. LD, letter to mother, 12 March 1951; LC.
91. LD, letter to mother, 29 March 1951; LC.
92. LD, letter to mother, 21 April 1951; LC.
93. LD, letter to father, 6 June 1951; LC.
94. LD, letter to mother, 26 June 1951; LC.
95. LD, letter to mother, 11 June 1951; LC.
96. EH, "My Love Affair with Music [1967]," in *The Body Is a Clear Place and Other Statements on Dance* (Princeton, NJ: Princeton Book Company, 1992), 79.

CHAPTER 3. NEW YORK BEGINNINGS

1. Dlugoszewski-Hawkins program note for a 1953 performance of *openings of the (eye)*.
2. In a 1983 interview LD named Varèse, Sultan, and Salzer as her teachers, and claimed to also have had "close associations" with Ben Weber, Elliott Carter, and Milton Babbitt. LD, interview with André Bernard, WNYC, 14 December 1983; NYPL-Sound.
3. "I suppose maybe some people are affirmed early, but I was so worried that someone would tell me I couldn't be a composer." LD, interview with Olivia Mattis, 29 December 1989; Stanford.
4. LD, letter to mother, 11 February 1950; LC.
5. Dlugoszewski retells a slightly different version of this story in her interview with Cole Gagne, *Soundpieces 2*, 58.
6. LD, interview with Olivia Mattis, 29 December 1989; Stanford.
7. LD, letter to Edgard Varèse, July 1965; Edgard Varèse Papers, PSS. Thanks to Anne Shreffler for helping me obtain access to Dlugoszewski's letters to Varèse.
8. LD told Virgil Thomson she had discovered Satie on her own in the Detroit Public Library. LD, letter to Virgil Thomson, 8 June 1959; Virgil Thomson Papers, Yale-Gilmore.
9. LD, interview with Olivia Mattis, 29 December 1989; Stanford.
10. LD, quoted in Walter Terry, article on Dlugoszewski, *BMI* magazine, May 1969.
11. LD, interview with André Bernard, WNYC, 14 December 1983; NYPL-Sound.
12. LD, interview with Olivia Mattis, 29 December 1989; Stanford.
13. Ibid. Brett Boutwell's forthcoming book on Feldman (University of Illinois Press, American Composers Series) documents Feldman's jealousy and his conflicts with other composers close to Cage, including Earle Brown and Philip Corner.

14. Despite ample evidence of Cage and Dlugoszewski's relationship, her name is completely absent from books on Cage, including Kenneth Silverman's otherwise exhaustive 483-page biography. See Kenneth Silverman, *Begin Again: A Biography of John Cage* (Evanston, IL: Northwestern University Press, 2010). Likewise, David Revill's 1992 biography, *The Roaring Silence: John Cage* (New York: Arcade Publishing, 1992), makes no mention of Dlugoszewski. I have found no acknowledgment whatsoever of her relationship with Cage in the early 1950s in any of the dozens of available publications on Cage's life and relationships.

15. Franko, *Martha Graham in Love and War*, 9.

16. Blackburn, "Eleanor Remembers Lucia Dlugoszewski."

17. Jamake Highwater, *Dance: Rituals of Experience* (New York: A&W Publishers, Inc., 1978), 197.

18. See Revill, *The Roaring Silence*, 133. David Tudor premiered Cage's *Music of Changes* on 1 January 1952, in a concert attended by John Ashbery and Frank O'Hara, also acquaintances of Dlugoszewski's. See David Lehman, *The Last Avant-Garde: The Making of the New York School of Poets* (New York: Anchor Books, 1999), 339.

19. Typescript dated 1/17/51; LC.

20. Typescript dated 1/20/51; LC.

21. Typescript dated 1/23/51; LC.

22. EH, letter to "Hank," 30 March 1951; LC.

23. EH, letter to "Hank," 21 April 1951; LC.

24. Keefer, "Erick Hawkins, Modern Dancer," 58.

25. "Lucia created a prepared piano more beautiful than Mr. Cage ever imagined," she wrote to her mother on 29 March 1951; LC.

26. Some of these hair combs have been preserved in Dlugoszewski's papers at the Library of Congress.

27. LD, letter to EH, 14 August 1951; LC.

28. In a 1993 interview with *Ballet Review* magazine, Dlugoszewski calls the fourth movement "Animal Innocence" and the fifth movement "Eros, the First Force"; LD, "*8 Clear Places*," *Ballet Review* 21, no. 4 (Winter 1993): 61–65.

29. A pencil draft of the piece is dated January 1952; LC. At the time of this writing, a recent (and first-ever) recording has been made of *openings of the (eye)* by the #Ensemble [Hashtag Ensemble], established in 2013 by the flutist Ania Karpowicz, in Warsaw, Poland.

30. Keefer, "Erick Hawkins, Modern Dancer," 233.

31. EH, "Dance as a Metaphor of Existence [1979]," in *The Body Is a Clear Place*, 118.

32. Jennifer Dunning, "Erick Hawkins: Celebrating the Body and the Spirit," *New York Times* (13 September 1981), 28.

33. Judith Malina, diary entry, 19 January 1952, in *The Diaries of Judith Malina, 1947–1957* (New York: Grove Press, Inc., 1984), 206.

34. See listings, "4 Programs of Dance," *New York Times* (13 January 1952), 256; also "The Week's Events: A Spate of Performances Mainly by Moderns," *New York*

Times (13 January 1952), 260. Around this time Dlugoszewski announced that she might have an opportunity to write music for Erdman; LD, letter to parents, 2 January 1952; LC.

35. Robert Sabin, "Dance Review," *Musical America*, January 1952.
36. Malina, diary entry, 20 January 1952; *The Diaries of Judith Malina*, 207.
37. LD, "What Is Sound to Music?," *Main Currents in Modern Thought* 30, no. 1 (Sept.–Oct. 1973): 5.
38. See Pierre Biner, *The Living Theatre* (New York: Horizon Press, 1972), 25f.
39. Malina, diary entry, 22 March 1952, 217.
40. Malina, diary entry, 6 February 1952, 208.
41. Malina, diary entry, 7 February 1952, 209.
42. Malina, diary entry, 10 February 1952, 209.
43. Aimee Scheff, "Picasso's *Desire*—What Is It?" *Theatre Arts* (April 1952): 36.
44. Biner, *The Living Theatre*, 31.
45. Grace Hartigan, journal entry of 13 March 1952, in *The Journals of Grace Hartigan 1951–1955*, ed. William T. La Moy and Joseph P. McCaffrey (Syracuse University Press, 2009), 26.
46. A similar phrase, substituting the word *world* for *ground*, appeared later in a descriptive annotation about the 1965 piece *Lords of Persia*, about which she wrote in the same document: "Structurally the score of *Lords of Persia* on all levels is springtime music in the way Buddhist and any other radical empiricists would extract aesthetic principles from such seasonal preoccupations structurally being springtime, the music is a constant *nageire*." Box including *Amor Elusive Empty August* and *Lords of Persia*; LC.
47. Malina, diary entry, 6 May 1952, 224.
48. Robert Sabin, "Living Theatre Concert, Cherry Lane Theatre, May 5," *Musical America* (May 1952), 27.
49. This piece might also be called *Moving Space Theater Piece* (for "everyday sounds"). Dlugoszewski claimed that she performed it in Detroit as early as 1949; LD, interview with Cole Gagne, *Soundpieces 2*, 59.
50. Postcard from LD to EH, postmarked 17 November 1952; LC.
51. LD, interview with Cole Gagne, *Soundpieces 2*, 59.
52. Malina, diary entry, 26 November 1952, 253f.
53. Keefer, "Erick Hawkins, Modern Dancer," 59f.
54. LD, interview with Cole Gagne, *Soundpieces 2*, 60.
55. Hal Rammel, CD liner notes, *Lucia Dlugoszewski: Disparate Stairway Radical Other* (NWCR 859), 1978 and 2000, Composers Recording, Inc., 2007, Anthology of Recorded Music, Inc.).
56. These handwritten "UBU MUSIC CUES" are held in The Living Theatre Papers; NYPL-Theatre.
57. Hal Rammel, quoting Tom Johnson, "Musician of the Month: Lucia Dlugoszewski," *High Fidelity/Musical America* (June 1975), MA-5, quoted in liner notes to *Lucia Dlugoszewski: Disparate Stairway Radical Other* (NWCR 859, 2000).

58. Hal Rammel, quoting interview with Joel Thome, 12 June 2000, quoted in liner notes to *Lucia Dlugoszewski: Disparate Stairway Radical Other*.

59. She also wrote: "I would let you crawl all over my ears to find the right place to sleep." LD, letter to EH, 20 August 1952; LC.

60. The film can be viewed on ubuweb: http://ubu.com/film/menken_noguchi.html; accessed 9 August 2019.

61. A copy of the promotional flyer is held in LC.

62. Almost all explanatory notes included in Dlugoszewski-Hawkins programs lack the name of a specific author, but are written in a style similar to Dlugoszewski's other writings, both public and private.

63. EH, "Art in Its Second Function," in *The Body Is a Clear Place*, 148.

64. Malina diary entry, 25 January 1953, 267.

65. Irving Sandler, as quoted in Amy Newman, *Challenging Art: Artforum 1962–1974* (New York, NY: Soho, 2000), 22–23.

66. Sandler, 23.

67. Malina, diary entry, 1 June 1956, 406.

CHAPTER 4. EXPANDING CREATIVITY AND COLLABORATION (1953–60)

1. Undated writing in LD's hand; LC.

2. Malina, diary entry, 29 October 1953, 300.

3. Mary Gabriel, *Ninth Street Women—Lee Krasner, Elaine de Kooning, Grace Hartigan, Joan Mitchell, and Helen Frankenthaler: Five Painters and the Movement That Changed Modern Art* (New York: Little, Brown, 2018), 504.

4. Routé and Kirsch, "Two New York Composers," 74.

5. Malina, diary entry, 1 April 1951, 153.

6. LD, letter to Lou Harrison, 19 February 1954; Lou Harrison Papers, UCSC.

7. The signature is handwritten and unclear; it could be "Julian" or "Judith." The dates "54/55" are penciled in on the card; Living Theatre Records, NYPL-Theatre.

8. "Hawkins will make any sacrifice, financial or otherwise, to have live music." Keefer, "Erick Hawkins, Modern Dancer," 254.

9. In August 1955 Beck and Malina asked Cage whether he thought French composer Pierre Schaeffer would let them use his *Symphonie pour un homme seul* (1949–50) as the soundtrack for the play. Draft of letter from Beck and Malina to Cage, dated 27 August 1955; Living Theatre Records, NYPL-Theatre.

10. LD, undated letter to Beck and Malina; Living Theatre Records, NYPL-Theatre.

11. Keefer, "Erick Hawkins, Modern Dancer," 306.

12. The score for *Double and Single Labyrinths* consists of a handwritten series of columns with words, pitches, and durations cascading down the page.

13. Malina, diary entry, 25 September 1955, 383.
14. LD, letter to EH, 14 December 1955; LC.
15. "The Week's Events," *New York Times* (24 November 1957).
16. LD, "Notes on New Music for the Dance," *Dance Observer* (November 1957), 133. (A half-page announcement of the *Here and Now with Watchers* premiere appeared on page 141 of this same issue.)
17. LD, 134.
18. LD, 135.
19. LD, 135.
20. John Cage, "Composition as Process," in *Silence: Lectures and Writings* (Middletown, CT: Wesleyan University Press, 1961), 41.
21. Clifford Gessler, "Controversial Dance Show Enchants Capacity Crowd," *Oakland Tribune* (5 June 1959), 28.
22. This handwritten list, dated 18 January 1954, concluded with a "rhythmic concept" drawn as "x U —," which was superimposed over (and under) her own name:

x U —   x U —
Dlu go sze wski, Lucia
x U —   x U —

She added this note: "Officially dedicated to the sweetheart of this rhythmic concept: Erick Hawkins (unofficially dedicated to Gluck, Messiaen, and the cummings who wrote *HIM*)"
23. LD, undated and unpublished typescript, "Theatre, Timbre, Time, and Transparency," held both in LC and NYPL.
24. She mentioned their first meeting at the premiere of *Here and Now with Watchers* in "What Is Sound to Music?," 4.
25. EH, letter to F.S.C. Northrop, 18 November 1957; LC.
26. Northrop, letter to EH, 27 November 1957; LC.
27. EH, letter to Northrop, 27 February 1958; LC.
28. EH, letter to Northrop.
29. Northrop, letter to EH, 3 March 1958; LC.
30. Northrop, letter to EH.
31. F. S. C. Northrop, *Philosophical Anthropology and Practical Politics* (New York: Macmillan, 1960), 313.
32. Gabriel, *Ninth Street Women*, 587f.
33. A folder labeled "Small Centers/Space Notation (1958)" at the Library of Congress holds a pencil draft of the score for what is presumably *Music for Small Centers*; the manuscript is dated "4/23/58," just some six weeks before the Five Spot engagement and one month after the Mills concert. The top two staves are labeled "legato attack" and the lower one (all three in treble clef throughout) is labeled "plucked strings."
34. Another version of this score bears the title *Violin Music for Left Ear in a Small Room* (1965), without the dedication, but with the parenthetical note: "in

12 parts the tiny distinction-airplane hetero structure" (which also appears on the dedicated version).

35. Keefer, "Erick Hawkins, Modern Dancer," 275f.

36. This manuscript is held in the Lillian and Frederick Kiesler Papers; AAA.

37. Routé and Kirsch, "Two New York Composers," 74. The reference to Salinger might be related to his use of the term *suchness* in his short story "Franny," first published in *The New Yorker* (31 January 1953), and later in the collection *Nine Stories* (April 1953). Dlugoszewski began using the term *suchness* in her piece titles around 1958. Kevin D. Lewis's 2011 doctoral thesis includes a careful examination about the possible meanings of "left ear" for Dlugoszewski, and how the notation for the "left ear" pieces might be interpreted. See Lewis, "'The Miracle of Unintelligibility': The Music and Invented Instruments of Lucia Dlugoszewski," DMA percussion thesis, University of Cincinnati, 2011.

38. LD, letter to Lillian Kiesler, undated; Lillian and Frederick Kiesler Papers, AAA.

39. LD, letter to Lillian Kiesler.

40. LD, letter to John Kirkpatrick, 15 May 1959; John Kirkpatrick Papers, Yale-Gilmore. She enclosed in this letter the "structural organization" of *Here and Now with Watchers* created for the Mills College of Education concert, and a number of other programs from her recent activities, including the Five Spot "manifestos" and "Curtain of Timbre" program.

41. For numbers 3, 4, and 5, "Curtain of Timbre" information was also included in the program.

42. Nancy K. Siff, "Composers' Showcase," *The Village Voice* (27 May 1959), 8.

43. Virgil Thomson, *American Music Since 1900* (New York: Holt, Reinhart, and Winston, 1970), 139.

44. LD, interview with Olivia Mattis, 29 December 1989; Stanford.

45. LD, letter to Thomson, 8 June 1959; Virgil Thomson Papers, Yale-Gilmore.

46. Clifford Gessler, "Controversial Dance Show Enchants Capacity Crowd," *Oakland Tribune* (5 June 1959), 28.

47. Gessler, 28.

48. Alfred Frankenstein, "Hawkins Dance Work Fascinating," *San Francisco Chronicle*, 2 June 1959.

49. According to the Erick Hawkins Dance Company official website (https://www.erickhawkinsdance.org/), the Company had been established in 1951.

50. According to papers held at the Library of Congress, Erick Hawkins and Martha Graham obtained a divorce in Mexico on 28 September 1959; the papers were translated and ratified in El Paso, Texas.

51. "Dad," letter to "Lucille," December 1959; LC.

52. Daisy Aldan, *A New Folder, Americans: Poems and Drawings* (1959), 127.

53. "The Newcomers: The Folder Poets," *Mademoiselle* (January 1960), 72–73.

54. Routé and Kirsch, "Two New York Composers," 75f.

55. LD quoted in: Allen Hughes, "And Miss Dlugoszewski Experiments—A Lot," *New York Times* (7 March 1971).

56. LD, interview with André Bernard, WNYC, 14 December 1983; NYPL-Sound.
57. LD, interview with Olivia Mattis, 29 December 1989; Stanford.

CHAPTER 5. THE DISPARATE ELEMENT (1960–70)

1. LD, interview with Cole Gagne, *Soundpieces 2*, 66.
2. LD, letter to Aldan, postmark November 1960; Daisy Aldan Papers, Yale-Beinecke.
3. Thanks to Laura Pettibone Wright for sharing a copy of LD and EH's marriage license.
4. EH, "Questions and Answers [1962]," in *The Body Is a Clear Place*, 49.
5. Keefer, "Erick Hawkins, Modern Dancer," 59.
6. To date, the best source of information on Dlugoszewski's instruments, including photographic documentation, is Kevin D. Lewis, "'The Miracle of Unintelligibility': The Music and Invented Instruments of Lucia Dlugoszewski," DMA thesis, College-Conservatory of Music, University of Cincinnati, 2011.
7. LD quoted in De View, "She Creates Music to Fill the World."
8. LD, in interview with Cole Gagne, *Soundpieces 2*, 62.
9. LD, quoted in Walter Terry, article on Dlugoszewski, *BMI* magazine, May 1969. An undated, unsigned typescript titled "Lucia Dlugoszewski / Composer and Inventor of the Timbre Piano" explained: "Her music is also a new departure from existing percussion music by emphasizing new techniques to achieve unusually delicate dynamics and remove the aggressive and brutal playing practices common among percussionists, in favor of perceptual and poetic values."
10. See Beal, *Johanna Beyer*, 41.
11. Nicolas Slonimsky asserted that because Dlugoszewski was "inspired by the example of Varèse's *Ionisations*, she invented or perfected a number of percussion instruments," but I have found no evidence for this claim. Nicolas Slonimsky, "Dlugoszewski, Lucia," in *Baker's Biographical Dictionary of Musicians*, 8th [revised] edition (New York: Schirmer Books, 1992), 438.
12. Undated program note for performance of *Suchness Concert / Otherness Concert* with *8 Clear Places*. Like Dlugoszewski's clusters of pieces with titles related to the ideas of *Music for Left Ear* and *Everyday Sounds*, *Suchness Concert* seems to have been fluidly combined with a number of other titles, including *Otherness Concert*, *Otherness Narrow Concert*, *Radical Narrowness Concert Other*, and *Radical Otherness Concert*.
13. LD quoted in Hughes, "And Miss Dlugoszewski Experiments—A Lot," *New York Times*, 7 March 1971.
14. Daisy Aldan Papers, Yale-Beinecke
15. LD, "8 Clear Places," *Ballet Review* 21, no. 4 (Winter 1993), 65.
16. In a handwritten list of the movements for *8 Clear Places*, Dlugoszewski named the second movement "pine tree in moon light" and the seventh "newly slow

shadow of she and he / sweet snowing shadow of she and he." Kevin Lewis calls the seventh movement "they moving."

17. Don McDonagh, *The Complete Guide to Modern Dance* (Middletown, CT: Wesleyan University Press, 1976), 299.

18. See Naima Prevots, *Dance for Export: Cultural Diplomacy and the Cold War* (Middletown, CT: Wesleyan University Press, 2012), 63f.

19. EH, "Art in Its Second Function," in *The Body Is a Clear Place*, 148f.

20. McDonagh, *The Complete Guide to Modern Dance*, 297.

21. McDonagh, 299f.

22. EH, "Questions and Answers," in *The Body Is a Clear Place*, 43.

23. Terry Trucco, "Erick Hawkins, Ever the Poet, Tries a New Vocabulary," *New York Times* (23 January 1994).

24. See John Cage, *Silence*, 41–53.

25. Ned O'Gorman, "New Ideas in Dance and Movies," *Jubilee: A Magazine of the Church and Her People* (August 1962), 48. O'Gorman went on to compare Dlugoszewski and Hawkins's work to another recent collaboration: "To watch them and then to watch the vulgar and shallow excursion into television of Stravinsky and Balanchine in the CBS production of *The Flood* is to know the depths to which the great can fall; it is to know too how the world can corrupt its geniuses."

26. Francis Mason, "A Conversation with Erick Hawkins and Lucia Dlugoszewski," *Ballet Review* 21, no. 4 (Winter 1993), 47f.

27. LD, paraphrasing Stein, in *Soundpieces 2*, 67. Dlugoszewski also valued this quality in late Schubert: "What Schubert does is he *continually* gives the unexpected." Emphasis hers. LD, interview with André Bernard, WNYC, 14 December 1983; NYPL-Sound.

28. A document titled "Project Description/Music by Lucia Dlugoszewski" (possibly for a grant application) included these "composers notes" on her piece from the early 1990s called *Radical Otherness Concert*.

29. Ticket/guest list for *Women of Trachis* in a file labeled "Productions: Theatre of Chance: Women of Trachis"; Living Theatre Records, NYPL-Theatre.

30. David E. James, *To Free the Cinema: Jonas Mekas and the New York Underground* (Princeton, NJ: Princeton University Press, 1992), 115.

31. Eugene Archer, "*Guns of the Trees*," *New York Times* (29 February 1964). A January 2020 article in the *New York Times* about a restoration and new screening of the film noted that "the action is punctuated with blasts of high-frequency noise," but failed to mention the name of the composer. See J. Hoberman, "The Bohemian Gloom and Gusto," *New York Times* (24 January 2020), C9.

32. "She and Mekas were apparently good friends and [he] was very generous in loaning me [her] recordings"; "Blue" Gene Tyranny, written communication with the author, 5 January 2018.

33. LD, letter to Thomson, 26 June 1962; Virgil Thomson Papers, Yale-Gilmore.

34. LD, "Is Music Sound?" *Jubilee* 10 (1962).

35. Cage, "History of Experimental Music in the United States," in *Silence*, 71.

36. LD, letter to Irving Sandler, 10 May 1962; Irving Sandler Papers, GRI.

37. LD, letter to Walter Sorell, 29 July 1962; Walter Sorell Research Files on Mary Wigman, NYPL-Dance. Sorell was the author of the book *Dance Has Many Faces* (1951).

38. LD, letter to Kenneth Wentworth, chairman of the Music Department, Sarah Lawrence College, 14 February 1963; LC.

39. LD, letter to Reinhardt, 9 June 1963: Ad Reinhardt Papers, AAA. The poem Dlugoszewski enclosed had the text "automobiles / opening the death / of rain," and included the graphic, geometric shapes and lines, in black ink, pencil, and charcoal shading; it also included performance instructions, written above the graphic representation of the poem at a slant: "Let one flute play / middle C softly for / ten seconds while one / piano strikes middle C / *mf* once holding the / pedal thirty seconds."

40. The premiere was reviewed (not entirely positively) in Claude Saurraute, "Une soirée d' avant-garde..." *Le Monde* (1 July 1963).

41. LD, letter to Daisy Aldan, 19 June 1964; Daisy Aldan Papers, Yale-Beinecke.

42. LD, letter to Peter Yates, 1 October 1964; Peter Yates Papers, UCSD.

43. Aside from this remark, Dlugoszewski's writings do not suggest that she was interested in the theoretical or compositional implications of just intonation.

44. "Erick Hawkins Dancers Program Series Next," *Albuquerque Tribune*, 29 October 1964.

45. LD, postcard to Reinhardt, postmarked 28 November 1964; Ad Reinhardt Papers, AAA.

46. "Dancers Set Show Monday in Chickasha," *Lawton Constitution Morning Press*, 22 November 1964.

47. LD, undated notebook entry; LC.

48. Strikethrough is LD's.

49. A copy of the undated report was found in Daisy Aldan Papers, Yale-Beinecke. All quotations about the tour are from this document.

50. One cannot help but wonder if Chester Dlugoszewski, LD's father, was the "automobile designer from Michigan" who was "seeing modern dance for the first time."

51. She also noted: "One young composition student said to me, 'your music reminds me of Xenakis and Ligeti, but I like to listen to your sounds more because they sound more beautiful.' That was nice! I think maybe it's because I love the Satie-Thomson tradition of playfulness that Xenakis and Ligeti are a little too European—'serious' to permit themselves!" LD, letter to Thomson [undated], Virgil Thomson Papers, Yale-Gilmore.

52. LD, letter to Thomson [undated], Virgil Thomson Papers, Yale-Gilmore.

53. LD, letter to Walter Sorell, "en route" [undated], letterhead from Terre Haute House (Indiana); Walter Sorell Research Files on Mary Wigman, NYPL-Dance.

54. LD, letter to Reinhardt, 10 June 1965; Ad Reinhardt Papers, AAA.

55. LD, letter to Charles Boultenhouse and Parker Tyler, 10 June 1965; Charles Boultenhouse and Parker Tyler Papers, NYPL-Manuscripts.

56. LD, letter to Schuman, 10 June 1965; Papers and Records of William Schuman, NYPL-Music; quoted by Steve Swayne, *Orpheus in Manhattan: William*

Schuman and the Shaping of America's Musical Life (New York: Oxford University Press, 2011): 212.

57. LD, letter to Thomson, 10 June 1965, Virgil Thomson Papers, Yale-Gilmore.

58. EH, letter to Sallie R. Wagner, 15 October 1967; Sallie R. Wagner Papers, LC.

59. She mentioned one woman in particular: "Your relation and friendship with Marie Springhart is all part of this." Several people, including dancer Bonnie Bird, have suggested that Erick Hawkins was homosexual. See Victoria Thoms, *Martha Graham: Gender and the Haunting of a Dance Pioneer* (Bristol, UK: Intellect, 2013), 150.

60. Japanese poet Masuo Basho (1644–1694) and Mu'Chi (Muqi), thirteenth-century Chinese Buddhist monk and painter.

61. Keefer, "Erick Hawkins, Modern Dancer," 273.

62. "Flower" quote in Keefer, "Erick Hawkins, Modern Dancer," 67f; Dlugoszewski, paraphrasing Stein, in *Soundpieces 2*, 67.

63. Beverly Brown Papers, NYPL-Dance. The following details about Dlugoszewski's class are from this collection.

64. A version of this chart is included in Renata Celichowska, *The Erick Hawkins Modern Dance Technique* (Hightstown, NJ: Princeton Book Co., 2000): 75. Celichowska called this dynamic chart "energy-level gradations," while Hawkins scholar Julia Keefer explained it as "the energy used to perform a movement from delicate to strong." Keefer, "Erick Hawkins, Modern Dancer," 67f.

65. Keefer, "Erick Hawkins, Modern Dancer," 275.

66. Walter Terry, "Lucia Dlugoszewski," *BMI: The Many Worlds of Music* (1969), 5.

67. Undated, unattributed program note for *Black Lake*. Hawkins also described *Black Lake* as a metaphor for the night sky: EH, "Art in Its Second Function," in *The Body Is a Clear Place*, 149.

68. Undated, unattributed program note for *Black Lake*.

69. Emphasis mine. (See chapter 3.)

70. A pencil notation in one of Dlugoszewski's many notebooks refers to this piece: "Gerry / Swift Diamond / 1970 / tpt solo"; LC.

71. LD, "About the Work," *Space Is a Diamond* [score], Margun Music.

72. LD, "About the Work."

73. Schwarz and Schuller, "Performance Notes," *Space Is a Diamond* [score], Margun Music.

74. LD, "About the Work," *Space Is a Diamond* [score], Margun Music. See also "Lucia Dlugoszewski's *Space Is a Diamond*," in Edward Stanley Bach, "A Performance Project on Selected Works of Five Contemporary Composers: Malcolm Arnold, Robert Henderson, Stan Friedman, John Elmsley, Lucia Dlugoszewski" (DMA thesis, University of British Columbia, 1991): 62–70.

75. William Bolcom, liner notes for "The New Trumpet" (Nonesuch, H-71275; 1972).

76. Thomson, *American Music Since 1910*, 139.

77. Sylvia Glickman and Martha Furman Schleifer, *From Convent to Concert Hall: A Guide to Women Composers* (Westport, CT: Greenwood Press, 2003), 256.

CHAPTER 6. AESTHETIC IMMEDIACY (1970–80)

1. LD, as quoted by Jennifer Dunning, "The Composer Who Energizes the Erick Hawkins Dancers," *New York Times* (7 December 1988).
2. LD, birthday poem for her father, 1 November 1943; LC.
3. Allen Hughes, "And Miss Dlugoszewski Experiments—A Lot," *New York Times* (7 March 1971).
4. John Gruen, "Lucia Dlugoszewski, Surfacing," *Vogue* (October 1970).
5. LD quoted in De View, "She Creates Music to Fill the World."
6. Announcements appearing in the *Ruston Daily Leader* (LA) (10 March 1970); "Hawkins Dance Company to Perform Today," *Cumberland News* (20 February 1971); "Lecture Arranged," *Northwest Arkansas Times* (20 March 1971).
7. Anna Kisselgoff, "Dance: Erick Hawkins Premiere at the Joyce," *New York Times* (11 October 1984). Keefer writes: "When creating these dances, Hawkins was inspired by the theme of nakedness. However, complete nakedness is never used. Men and women wear G-strings or dance belts, because Hawkins wants sensuousness, not pornography or eroticism. The audience should see line and form, not genitals." Keefer, "Erick Hawkins, Modern Dancer," 314.
8. Accessed online at https://www.allmusic.com/album/angels-of-the-inmost-heaven-mw0000882802; 23 June 2019. The 1975 recording of *Densities*, conducted by Gerard Schwarz, appeared on *New American Music Vol. 2*; Smithsonian Folkways.
9. Dean Suzuki, "Review of *New American Music Vol. 2*," *OP*, "L" issue (July–August 1982).
10. See Chou Wen-Chung, "Varèse: A Sketch of the Man and His Music," *Musical Quarterly* 52/2 (April 1966), 157f.
11. Keefer, "Erick Hawkins, Modern Dancer," 256.
12. Leighton Kerner, "Music," *The Village Voice* (11 May 1972), 49.
13. Kerner, 49.
14. EH, letter to Thomson, 24 August 1971; Virgil Thomson Papers, Yale-Gilmore.
15. EH, letter to Thomson, 8 December 1971; Virgil Thomson Papers, Yale-Gilmore.
16. LD, letter to Thomson, undated; Virgil Thomson Papers, Yale-Gilmore.
17. Ruth Stephan, letter to Arizona Poetry Center, 24 September 1972; Arizona Poetry Center, University of Arizona.
18. Ruth Stephan, letter to Arizona Poetry Center, 23 September 1972; Arizona Poetry Center, University of Arizona.
19. After seeing a recitation of Spanish poetry with a piano accompaniment by Aaron Copland during her early days in New York, she speculated in a letter to her

father: "I've been thinking I could write my own poetry and write my own music for accompaniment—my goodness it will be like an opera." LD, letter to father, 6 February 1950; LC.

20. Ashbery's set called *The Poems* (1955–56) includes two poems titled "Heidi." Ashbery and Dlugoszewski had been acquaintances since the early 1950s; according to David Lehman, Ashbery had a strong connection to music; see Lehman, *The Last Avant-Garde*, 124f.

21. Allen Hughes, "Composers Honor Frank O'Hara with Vocal Works," *New York Times* (28 April 1972).

22. Gene Santoro, *Myself When I Am Real: The Life and Music of Charles Mingus* (New York: Oxford University Press, 2000), 308f.

23. This description of the journal's aims is printed on the same page as the table of contents and the editorial and publication information.

24. LD, "What Is Sound to Music?," *Main Currents in Modern Thought*, 30, no. 1 (Sept.–Oct. 1973): 4f.

25. LD, "What Is Sound to Music?," 3.

26. Typescript from 1972 included in Virgil Thomson Papers, Yale-Gilmore. Nothing is known about the "project for a large dance-vocal and orchestral work" mentioned by Thomson.

27. LD, letter to Thomson, 18 November 1973; Virgil Thomson Papers, Yale-Gilmore.

28. Joel Thome, interview with the author, 15 September 2019; LD, letter to Virgil Thomson, 18 November 1973; Virgil Thomson Papers, Yale-Gilmore.

29. Joel Thome, written communication with Laura Pettibone Wright, 19 April 2018. He added: "Amazingly, my father purchased our first [white baby grand] piano from her father. My dad also looked in on Chester's health during his final year."

30. Joel Thome, interview with the author, 15 September 2019.

31. LD, interview with André Bernard, WNYC, 14 December 1983; NYPL-Sound. The Library of Congress holds a messy, seventy-eight-page pencil manuscript of the piece, dated "April 20 1974."

32. EH, letter to Noguchi, 26 May 1974; Isamu Noguchi Papers, Isamu Noguchi Foundation and Garden Museum, Long Island City, New York.

33. Paul Hume [clipping, no title], *Washington Post* (25 May 1976); Lillian and Frederick Kiesler Papers, AAA.

34. Jamake Highwater [clipping, no title], *Soho Weekly News* (3 June 1976); Lillian and Frederick Kiesler Papers, AAA.

35. Review by Heuwell Tircuit, 12 October 1979; clipping held in file at LC; publication information not available. It is likely that the review appeared in the *San Francisco Chronicle*.

36. Stanley Silverman, written communication with the author, 3 April 2018.

37. LD, "What Is Sound to Music?," 10.

38. Program for 5 December 1975 concert accessed at the New York Philharmonic Leon Levy Digital Archives, 14 February 2020; https://archives.nyphil.org

/index.php/artifact/193c3c2f-524f-403b-992b-0c5d2826d156-0.1/fullview#page/1/mode/2up.

39. EH, letter to Thomson, 10 March 1975; Virgil Thomson Papers, Yale-Gilmore.

40. Gerard Schwarz, with Maxine Frost, *Behind the Baton: An American Icon Talks Music* (Milwaukee, WI: Hal Leonard Corporation, 2017), 40.

41. Tom Johnson, "Musician of the Month," *High Fidelity/Musical America* (June 1975).

42. Notes reproduced inside the cover of the bound manuscript of *Abyss and Caress* included structural sketches of the piece, labeling compositional elements in odd ways, like "map of leaping change and memory swipes"; "curve of leaping change through 15 movement arrivals"; and maps of "keystone stresses and balances and phrase severances and negative arrival fulcrums."

43. "What's Doing? Concert Tomorrow," *Berkshire Eagle* (17 August 1976).

44. Irwin Shainman, "A Musical Dichotomy: Academic and Regional Opera Music Are Worlds Apart," *Berkshire Eagle* (4 September 1976), 8.

45. Virgil Thomson, letter to the NEA, 28 October 1976; Virgil Thomson Papers, Yale-Gilmore.

46. Prints of the photo shoot, which took place on 12 May 1977, can be viewed at the New York Philharmonic Leon Levy Digital Archives, https://archives.nyphil.org/index.php/search?search-type=singleFilter&search-text=%2ADlugoszewski&doctype=visual; accessed 24 May 2020.

47. Program note written in 1978.

48. Program note written in 1978.

49. Tom Johnson, "Nigel Rollings Has Some Good Ideas," *Village Voice* (25 September 1978).

50. Tom Johnson, "Confronting the Ears Head On," *Village Voice* (15 August 1974).

51. Jamake Highwater, "Discovering Dlugoszewski," *Soho Weekly News* (11 May 1978).

52. Ned Rorem, "The World's Most Influential Music Teacher, Other Women in the Art: Thoughts from a Prizewinning Composer on What Women Add to Serious Music," *Vogue* (September 1979), 324.

53. Ned Rorem, *An Absolute Gift* (New York: Simon and Schuster, 1978), 110.

54. The original piece was allegedly nominated for a Pulitzer Prize in 1971. The Pulitzer winner that year was Mario Davidovky's *Synchronisms No. 6* for piano and electronic sound (1970).

55. Hal Rammel, "Notes," *Lucia Dlugoszewski: Disparate Stairway Radical Other*. Recording NWCR 859 (1978 and 2000, Composers Recording, Inc.; 2007, Anthology of Recorded Music, Inc.).

56. Jerry Schwartz and Cheryl Bray, "Music: Classical," *Atlanta Journal and Constitution* (14 October 1978); and Andrew Stiller, "New Music," *Buffalo Evening News* (22 September 1978). Stiller oddly added a gendered comment on the piece: "Aside from its purely musical merits there is an intriguing psycho-sexual aspect–possibly unintentional but certainly not fortuitous or irrelevant—to this

piece in which percussionist Dlugoszewski dialogues with six (male) brass players. When, comes the revolution, half those brass parts are played by women, and female percussionist-composers are a dime a dozen, this resonance will probably be lost forever."

57. Rzewski's *The People United Will Never Be Defeated* (1975) is a set of thirty-six piano variations based on the Chilean revolutionary song "El pueblo unido jamás será vencido" by Sergio Ortega and Quilapayún. It was first recorded by pianist Ursula Oppens in 1979.

58. Here she seems to be sarcastically quoting Rzewski, who turned from the theatrical-anarchic free improvisation aesthetic of his work with the ensemble Musica Elettronica Viva in the late 1960s toward a more composer-centric "New Romantic" virtuosity in the 1970s.

59. This entry was labeled "Aesthetic diary" and dated "Feb 10, 1979 7:35 a.m."

60. Keefer quoting 1977 interview with LD; Keefer, "Erick Hawkins, Modern Dancer," 75f.

61. Keefer, 75.

62. LD, letter to Aaron Copland, 11 April 1979; Aaron Copland Papers, LC. For earlier references to Dlugoszewski's contact with Copland, see letters to her parents, 19 May 1950 and 6 November 1950, discussed in chapter 2.

63. LD, letter to Copland, 12 April 1979; Aaron Copland Papers, LC.

64. LD, in *Soundpieces 2*, 79.

65. Other noteworthy board members included Walter Abish, Robert Bly, Meredith Monk, and Gregg Smith.

66. LD, letter to Highwater, 3 May 1977; Jamake Highwater Papers, NYPL-Manuscripts.

67. Jamake Highwater, *Dance: Rituals of Experience* (New York: A&W Publishers, Inc., 1987), 198.

68. A typescript of this essay was found in the Jamake Highwater Papers, NYPL-Manuscripts; an additional copy is held in the Lillian and Frederick Kiesler Papers, AAA.

69. See Joan Giroux, *The Haiku Form* (Rutland, VT: Tuttle Publishing, 1974), 89. J. D. Salinger included a reference to this poem in his short story "Teddy" (1953). (See chapter 4, footnote 37.)

CHAPTER 7. RAGE (1980–87)

1. LD, Undated note; LC.

2. Found in a notebook titled "April 5 1981 Aesthetic Diary/Delicacy of Quidditas." (Other notebooks contained similar statements, such as, "For Lucia life is not intense enough deep enough.")

3. One such "Sky Watch," "This Week at 2 A.M.," published in the *New York Times*, was pasted into a notebook with a handwritten date of Nov. 15, 1987, with Dlugoszewski's handwritten annotation: "this twilight / I will go to the river / to

search the beauty of river [?] tear / 3rd muga day / sun sets 4:38 PM / venus sets 5:48 PM."

4. She recycled this idea frequently, as in this typical entry, dated "4th Wabin 8:50 P.M. Dec. 1985": Lucia you are / constantly descending / into the most secret / part of yourself / and you tell all / about what you / find there / with fiercest / unflinching / as though / no one / were / listening."

5. Entry in notebook labeled: "Aug 20, 1980 Book I Startle Transparent Terrible Freedom Full orchestra."

6. All written 3 February 1981, 8 p.m.

7. Phrase written repeatedly in notebook titled "Feb 18 1981 Book VI Final Aesthetic Startle Transparent Terrible Freedom Structure final."

8. See Susan Balée, "Autobiography: General Essay," in *The Oxford Encyclopedia of American Literature* vol. 3, ed. Jay Parini (Oxford: Oxford University Press, 2004), 95.

9. Balée, 95.

10. "March 19 1981 6 p.m."; Entry in notebook labeled "March 16 1981 Startle Transparent Hearing III Final."

11. Joel Thome, interview with the author, 15 September 2019.

12. Page dated 11 November 1983; another "credo" was dated 18 November 1983, and included the following: "Lucia / quick / light / deep depth / powerful / meaning / imagination [...] Lucia / Noguchi / gross-subtle / the lightness of Zen / shallow—profound / the heaviness of Duende [...] Lucia / swift / sudden / deep / vulnerable / transparency utterly alive."

13. This entry referred to "Nov 18, 1983 credo" but also included the date of "May 12, 1984."

14. Found in the Jamake Highwater Papers, NYPL-Manuscripts.

15. The Boehm Quintette musicians who premiered the piece were Sheryl Henze, flute; Phyllis Bohl, oboe; Don Stewart, clarinet; Joseph Anderer, horn; and Matthew Shubin, bassoon.

16. Joanne Sheehy Hoover, "Boehm Quintette," *Washington Post* (12 January 1980).

17. Matthew Shubin, written communication with the author, 24 August 2019.

18. Program found in Jamake Highwater Papers, NYPL-Manuscripts.

19. Jamake Highwater, "Discovering Dlugoszewski," *Soho Weekly News* (11 May 1978).

20. Leonard Marcus, "An Enlightening Surprise," *High Fidelity* (December 1980): 54. *Fire Fragile Flight* shared the Koussevitzky award with German composer Aribert Reimann's *Lear*, which Marcus called "one of the most talked-about new European works in years." Sofia Gubaidulina was the next woman to win the prize, in 1989, for her violin concerto titled *Offertorium*.

21. LD, letter to Isamu Noguchi, 28 October 1986; Isamu Noguchi Foundation and Garden Museum, Long Island City, New York.

22. EH, letter to Sallie R. Wagner, 11 June 1981; Sallie R. Wagner Papers, LC.

23. EH, letter to Sallie R. Wagner, 11 October 1981; Sallie R. Wagner Papers, LC.

24. LD, letter to Jamake Highwater, "Thurs. AM" [ca. 1981–82: *The Primal Mind* was published in 1982]; Jamake Highwater Papers, NYPL-Manuscripts.

25. LD, letter to Highwater, 19 November 1981; Jamake Highwater Papers, NYPL-Manuscripts. Many people I spoke with in the course of my research mentioned Dlugoszewski and Hawkins's chronic financial difficulties.

26. The Alice Tully Hall performance of *Heyoka*, which took place on 14 September 1981, was discussed in Jennifer Dunning, "Erick Hawkins—Celebrating the Mind and Spirit," *New York Times*, 13 September 1981.

27. LD, letter to Highwater, 19 November 1981; Jamake Highwater Papers, NYPL-Manuscripts.

28. "Chamber Music Society Postpones *Wilderness*," *New York Times* (22 November 1981).

29. Leighton Kerner, "Two Meaningful Pieces," *Village Voice* (17 August 1982), 68.

30. This typescript, found in Lillian Kiesler's papers, was dated November 1982 and labeled "for Columbia College"; AAA.

31. The typescript for the program note was dated 31 August 1983; I have found no printed program that indicates that the essay was ever used, or indeed if the piece was ever performed. Copies of the typescript are held in the Jamake Highwater Papers, NYPL-Manuscripts; and in the Lillian and Frederick Kiesler Papers, AAA.

32. LD, interview with André Bernard, WNYC, 14 December 1983; NYPL-Sound.

33. LD, linter notes for the album *David Taylor, Bass Trombone* (New World Records 80494; 1996).

34. LD, letter to EH, 14 March 1985; LC. Emphasis hers.

35. LD, letter to EH, 12 March 1985; LC.

36. LD, letter to EH, 12 March 1985; LC.

37. LD, letter to EH, 12 March 1985; LC.

38. LD, letter to EH, 14 March 1985; LC.

39. LD, letter to EH, 15 March 1985; LC.

40. LD, letter to EH, 18 March 1985; LC.

41. LD, undated letter to Highwater (prior to March 4, probably 1985); LC.

42. All of this section was taken from an undated letter to Highwater (prior to March 4); LC.

43. LD, letter to EH, 20 February 1986; LC.

44. LD, letter to EH, 26 February 1986; LC.

45. The first of these was labeled "Washington Square 6:30 PM March 24, 1986," and its text read: "*first birthday present* to sweetest Lillian / on the eve of the eve of her birthday / from Lucia Dlugoszewski / who loves her forever! / *hanging from the sudden southeast / the tear of sirius*!" The last of the set I found read: "morton pier *midnight* March 25, 1986 / fourth and last birthday present of vulnerable departing Sirius / on the eve of my wildly creative special Lillian / the gloriously beautiful life love! / *A river of unshed sirius tears / in laser-careful passing / Through a single pore / of my body*! / And everything is suddenly / vivid / and / unforgettable!" Emphasis hers.

46. Diary entry dated "7:30 AM–8 PM Dec 27 1986."

47. Diary entry dated 27 December 1986. On another occasion, on 14 February (probably 1988), Dlugoszewski and Hawkins went to see John Huston's film of James Joyce's *The Dead*.

48. Dlugoszewski seems to have been obsessed with the idea of Motherwell at this time. A diary entry from December 1986 included his name as the center of one of her "word cycles": "grace frenzy Motherwell / of Motherwell evening / grace frenzy path of Motherwell / grace frenzy fractured Motherwell / fractured grace frenzy Motherwell / fractured frightened sudden grace frenzy Motherwell / grace frenzy hermetic energy Motherwell."

49. Diary entry dated 24 March 1987.

50. Similar messages to herself included "You alone have that dislocated intense other to destroy with originality like the unspeakable deserted corridors of Shinto"; "Duende—Lucia: most austere terrible alone courage autonomy"; and "Lucia: terrify yourself daily with the Haiku poet's anxiety of nothingness"; and dozens more.

51. Diary entry dated 30 September 1987, "4:50 PM still in plane on the ground in Newark waiting for weather improvement in Detroit / dangerous delicacy of imagination most ferociously Radical Quidditas / a paradox of energies at the same time / leap out into unknown / deepening / pierce / penetrating / to the unspeakable abyss hear of what is."

52. LD, interview with Cole Gagne, in *Soundpieces 2*, 79.

CHAPTER 8. LOSSES (1988–2000)

1. LD, undated note; LC.

2. Handwritten note, labeled "Jennie Dlugoszewski Orvis, Memorial Service, March 5, 1988"; LC.

3. This longer entry of 27 December 1988 also made reference to her watching a 1982 movie called *Six Weeks*, staring Dudley Moore and Mary Tyler Moore, about a girl dying of leukemia. The entry ended with a meditation on "wigilia": "Through my Jolas myth of wigilia / quick abyss Wigilia receding / pierce waiting to be born / (not quite remembering my words) / + reading 1987 Dec notebook / + suddenly pierced / with the aesthetic being / of my pathless way."

4. Undated entry from "Radical Quidditas" notebook (late 1980s).

5. A confusing set of real estate documents suggests that Dlugoszewski sold her mother's house to the Hawkins Dance Foundation in January 1997, and that the Foundation then sold it for $127,000 in May 2000 following Dlugoszewski's own death in April of that year.

6. Jennifer Dunning, "The Composer Who Energizes the Erick Hawkins Dancers," *New York Times* (7 December 1988).

7. Katherine Duke, who was originally from Charlotte, North Carolina, first met Dlugoszewski at a summer intensive workshop in Lake Placid, New York, in August of 1983. Duke joined the Hawkins Company that same year and was given

her debut solo role in 1988 in the piece *Early Floating*. She became a close friend of Dlugoszewski's and has been a major liaison between the legacy of the Erick Hawkins Dance Company and the Library of Congress's acquisition of Dlugoszewski's materials.

8. James R. Oestreich, "Music in Review," *New York Times* (29 June 1991).

9. The concert took place at the Laurie Wagman Recital Hall on 26 September 1991.

10. She described the title as such: "Radical meaning extreme; Strange for otherness; Quidditas just for the innocence of each sound; Dew Tear, some evening-star nature meditation to clean up my act; and Duende, to give me courage." Dlugoszewski also said that the piece was a commission from the American Composers Orchestra. LD, interview with Cole Gagne, *Soundpieces 2*, 80.

11. LD, interview with Cole Gagne, in *Soundpieces 2*, 79.

12. LD, "*8 Clear Places*," 65.

13. A pencil-draft of the (incomplete) manuscript was given to me by John Ransom Phillips, dated as "July 1991 John Phillips Barn Columbia County; Dec. 1991 Jan. Feb. 1992–Feb 1993 NYC 15 East 11st."

14. John Ransom Phillips, interview with the author, 5 May 2018.

15. "Erick Hawkins to Get Scripps Dance Award," *New York Times* (26 November 1987); "Erick Hawkins Given $25,000 Dance Award," *New York Times* (17 June 1988).

16. LD, letter to Anna Kisselgoff (dance critic for the *New York Times*), 13 December 1994; LC. Dlugoszewski also wrote to Kisselgoff: "Bill Clinton also wrote me a beautiful letter about Erick's death but it arrived unfortunately a day after the memorial."

17. John Ransom Phillips, interview with the author, 5 May 2018.

18. Reported in Jennifer Dunning, "Erick Hawkins Is Remembered with Film, Poetry and Laughter," *New York Times* (6 December 1994); and in "Erick Hawkins Remembered," *Ballet Review* (Summer 1996), 88.

19. "Though he has completely recovered from a stroke suffered six years ago, Mr. Hawkins's speech and steps have slowed, and at times he seems frail," wrote Terry Trucco, "Erick Hawkins, Ever the Poet, Tries a New Vocabulary," *New York Times* (23 January 1994).

20. LD, letter [draft] to Anna Kisselgoff, 13 December 1994; LC.

21. "Erick Hawkins Remembered I," *Ballet Review* (Summer 1996), 88–94; and "Erick Hawkins Remembered II," *Ballet Review* (Fall 1996), 78–87.

22. Helen and Elliott Carter, letter to LD, undated; Elliott Carter Collection, PSS. Thanks to Anne Shreffler for locating and transcribing this letter for me.

23. On the 25th of December, she wrote Phillips several poems. They included both graphic elements and musical notation, and exalted in Sirius. Musical suggestions cascading down the right side of the page instructed: "Let one piccolo play highest A for 20 seconds *mf* then light a match blow it out quickly; then wait in darkness for 25 seconds / then let two piccolos play high A and high A# for 17 seconds and let nothing happen for 20 seconds and then let one violin pizzicato

low A and wait 17 seconds then do it again." This poem was dedicated "To John, Easthouse Dec 25 1994 while watching sirius rise at twilight 5 PM and also remembering August 24 1994 at dawn 5:20 AM watching the first sirius of the year rise after the night Erick Hawkins was rushed to emergency. Love Lucia Dlugoszewski." She wrote several other poems for Phillips that same night; John Ransom Phillips, private papers.

24. Documented in: Barbara MacAdam, "Lucy in the Barn—The Creative Process: A Tribute to Composer Lucia Dlugoszewski," *John Ransom Phillips: New Paintings*. Pond Art Foundation, Inc., 1994.

25. Phillips's letter to John and Susie O'Neill was undated; John Ransom Phillips, private papers.

26. LD, letter to David Liptak, chair of a conductor search committee at the Eastman School of Music, 28 December 1995; LC.

27. LD, letter to Anna Kisselgoff, 13 December 1994; LC.

28. Blackburn, "Eleanor Remembers Lucia Dlugoszewski."

29. Fax from David Guion to Baryshnikov ("Misha") and Christina Sterner, 13 June 1995; Baryshnikov Papers, NYPL-Dance. Not all critics were kind. In reviewing the piece for the *Wall Street Journal*, Joan Acocella wrote: "Mr. Hawkins was into Eastern religions and therefore showed a certain aggressive naivety, whereby, for example, we were supposed to stare in holy awe if he raised his arm and held it there.... Like much of Mr. Hawkins's work, the piece is thin." Quoted in Diane Hubbard Burn, "Hawkins, Erick," in *International Dictionary of Modern Dance*, Taryn Benbow-Pfalzgraf, ed. (Farmington Hills, MI: St. James Press, 1998), 348.

30. LD, letter to "Misha" and Christina [Sterner], 2 July 1997; Baryshnikov Papers, NYPL-Dance.

31. The premiere of *Disparate Stairway Radical Other* was listed on a Pulitzer Prize application as having taken place at Dartmouth College on 20 February 1997.

32. LD, interview with Cole Gagne, *Soundpieces 2*, 69.

33. LD, "Composer's notes on *Journey of a Poet*"; LC.

34. Hal Rammel, "Notes," *Lucia Dlugoszewski, Disparate Stairway Radical Other* (2000), NWCR 859.

35. LD, notes included in score for *Depth Duende Scarecrow Other*; LC.

36. LD, letter to Lillian Kiesler, 26 November 1997; Lillian and Frederick Kiesler Papers, AAA.

37. Lillian and Frederick Kiesler Papers, AAA.

38. Lillian and Frederick Kiesler Papers, AAA.

39. Lillian and Frederick Kiesler Papers, AAA.

40. LD, letter to Lillian Keisler, 26 November 1997; Lillian and Frederick Kiesler Papers, AAA. Several friends of Dlugoszewski's told me that she had a serious relationship with at least one man following Hawkins's death: according to some, he was a poet; according to others, he was an African American New York City subway driver.

41. Katherine Duke, written communication with the author, 23 August 2019.

42. A poster/program for this event was found in Lillian Kiesler's papers; AAA.

43. Hal Rammel, liner notes, 2000 recording. In March 2021, Italian pianist Agnese Toniutti released a new recording of *Exacerbated Subtlety Concert (Why Does a Woman Love a Man?)* on an album titled *Subtle Matters* (Neuma Records).

44. Kate Mattingly, "Giddy Up," *Village Voice* (9 March 1999).

45. Anna Kisselgoff, "A Photo Album for an Acrobat: Erick Hawkins Dance Company," *New York Times* (31 March 1999).

46. Deborah Jowitt, "Of Marvels," *Village Voice* (30 March 1999). See also "*Motherwell Amor*: Reviving the Past—Inspiring the Future," *UNLV Dance* (January 2016), 4–5. *Radical Ardent* had a five-night run at the 92nd Street Y in March 1999.

47. "Composing Brought about by Mother's Challenge"; undated, unattributed newspaper article (ca. 1939) included in Dlugoszewski's childhood scrapbook; LC.

48. Gerard Schwarz, with Maxine Frost, *Behind the Baton*, 37.

49. Schwarz with Frost, 37.

50. Blackburn, "Eleanor Remembers Lucia Dlugoszewski."

51. William Trigg, written communication with the author, 4 September 2019.

52. LD, handwritten, one-page letter titled "Something from Lucia to John [Ransom Phillips]," 22 April 1994; John Ransom Phillips, private papers.

53. Jennifer Dunning, "Lucia Dlugoszewski, 68, Composer; Directed Hawkins Dance Troupe," *New York Times* (13 April 2000).

54. Jennifer Dunning, "Dance Review: A Premiere Engagement Is Turned into a Memorial," *New York Times* (13 April 2000). Hawkins once reported that Motherwell told Dlugoszewski that she was his favorite composer. EH, letter to Sallie R. Wagner, 24 December 1980; Sallie R. Wagner Papers, LC.

55. Dunning.

56. Signed "Sol Adler, Executive Director, 92nd Street Y, Joan Finkelstein, Director, 92nd Street Y Harkness Dance Center." Both Kisselgoff's obituary and the 92nd Street Y tribute were published in the *New York Times* on 13 April 2000.

57. Dunning, "Dance Review: A Premiere Engagement Is Turned into a Memorial." *Motherwell Amor* was revived for a performance at the Levy Gorvy Gallery on 10 December 2015; in a film of the performance the dancers are accompanied by a brass quintet and William Trigg playing percussion against a backdrop of Motherwell's series of paintings titled *Elegy to the Spanish Republic* (1948–67).

58. "Dlugoszewski Memorial," *New York Times* (6 December 2000), C19. According to Katherine Duke, Dlugoszewski was laid to rest at the Forest Green Cemetery in Old Bridge (Morganville), New Jersey; interview with the author, 21 August 2018.

59. Source: *The Complete Poems of Emily Dickinson*, edited by Thomas H. Johnson (Boston: Little, Brown and Co., 1961), Cambridge, MA: The Belknap Press of Harvard University Press, Copyright © 1951, 1955, 1979, 1983 by the President and Fellows of Harvard College. Used by permission. (Emphasis is Dlugoszewski's.)

60. LD, excerpt from essay titled *Amor Elusive Empty August*, dated 1 August–24 December 1979.

OUT FROM THE SHADOWS: A CONCLUSION

1. LD, composition notebook (ca. 1970); LC.
2. I am grateful to Dr. Diane Bridgeman for helping me to understand various facets of Dlugoszewski's behavior and personality.
3. Kyle Gann, "'Magnificent—in a Mysterious Way': Varèse's Impact on American Music," in *Edgard Varèse: Composer, Sound Sculptor, Visionary*, ed. Felix Meyer and Heidy Zimmermann (Woodbridge, UK: Boydell, 2006), 427.
4. Austin Clarkson, "The Varèse Effect: New York City in the 1950s and 60s," in Meyer and Zimmermann, *Edgard Varèse*, 378.
5. Hal Rammel, "Notes," *Lucia Dlugoszewski: Disparate Stairway Radical Other* (NWCR 859; 1978 and 2000; Composers Recording, Inc., 2007).
6. Oral history interview with Philip Corner (20 September 2015); interviewers Luciano Galliano and Toshie Kakinuma (accessed online, 26 January 2020; http://www.kcua.ac.jp/arc/ar/philipcorner_en/).
7. Yvonne Rainer as quoted in Cynthia Novack, *Sharing the Dance: Contact Improvisation and American Culture* (Madison: University of Wisconsin Press, 1990), 32.
8. Lois V Vierk, written communication with the author, 4 May 2018.
9. Dlugoszewski, in *Soundpieces 2*, 76.
10. Dlugoszewski, 76.
11. Typescript dated January 1980 and labeled "Chronology leading to *Pierce Sever*, 1957–1980"; found in Lillian Kiesler's Papers, AAA.
12. Typescript "Chronology leading to *Pierce Sever*."
13. He added: "It is apparent that, after a lifetime devoted to the music of post modernism, Lucia continues to blaze new territory." Mikhail Baryshnikov, letter to National Endowment for the Arts Specialist for Dance Jonelle Ott, 4 November 1999; Baryshnikov Papers, NYPL-Dance.
14. Dr. Stephen Buckley, letter to *The New Yorker* (1 July 2019), 3. Buckley's letter was in response to an article by music critic Alex Ross, "Antonio Salieri's Revenge," *The New Yorker*, 3 June 2019.
15. Dlugoszewski, in *Soundpieces 2*, 80.

APPENDIX 2. LUCIA DLUGOSZEWSKI– ERICK HAWKINS COLLABORATIONS

1. This list is adapted from Renata Celichowska, *The Erick Hawkins Modern Dance Technique* (Princeton, NJ: Princeton Book Company, 2000), 150–59.

SOURCES AND BIBLIOGRAPHY

PRIMARY SOURCES

Archive of American Art, Smithsonian Institution
    Dore Ashton Papers
    Lillian and Frederick Kiesler Papers
    Ad Reinhardt Papers
Archive of Recorded Sound, New York Public Library
Archive of Recorded Sound, Stanford University
    Olivia Mattis Collection
Beinecke Rare Book and Manuscript Library, Yale University
    Daisy Aldan Papers
Billy Rose Theatre Division, New York Public Library
    Living Theatre Records
Detroit Historical Society
Getty Research Institute
    Irving Sandler Papers
Harry Ransom Humanities Research Center, University of Texas, Austin
    Daisy Aldan Papers
Harvard University Archives
Isamu Noguchi Foundation and Garden Museum, Long Island City, New York
Irving S. Gilmore Music Library, Special Collections, Yale University
    Betsy Jolas Papers
    John Kirkpatrick Papers
    Virgil Thomson Papers

Jerome Robbins Dance Division, New York Public Library
- Mikhail Baryshnikov Archive
- Beverly Brown Papers
- Walter Sorell Research Files on Mary Wigman
- Walter Terry Papers

Library of Congress, Special Collections, Music Division, Washington, D.C. (LC)
- Aaron Copland Papers
- Lukas Foss Papers
- Erick Hawkins and Lucia Dlugoszewski Papers
- Sallie R. Wagner Papers

McHenry Library Special Collections and Archive, University of California, Santa Cruz
- Lou Harrison Papers

Manuscripts and Archives Division, New York Public Library
- Charles Boultenhouse and Parker Tyler Papers
- Jamake Highwater Papers

Music Division, New York Public Library
- Henry Cowell Papers
- Louis Horst Collection
- Papers and Records of William Schuman
- Ted Shawn Collection

New York Philharmonic, Leon Levy Digital Archives

92nd Street Y Archives of Events and Performances

Paul Sacher Stiftung
- Elliott Carter Collection
- Edgard Varèse Collection
- Louise Varèse Collection

John Ransom Phillips Private Collection

University of Arizona Poetry Collection
- Ruth Stephan Papers

University of California, San Diego, Mandeville Special Collections and Archives
- Peter Yates Papers

Wayne State University, Office of Alumni Relations Records

INTERVIEWS AND CORRESPONDENCE

Katherine Duke, 21 August 2018
Michael Hinton, July 2019
Josiah McElheny, September 2019
Bethany Morgan, 20–21 July 2020
Linda Quan, 13 October 2020
John Ransom Phillips, 5 May 2018 and 20 August 2019
Matthew Shubin, 23 August 2019
Stanley Silverman, 3 April 2018
Mike Silverton, 23 August 2019
James Thoma, 17 July 2019
Joel Thome, 15 September 2019
Bill Trigg, 4 September 2019
"Blue" Gene Tyranny, 5 January 2018

SECONDARY SOURCES

Aldan, Daisy, ed. *A New Folder: Americans: Poems and Drawing*. New York: Folder Editions, 1959.
Ammer, Christine. *Unsung: A History of Women in American Music*. Westport, CT: Greenwood Press, 1980.
Ashton, Dore. *The Life and Times of the New York School*. Bath, UK: Adams and Dart, 1972.
———. *The New York School: A Cultural Reckoning*. Berkeley: University of California Press, 1992.
Atlas, James. *The Shadow in the Garden: A Biographer's Tale*. Pantheon, 2017.
Bach, Edward Stanley. "A Performance Project on Selected Works of Five Contemporary Composers: Malcolm Arnold, Robert Henderson, Stan Friedman, John Elmsley, Lucia Dlugoszewski." DMA thesis, University of British Columbia, 1991.
Badaczewski, Dennis. *Poles in Michigan*. East Lansing: Michigan State University Press, 2002.
Bak, Richard. *Detroitland: A Collection of Movers, Shakers, Lost Souls, and History Makers from Detroit's Past*. Detroit, MI: Painted Turtle, 2011.
Balée, Susan. "Autobiography: General Essay." In *The Oxford Encyclopedia of American Literature*. Vol. 3, edited by Jay Parini. Oxford: Oxford University Press, 2004.
Beal, Amy C. *Johanna Beyer*. Champaign: University of Illinois Press, 2015.
Billings, William. "To All Musical Practitioners," in *The New England Psalm Singer* [Boston, 1770], *The Complete Works of William Billings*, vol 1., edited by Karl

Kroeger. Boston: The American Musicological Society and the Colonial Society of Massachusetts, 1981.

Biner, Pierre. *The Living Theatre.* New York: Horizon Press, 1972.

Blackburn, Philip. "Eleanor Remembers Lucia Dlugoszewski." Interview with Eleanor Hovda. *American Mavericks*, 5 May 2003. St. Paul, MN: American Public Media, 2018.

Block, Adrienne Fried. *Amy Beach, Passionate Victorian: The Life and Work of an American Composer 1867–1944.* New York: Oxford University Press, 1998.

Bowers, Jane, and Judith Tick, eds. *Women Making Music: The Western Art Tradition, 1150–1950.* Champaign: University of Illinois Press, 1986.

Brown, Norman O. *Love's Body.* New York: Random House, 1966.

Cage, John. *Silence: Lectures and Writings.* Middletown, CT: Wesleyan University Press, 1961.

Celichowska, Renata. *The Erick Hawkins Modern Dance Technique.* Hightstown, NJ: Princeton Book Co., 2000.

Clarkson, Austin. "The Varèse Effect: New York City in the 1950s and 60s." In *Edgard Varèse: Composer, Sound Sculptor, Visionary*, edited by Felix Meyer and Heidy Zimmermann, 371–381. Woodbridge, UK: Boydell Press, 2006.

Cohen, Aaron I. "Dlugoszewski, Lucia." In *International Encyclopedia of Women Composers.* Second edition, 1:199–200. New York: Books and Music Inc., 1987.

Connors, Brenda. *Enlightenment: A Laban Movement Analysis of Select Sections of the Choreography of Erick Hawkins.* Certificate Project, Weekend Program 1996–98, New York City, 2000. ["final draft/copy" held in the Library of Congress Performing Arts Reading Room]

De View, Lucille. "She Creates Music to Fill the World." *Detroit News* (11 July 1972): 4D.

Dickinson, Emily. *The Complete Poems of Emily Dickinson.* Edited by Thomas H. Johnson. Boston: Little, Brown and Co., 1961.

Dlugoszewski, Lucia. "The Aristocracy of Play." *Parnassus* 5 (Spring/Summer 1977).

———. "Composer/Choreographer." *Dance Perspectives* 16 (1963): 21–25.

———. "*8 Clear Places.*" *Ballet Review* 21, no. 4 (Winter 1993): 61–65.

———. "Erick Hawkins: Heir to a New Tradition." In *On the Dance of Erick Hawkins*, edited by M. L. Gordon Norton. New York: Foundation for Modern Dance [undated; 1974?]

———. "Is Music Sound?" *Jubilee* 10 (1962).

———. "Notes on New Music for the Dance." *Dance Observer* 24 (November 1957): 133–135.

———. "Tribute." In *The Erick Hawkins Modern Dance Technique.* By Renata Celichowska. Hightstown, NJ: Princeton Book Co., 2000): xvii–xxviii.

———. "What Is Sound to Music?" *Main Currents in Modern Thought* 30, no. 1 (Sept.–Oct. 1973): 3–11.

Dunning, Jennifer. "The Composer Who Energizes the Erick Hawkins Dancers," *New York Times* (7 December 1988).

———. "Dance Review: A Premiere Engagement Is Turned into a Memorial." *New York Times* (13 April 2000).
———. "Erick Hawkins: Celebrating the Body and the Spirit. *New York Times* (13 September 1981): 28.
———. "Lucia Dlugoszewski, 68, Composer; Directed Hawkins Dance Troupe." *New York Times* (13 April 2000).
Eiseley, Loren C. *The Unexpected Universe*. Harcourt, Brace and World, 1969.
Franko, Mark. *Martha Graham in Love and War: The Life in the Work*. Oxford: Oxford University Press, 2012.
Gabriel, Mary. *Ninth Street Women: Lee Krasner, Elaine de Kooning, Grace Hartigan, Joan Mitchell, and Helen Frankenthaler: Five Painters and the Movement That Changed Modern Art*. New York: Little, Brown, 2018.
Gagne, Cole. *Soundpieces 2: Interviews with American Composers*. Metuchen, NJ: Scarecrow Press, 1993.
Gann, Kyle. "'Magnificent—in a Mysterious Way': Varèse's Impact on American Music." In *Edgard Varèse: Composer, Sound Sculptor, Visionary*, edited by Felix Meyer and Heidy Zimmermann. Woodbridge, UK: Boydell Press, 2006): 426–432.
Giroux, Joan. *The Haiku Form*. Rutland, VT: Tuttle Publishing, 1974.
Glickman, Sylvia, and Martha Furman Schleifer. *From Convent to Concert Hall: A Guide to Women Composers*. Westport, CT: Greenwood Press, 2003.
Gruen, John. "*Vogue*'s Spotlight Underground: Lucia Dlugoszewski, Surfacing." *Vogue* (1 October 1970).
Hartigan, Grace. *The Journals of Grace Hartigan 1951–1955*, edited by William T. La Moy and Joseph P. McCaffrey. Syracuse, NY: Syracuse University Press, 2009.
Hawkins, Erick. *The Body Is a Clear Place and Other Statements on Dance*. Princeton, NJ: Princeton Book Company, 1992.
———. "Machine versus Tool." *Ballet Review* 21, no. 4 (Winter 1993): 54–59.
Highwater, Jamake. *Dance: Rituals of Experience*. New York: A&W Publishers, Inc., 1978.
———. "Discovering Dlugoszewski." *Soho Weekly News* (11 May 1978): 37.
———. "Dlugoszewski Ascending." *New York Arts Journal* 18 (1980).
———. *The Primal Mind: Visions and Reality in Indian America*. New York: New American Library, 1982.
Highwater, Jamake, and Sara Jobin. "Dlugoszewski, Lucia." In *The Norton/Grove Dictionary of Women Composers*, edited by Julie Anne Sadie and Rhian Samuel, 145–147. New York: W.W. Norton, 1995.
Hoover, Joanne Sheehy. "Boehm Quintette." *Washington Post* (12 January 1980).
Hughes, Allen. "And Miss Dlugoszewski Experiments—A Lot." *New York Times* (7 March 1971).
———. "Composers Honor Frank O'Hara with Vocal Works." *New York Times* (28 April 1972).
———. "Concert: New Music Unit." *New York Times* (27 April 1980).

James, David E. *To Free the Cinema: Jonas Mekas and the New York Underground.* Princeton, NJ: Princeton University Press, 1992.

Johnson, Steven, ed. *The New York Schools of Music and Visual Arts.* New York: Routledge, 2002.

Johnson, Tom. "Confronting the Ears Head On." *Village Voice* (15 August 1974).

———. "Musician of the Month: Lucia Dlugoszewski." *High Fidelity/Musical America* (June 1975): 4–5.

———. "Nigel Rollings Has Some Good Ideas." *Village Voice* (25 September 1978).

Jowitt, Deborah. "Of Marvels." *Village Voice* (30 March 1999).

———. "Shedding Light." *Village Voice* (14 March 1995): 83.

Keefer, Julia L. "Erick Hawkins, Modern Dancer: History, Theory, Technique, and Performance." PhD dissertation, New York University, 1979.

Kerner, Leighton. "Lucia Dlugoszewski Caresses the Abyss." *Village Voice* (15 December 1975).

———. "The Meaningfulness of It All." *Village Voice* (3 August 1982): 62.

———. "Music," *The Village Voice* (11 May 1972), 49.

———. "Music to Dance To." *Village Voice* (28 March 1995): 82.

———. "Two Meaningful Pieces." *Village Voice* (17 August 1982): 68.

Kimber, Marian Wilson. "The 'Suppression' of Fanny Mendelssohn: Rethinking Feminist Biography." *Nineteenth-Century Music* 26, no. 2 (Fall 2002): 113–129.

Kisselgoff, Anna. "Dance: Erick Hawkins Premiere at the Joyce," *New York Times* (11 October 1984).

———. "Dance Review: A Spirit of Experiment and a Cameo by Baryshnikov." *New York Times* (15 February 1996).

———. "A Photo Album for an Acrobat: Erick Hawkins Dance Company," *New York Times* (31 March 1999).

Lee, Hsiao-Fang. "Erick Hawkins: Choreographic Analysis." MA thesis, American University, 1998.

Lehman, David. *The Last Avant-Garde: The Making of the New York School of Poets.* New York: Anchor Books, 1999.

Lerner, Gerda. *The Majority Finds Its Past: Placing Women in History.* New York: Oxford University Press, 1979.

Lewis, Kevin D. "'The Miracle of Unintelligibility': The Music and Invented Instruments of Lucia Dlugoszewski." DMA thesis, College-Conservatory of Music, University of Cincinnati, 2011.

———. "'The Miracle of Unintelligibility': The Music and Invented Instruments of Lucia Dlugoszewski," *Percussive Notes* 49, no. 5 (September 2011): 52–53.

Lloyd-Jones, Rebecca. "A Space for Women as Women: Exploring a Gendered Feminine Percussion Practice through the work of Lucia Dlugoszewski" [unpublished conference paper, 2018].

Loomis, Bill. *On This Day in Detroit History.* Charleston, SC: The History Press, 2016.

MacAdam, Barbara. "Lucy in the Barn—the Creative Process: A Tribute to Composer Lucia Dlugoszewski." In *John Ransom Phillips: New Paintings.* Art Pond Foundation, Inc., 1994.

Malina, Judith. *The Diaries of Judith Malina, 1947–1957*. New York: Grove Press, 1984.
Marcus, Leonard. "An Enlightening Surprise." *High Fidelity* (December 1980): 54.
Mason, Francis. "A Conversation with Erick Hawkins and Lucia Dlugoszewski." *Ballet Review* 21, no. 4 (Winter 1993): 47–53.
Martelle, Scott. *Detroit (A Biography)*. Chicago: Chicago Review Press, 2012.
McDonagh, Don. *The Complete Guide to Modern Dance*. New York: Doubleday, 1976.
McIntosh, Fergus. "Metaphysical Music: A Composer [Ethel Smyth] Finally Gets Her Due." *The New Yorker* (14 May 2018): 16.
"*Motherwell Amor*: Reviving the Past—Inspiring the Future," *UNLV Dance* (January 2016): 4–5.
Nattiez, Jean-Jacques, ed. *The Boulez-Cage Correspondence*. Translated and edited by Robert Samuels. Cambridge: Cambridge University Press, 1993.
"The Newcomers: The Folder Poets," *Mademoiselle* (January 1960): 72–73.
Newman, Amy. *Challenging Art: Artforum 1962–1974*. New York: Soho Press, 2000.
Nicholls, David. "Getting Rid of the Glue: The Music of the New York School." *Journal of American Studies* 27, no. 3 (December 1993): 335–353.
Nin, Anaïs. *Diary 1947–55*. Edited by Gunther Stuhlmann. New York: Harcourt, Brace, Jovanovich, 1974.
Northrop, F. S. C. *The Meeting of East and West: An Inquiry Concerning World Understanding*. New York: Macmillan, 1946.
———. *Philosophical Anthropology and Practical Politics*. New York: Macmillan, 1960.
Novack, Cynthia. *Sharing the Dance: Contact Improvisation and American Culture*. Madison: University of Wisconsin Press, 1990.
Oestreich, James R. "Music in Review," *New York Times* (29 June 1991).
O'Gorman, Ned. "New Ideas in Dance and Movies." *Jubilee: A Magazine of the Church and Her People* (August 1962).
Palazzolo, Gamulka. *Horn Man: The Polish-American Musician in Twentieth-Century Detroit*. Detroit: The American-Polish Society, 2003.
Poremba, David Lee. *Detroit in Its World Setting: A Three-Hundred Year Chronology 1701–2001* (Detroit: Wayne State University Press, 2001.
Prevots, Naima. *Dance for Export: Cultural Diplomacy and the Cold War*. Middletown, CT: Wesleyan University Press, 2012.
Rammel, Hal. "Notes." *Lucia Dlugoszewski: Disparate Stairway Radical Other*. Recording NWCR 859 (1978 and 2000, Composers Recording, Inc.; 2007, Anthology of Recorded Music, Inc.)
Revill, David. *The Roaring Silence—John Cage: A Life*. New York: Arcade Publishing, 1992.
Robinson, Suzanne. *Peggy Glanville-Hicks: Composer and Critic*. Champaign: University of Illinois Press, 2019.
Rorem, Ned. *An Absolute Gift*. New York: Simon and Schuster, 1978.

———. "The World's Most Influential Music Teacher, Other Women in the Art: Thoughts from a Prizewinning Composer on What Women Add to Serious Music." *Vogue* (September 1979): 324.

Rosenman, Ellen Bayuk. *A Room of One's Own: Women Writers and the Politics of Creativity*. New York: Twayne Publishers, 1995.

Routé, Luther, and John Kirsch. "Two New York Composers: Interviews with Ben Weber and Lucia Dlugoszewski." *Wagner Literary Magazine* #2 (1960–61): 67–78.

Sabin, Robert. "Living Theatre Concert, Cherry Lane Theatre, May 5," *Musical America* (May 1952): 27.

Santoro, Gene. *Myself When I Am Real: The Life and Music of Charles Mingus*. New York: Oxford University Press, 2000.

Sarraute, Claude. "Une soirée d'avant-garde." *Le Monde* (1 July 1963).

Scheff, Aimee. "Picasso's *Desire*—What Is It?" *Theatre Arts* (April 1952): 36–37.

Schwarz, Gerard, with Maxine Frost. *Behind the Baton: An American Icon Talks Music*. Milwaukee, WI: Hal Leonard Corporation, 2017.

Shainman, Irwin. "A Musical Dichotomy: Academic and Regional Opera Music Are Worlds Apart." *Berkshire Eagle* (4 September 1976): 8.

Siff, Nancy K. "Composers' Showcase," *Village Voice* (27 May 1959): 8.

Silverman, Kenneth. *Begin Again: A Biography of John Cage*. Evanston, IL: Northwestern University Press, 2010.

Silverton, Mike. "A Tribute to Lucia Dlugoszewski." *Twentieth Century Music* (2000), 17.

———. "A Friend's Tribute to Lucia Dlugoszewski" (unpublished; 2000).

Slonimsky, Nicolas. "Dlugoszewski, Lucia." In *Baker's Biographical Dictionary of Musicians*. 8th [revised] edition, 438. New York: Schirmer Books, 1992.

Sprague, Katharine Bosman. "A Portrait of Erick Hawkins." MA Thesis, University of California Los Angeles, 1989.

Suzuki, Dean. "Review of *New American Music Vol. 2*," *OP Magazine*, "L" issue (July–August 1982).

Swayne, Steve. *Orpheus in Manhattan: William Schuman and the Shaping of America's Musical Life*. New York: Oxford University Press, 2011.

Terry, Walter. *The Dance in America*. Revised edition. New York: Harper and Row Publishers, 1971.

———. "Lucia Dlugoszewski." *BMI: The Many Worlds of Music*. (1969): 5.

Thoms, Victoria. *Martha Graham: Gender and the Haunting of a Dance Pioneer*. Bristol, UK: Intellect, 2013.

Thomson, Virgil. *American Music Since 1910*. New York: Holt, Reinhart, and Winston, 1970.

Tick, Judith. *Ruth Crawford Seeger: A Composer's Search for American Music*. New York: Oxford University Press, 1997.

Trucco, Terry. "Erick Hawkins, Ever the Poet, Tries a New Vocabulary." *New York Times* (23 January 1994).

Tyranny, "Blue" Gene. "88 Keys to Freedom: Segues through the History of American Piano Music." *New Music Box* (1 October 2003).

von Bredow, Moritz. *Rebellische Pianistin: Das Leben der Grete Sultan zwischen Berlin und New York*. Mainz, Germany: Schott Verlag, 2012.

Ward, Charles. "Avante-garde [*sic*] Composer Dlugoszewski Featured Festival Artist." *Houston Chronicle* (25 October 1986).

Wen-Chung, Chou. "Varèse: A Sketch of the Man and His Music." *Musical Quarterly* 52, no. 2 (April 1966): 151–170.

"What's Doing? Concert Tomorrow." *Berkshire Eagle* (17 August 1976).

Wolff, Christian. *Occasional Pieces: Writings and Interviews, 1952–2013*. New York: Oxford University Press, 2017.

Wright, Laura Pettibone, with Catherine Tharin. "Erick Hawkins' Collaborations in the Choreographing of *Plains Daybreak*." *Dance: Current Selected Research* 9 (August 2018).

Yetzke, Angie. "Escaping Martha . . . the Life and Truths of Erick Hawkins." Unpublished seminar paper, University of Wisconsin, Milwaukee, 2011.

INDEX

Acocella, Joan, 205n29
Addams, Jane, 20, 23
Ajemian, Maro, 30, 31, 40
Albers, Josef, 29
Aldan, Daisy, 79–81, 82, 84, 89, 92, 97
Allen, Beatrice, 77
American Brass Quintet, 111
American School of Ballet, 41
Amirkhanian, Charles, 179n26
Anderson, Jack, 129
Andy, Katja (Käte Aschaffenburg), 26, 27, 32
Aquinas, Thomas, 129
Armstrong, Louis, 10
Arrau, Claudio, 35, 36
Artaud, Antonin, 76
Ashbery, John, 56, 58, 62, 80, 112, 135, 145
Atlas, James, 8
Auden, W. H., 25
"Aunt Kaye," 18–19

Babbitt, Milton, 70, 98, 120, 121, 145, 187n2
Bach, Johann Sebastian, 17, 25, 26, 87, 88, 126, 152
Badaczewski, Dennis, 13
Balanchine, George, 42, 66, 163, 194n25
Baldwin, James, 29
Balée, Susan, 132
Ballet Caravan, 41
Ballet Review, 148, 150, 151
Baraka, Amiri. *See* Jones, LeRoi
Barber, Samuel, 124
Barron, Louis and Bebe, 60
Bartók, Béla, 30, 39, 114

Baryshnikov, Mikhail, 150, 153, 164
Basho, 101, 122, 130, 131, 140
Baumgarten, Julia, 155
Beach, Amy, 16
Beck, Julian, 55, 56, 63–64
Beethoven, Ludwig van, 17, 18, 25, 39, 152
Belafonte, Harry, 150
Benichou, Pascal, 155, 156
Benoit, Hubert, 102
Berger, Arthur, 98
Berginc, Charles, 120
Berio, Luciano, 118
Berkshire Foundation, 26–27, 28, 30, 35, 38, 43, 45, 46
Bernard, André, 140
Bernstein, Leonard, 30, 123
Beutel, Carl: Carl Beutel Piano School, 17, 25, 34
Beyer, Johanna Magdalena, 3, 4, 7, 84
Billings, William, 6
Biner, Pierre, 55
Bird, Bonnie, 196n59
Birtwistle, Harrison, 118
Blake, Braxton, 137
Block, Adrienne Fried, 16
Blyth, R. H., 102, 129, 130, 140
Boehm Quintette, 127, 134
Bohl, Phyllis, 201n15
Bolcom, William, 106
Borakove, Ellen, 159
Boulanger, Nadia, 26
Boulez, Pierre, 40, 47, 70, 88, 97, 98, 108, 118, 120, 121, 123, 126, 129, 152

Boultenhouse, Charles, 80, 97
Braxton, Anthony, 6
Bredshall, Edward, 17, 26, 27, 31
Bridgeman, Diane, 207n2
Briskin, David, 151
Britten, Benjamin, 137
Brooklyn Academy of Music, 66, 100, 123
Brooklyn Music School, 28, 35, 37–38, 43
Brown, Beverly, 102–3
Brown, Carolyn, 89
Brown, Earle, 60, 66, 88, 89, 121, 187n13
Brown, Norman O., 98, 101, 102
Brown, Trisha, 136
Brubeck, Dave, 150
Buddhism. *See* Zen Buddhism
Bujold, Lara, 155
Burgmüller, Friedrich, 17
Bursack, David J., 154

Cage, John, 1, 27, 51, 52, 53, 57, 60, 62, 64, 84, 90, 96, 104, 109, 121, 122, 126, 129, 153, 163; Dlugoszewski's criticism of, 46, 47–48, 54, 67, 86, 88–89, 92, 98, 103, 140; early relationship with Dlugoszewski, 29–45; *Music of Changes,* 49, 98; prepared piano, 30, 31, 43, 51, 52, 98, 104, 184n30, 188n25; *Sonatas and Interludes,* 31, 40, 56, 184n30
Cahan, Cora, 151
Calder, Alexander, 59
Campbell, Joseph, 55, 129
Carnegie Hall: Carnegie Recital Hall, 30, 31, 40, 137, 138
Carroll, Edward, 124
Carter, Elliott, 88, 121, 145, 151, 187n2
Carter, Helen, 151
Cather, Willa, 122
Catholicism, 11, 13, 147
Caturla, Alejandro Garcia, 43
Cedar Tavern, 28, 58, 73
Chaplin, Charlie, 35
Charlip, Remy, 89
Chavez, Carlos, 183n66
Chekov, Anton, 24, 26
Cherry, Herman, 78
Cherry Lane Theatre, 55, 56, 58
Chopin, Frédéric, 11, 17, 18, 25
Churchill, Winston, 21

Clark, Frances, 55
Clarkson, Austin, 163
Clinton, Bill, 149, 150, 204n16
Clinton, Hillary, 150
Cocteau, Jean, 64, 130
Coleman, Ornette, 6, 163
Coltrane, John, 73
Composers Recordings Inc. (CRI), 124, 127, 156
Coolidge, Calvin, 10
Coomaraswamy, Ananda (*The Dance of Shiva*), 102
Copland, Aaron, 5, 33–34, 39, 98, 121, 124, 127, 197n19
Corner, Georgia, 155
Corner, Philip, 187n13, 207n6
Corso, Gregory, 80
Cowell, Henry, 43, 56, 90
Crawford (Seeger), Ruth, 32, 47, 114, 183n66
Crawley, Robert, 96
Creeley, Robert, 80
Crumb, George, 118
Cruz, Celia, 150
Cummings, E. E., 32, 49, 67
Cunningham, Merce, 29, 30, 33, 43–44, 53, 62, 64, 66, 103, 104, 136, 153; rivalry with Erick Hawkins, 48–49, 94, 96
Curie, Marie, 36
Czerny, Carl, 17

Dahl, Linda, 3, 6
Davidovsky, Mario, 121, 199n54
Davies, Dennis Russell, 116, 117
Davies, Peter Maxwell, 106
Davis, Peter G., 134, 145
Dean, Laura, 136
de Beauvoir, Simone, 100
Debussy, Claude, 25, 30, 53, 110, 114
De Creeft, José, 34, 39, 83
de Kooning, Elaine, 89
de Kooning, Willem, 73, 80, 145
Dello Joio, Norman, 124
Del Tredici, David, 121
Denishawn School of Dance, 163
Deren, Maya, 63
Detroit City College, 24
Detroit Conservatory of Music, 17

Detroit Musicians League/Association, 18, 25
Dickens, Charles, 12, 88
Dickinson, Emily, 128, 160–61
Didion, Joan, 122
Dillard, Annie, 122, 129, 130
Dinesan, Isak, 122
Dlugoszewski, Chester ("Czesio"), 10, 11, 12, 14, 15–16, 79, 108, 112, 124, 142, 143, 147, 195n50
Dlugoszewski (née Goralewski), Jennie ("Jolas"), 10, 11, 12, 13–14, 29, 38, 124, 131, 140–46, 147
Dlugoszewski, Lucia: aging of, 128, 135, 143; choreography of, 138, 155–57; conflicts with Erick Hawkins, 45, 82, 98–101, 105, 122, 136, 151; "curtain of timbre," 65, 73, 74, 76, 89, 164; death of, 158–60; difficulty finishing pieces, 3, 157–58; "disparate element," 3, 83, 87, 153–54, 165; early relationship with Hawkins, 40–41, 43–44, 49–51, 52, 61; effects of sexism on, 3–6, 26, 84, 94, 99–101, 109, 115, 117, 120–21, 126, 135; insomnia of, 108, 122, 125–26, 132–33, 143; percussion instruments of, 30, 32, 83–84, 86, 94, 124; poetry of, 16, 19–20, 24, 25, 49–51, 80, 128, 146, 152, 160; possible marriage to Ralph Dorazio, 36–37, 82; star watching of, 115–16, 126, 129, 131, 141, 143–44, 149; timbre piano of, 2, 43, 44, 51, 52, 55, 56, 65, 75, 83, 84, 89, 97, 104, 109, 117, 129, 139, 140, 156, 159; and *Wigilia* 13, 40, 122, 140, 144, 203n3
Dlugoszewski, Lucia, musical works of: *5 Radiant Grounds,* 89; *8 Clear Places,* 83–88, 89, 92, 99, 148; *Abyss and Caress,* 109, 118–21, 124, 129, 133; *Amor Elusive Empty August,* 109, 127, 128, 134; *Amor Now Tilting Night,* 121–22; *Archaic Timbre Piano Music,* 65, 73, 75; *Balance Naked Flung,* 104; *Beauty Music,* 97; *Bell Buoy No. 13,* 18; *Bell's Story of Christmas, The,* 18; *Black Lake,* 83, 104, 105, 111, 129, 157; *Cantilever,* 83, 91, 92, 100, 111; *Chromium Nitrate,* 18; *Cicada Terrible Freedom,* 137–38; *Clarinet Music for Left Ear in a Small Room,* 75; *Dazzle on a Knife's Edge,* 83; *Densities: Nova, Corona, Clear Core (Angels of the Inmost Heaven),* 8, 106, 109, 110–11, 120, 124, 146; *Depth Duende Scarecrow Other (Symphony for Seven Instruments),* 154; *Disparate Stairway Radical Other,* 153–55; *Duende Newfallen,* 139–40; *Duende Quidditas,* 140; *Double and Single Labyrinths,* 65, 73; *Early Floating,* 83, 89, 204n7; *Everyday Sounds for bright by e.e. cummings,* 77; *Everyday Sounds for e.e. cummings with Transparencies,* 58; *Evolutionary Joe,* 18; *Exacerbated Subtlety Concert (Why Does a Woman Love a Man?),* 156, 157; *Fire Fragile Flight,* 109, 116–18, 120, 121, 154; *Flower Music for Left Ear in Small Room,* 75; *Geography of Noon,* 83, 93, 94, 100, 129; *Halloween Symphony,* 1, 18; *Heidi Songs, The,* 112; *In Memory of My Feelings,* 113; *Here and Now with Watchers,* 65–73, 75, 76, 77–79, 83, 85, 92, 111, 128, 163; *Lords of Persia,* 83, 100, 104, 105, 189n46; *Moving Space Theater Piece (for "everyday sounds"),* 189n49; *Music for Left Ear,* 75; *Music for Left Ear in a Small Room,* 75, 76, 97; *Music for Small Centers,* 73, 74; *Orchestra Structure for the Poetry of Everyday Sounds,* 58; openings of the (eye), 42, 44, 52–54, 61–62, 67, 68, 77, 83, 85; *Otherness Concert,* 84, 148; *Otherness Narrow Concert,* 148; *Percussion Airplane Hetero,* 97; *Percussion Flowers,* 97; *Percussion Kitetails,* 97; *Pierce Sever,* 109, 125, 129–30; *Radical Narrowness Concert [Other],* 148, 149, 154; *Radical Otherness Concert,* 148; *Radical Quidditas for an Unborn Baby,* 148; *Radical, Strange, Quidditas, Dew Tear, Duende,* 148; *Ritual of the Descent,* 77; *Song of Young Writers,* 1, 18–19; *Space is a Diamond,* 105–6, 111, 146; *Space of March and April and May Has Turned the Ground on Its Tender Side and Everyone Has to Turn the Same Way,* 56, 105; *Spring Azure,* 83, 92; *Structure for the Poetry of Everyday Sounds,* 54, 57; *Suchness*

Dlugoszewski, Lucia, musical works of (*continued*)
  Concert, 83–85, 148; *Suchness of Nine Concerts,* 104; *Suchness with Radiant Ground,* 97; *Sudden Snake Bird,* 83; *Swift and Naked,* 134; *Swift Music,* 97; *Tender Theatre Flight Nageire,* 123–25, 127; *Threshold of Changing Twins,* 65; *Tightrope,* 83, 104; *To Everybody Out There,* 83, 93; *Transparencies for Everyday Sounds,* 1–50, 58; *Transparencies for Flute,* 58; *Transparencies for Harp,* 58; *Transparencies for Harp and Violin,* 58; *Transparencies for String Quartet,* 58; *Violin Music for Left Ear in a Small Room,* 75; *Wilderness Elegant Tilt,* 136–37, 157
Dlugoszewski, Lucia, choreographic works of: *A Fountain in the Middle of the Room,* 156; *Last Love Duet,* 157; *Motherwell Amor,* 159–60; *Radical Ardent,* 157; *Taking Time to be Vulnerable,* 156; *Why Does a Man Dance,* 157
Dlugoszewski, Lucia, writings by: "Is Music Sound," 90, 114; "Notes on New Music for the Dance," 66–67; "Theatre, Timbre, Time, and Transparency," 69; "What American Democracy Means to Me," 21–22; "What is Sound to Music?," 113–16, 119
Dorazio, Mary (née Norton), 34, 37, 38, 40, 57, 60, 76, 110, 152, 153
Dorazio, Ralph, 39, 53, 54, 57, 60, 61, 62, 63, 65, 78, 83, 85, 93, 100, 110, 151; possible marriage to Dlugoszewski, 36–37, 82
downtown/uptown dichotomy, 7, 163–64
Duchamp, Marcel, 29
Duke, Katherine, 131, 148, 151, 155, 156
Duncan, Isadora, 163
Dunning, Jennifer, 148, 159–60

Eckhardt, Meister, 129
Edmunds, John, 92
Edwards, Frank, 36
Eighth Street Artist's Club ("The Club"), 28, 58, 62, 73, 89, 90
Einstein, Albert, 36, 98, 130, 139
Eiseley, Loren C., 128, 130, 132, 138, 140, 147

Eliot, T. S., 55
Emerson, Ralph Waldo, 98
Enesco, George, 30
Engstrom, Robert, 151
Erdman, Jean, 53, 55, 151, 189n34
Erick Hawkins Dance Company, 1, 5, 79, 81, 88, 102, 148, 149, 152, 153, 159; Dlugoszewski's direction of, 155–57; touring, 92–97, 109, 110. *See also* Hawkins, Erick

Feldman, Barbara Monk, 179n26
Feldman, Morton, 47, 48, 53, 57, 60, 62, 89, 123
Finckel, Chris, 134
Finkelstein, Joan, 156, 159
Finney, Ross Lee, 136
Fischer, Edwin, 26
Fisher Body (General Motors), 10, 12, 16, 34
Fishwick, William, 20
Fitzgerald, F. Scott, 10
Five Spot Cafe, 73, 74, 75, 77, 81, 86
Fontanne, Lynn (and Alfred Lunt), 30
Foss, Lukas, 112, 123, 124, 145
Frankenstein, Alfred, 1, 79
Frankenthaler, Helen, 80
Franko, Mark, 48
Freud, Sigmund, 98
Frick Museum, 33

Gagne, Cole, 5
Galileo, Galilei, 33
Gann, Kyle, 4, 162
Geist, Sidney, 86, 89, 90
Gideon, Miriam, 5, 179n18
Ginsberg, Allen, 80, 89
Giuffre, Jimmy, 113
Glackin, William C., 96
Glanville-Hicks, Peggy, 5, 39
Glass, Philip, 136
Goethe, Johann Wolfgang von, 24, 98, 122
Goode, Daniel, 179n26
Goodman, Paul, 5, 64, 89
Goodman, Vera, 89
Gottschalk, Louis Moreau, 66
Graham Ashton Brass Ensemble, 160
Graham, Martha, 35, 40, 41–42, 48–49, 54, 55, 82, 83, 92, 94, 101, 124, 163; *Appalachian Spring,* 42, 48, 163; *Cave of the*

Heart, 54; *El Penitente*, 48; *Herodiade*, 54; *Judith*, 97
Graves, Morris, 88
Green, Charles E., 94, 96
Greenwich Music School, 35, 37
Grieg, Edvard, 17
Grinnell Brothers Radio-Television Show, 18
Gruen, John, 109
Gubaidulina, Sofia, 201n20
Guest, Barbara, 62, 80
Guggenheim Fellowship, 108, 115
Guion, David, 153
Guston, Philip, 80

haiku, 88, 101, 104, 114, 122, 130, 146
Handel, George Friedric, 25
Hardy, Thomas, 98
Harkness Dance Project (92nd Street Y), 156
Harris, Conrad, 154
Harris, Julie, 150
Harrison, Lou, 33, 35, 43, 53, 56, 62, 64
Hartigan, Grace, 56, 80
Harvard University, 41, 53
Hauer, Josef Mattias, 66
Hawkins, Erick: conflicts with Dlugoszewski, 45, 82, 98–101, 105, 122, 136, 151; correspondence with Northrop, 70–72; death of, 150–51; early life, 41–42; early relationship with Dlugoszewski, 40–41, 43–44, 49–51, 52, 61; and Martha Graham, 41–42, 48, 79, 82, 83, 94; rivalry with Merce Cunningham, 48–49, 94, 96
Hawkins, Erick, choreographic works of: *8 Clear Places*, 83–88, 89, 92, 99, 148; *Angels of the Inmost Heaven*, 8, 106, 109, 110–11, 120, 124, 146; *Black Lake*, 83, 104, 105, 111, 129, 157; *Body is a Clear Place and Other Statements on Dance, The*, 61, 86, 99; *Bridegroom of the Moon*, 53; *Cantilever*, 83, 91, 92, 100, 111, 157; *Each Time You Carry Me This Way*, 149, 157; *Early Floating*, 83, 89, 204n7; *Geography of Noon*, 83, 93, 94, 100, 129; *Here and Now with Watchers*, 65–73, 75, 76, 77–79, 83, 85, 92, 111, 128, 163; *Heyoka*, 136; *Intensities of Space and Wind*, 157; *Journey of a Poet*, 153; *Killer of Enemies: The Divine Hero*, 157; *Lives of Five or Six Swords*, 53; *Lords of Persia*, 83, 100, 104, 105, 189n46; *New Moon*, 157; *Of Love*, 124; *openings of the (eye)*, 42, 44, 52–54, 61–62, 67, 68, 77, 83, 85; *Showpiece*, 41; *Spring Azure*, 83, 92; *Sudden Snake Bird*, 83; *Threshold of Changing Twins*, 65; *Tightrope*, 83, 104; *To Everybody Out There*, 83, 93. See also Erick Hawkins Dance Company
Haydn, Josef, 17, 30, 31
Hegel, Georg Wilhelm Friedrich, 98
Hellermann, William, 106, 129
Henahan, Donal, 145
Henry, Pierre, 64
Henry Street Settlement House, 37
Hensel, Fanny (Mendelssohn), 4
Hereford, Julius, 27, 30
Herrigel, Eugen, 102
Highwater, Jamake, 1, 26, 48, 117, 123, 128–29, 131, 134, 135, 136–37, 141–42, 148; *Dance: Rituals of Experience*, 129; *Primal Mind, The*, 136, 137
Hofmann, Hans, 29
Holland, Bernard, 145
Holmes, Sherlock, 23
Hovda, Eleanor, 48, 115, 153, 157
Hovhaness, Alan, 43, 53, 55, 62, 56
Hovhaness, Serafina, 55
Hovsepian, Vanig, 56
Howard, Randy, 151
Hughes, Allen, 109, 113, 145
Hunter College, 32, 86, 102
Hunter Playhouse, 53, 55, 61, 66, 86, 92
Hutchinson, Brenda, 179m26

Ibert, Jacques, 25
International Composers Guild, 31
International Society for Contemporary Music (ISCM), 32, 84, 92–93, 96
Ives, Charles, 47, 119

James, David E., 90
Jarry, Alfred, 57
Jenkins, Paul, 89
Jenkins, Speight, 135
Johnson, L. Russell, 20

Johnson, Tom, 59, 120, 122–23
Jolas, Betsy, 5, 179n18
Jones, LeRoi (Amiri Baraka), 80, 89
Jones, Margaret, 154
Jowitt, Deborah, 156
Joyce, James, 60, 87, 88, 121, 122, 127, 129, 130, 138, 140, 164
Joyce Theater, 110, 149, 151
Judson Dance Theater, 163
Juilliard School, 30, 84

Kant, Immanuel, 98
Kaprow, Allan, 89
Kavouras, Louis, 155, 160
Keats, John, 122
Keefer, Julia, 51, 75, 111, 126
Kelly, Gene, 150
Kennedy, John, 179n26
Kerner, Leighton, 111, 134, 138, 145, 160
Kerouac, Jack, 80
Kiesler, Frederick, 37, 76, 80, 92, 97
Kiesler, Lillian, 76, 129, 131, 143, 151, 155, 156
Kirkpatrick, John, 77
Kirstein, Lincoln, 41
Kisselgoff, Anna, 110, 150, 152, 156, 159
Kitchen, The, 131, 134
Klee, Paul, 88
Kline, Franz, 80
Knickerbocker, R. H., 21
Koch, Kenneth, 80
Kokubo, Ted, 20
Kolb, Barbara, 123
Koussevitzky International Recording Award, 108, 117, 135
Krenek, Ernst, 98
Kreutzberg, Harald, 41
Kuhn, Chester, 24

Lang, Nancy, 66
Langlitz, David, 124
Lawrence, D. H., 98, 129
Lawson, Dorothy, 154
Leach, Mary Jane, 179n26
League of Composers, 26, 40
Lee, Ralph, 151
Lerner, Gerda, 6
Lessing, Doris, 122
Lewis, John L., 29

Lewis, Kevin D., 192n37, 193n6
Library of Congress, 7, 16, 131, 134
Ligeti, György, 195n51
Lincoln Center, 94, 163; Lincoln Center Chamber Music Society, 116, 131, 137, 157
Liszt, Franz, 17
Living Theatre, The, 1, 2, 28, 54, 55–59, 64, 81, 87, 89, 104; *Desire Trapped by the Tail* (Picasso), 55, 56; *Ubu the King* (Jarry), 57–59; *Women of Trachis* (Sophocles), 89
Lorca, Federico García, 139
Lovisco, Mr., 34, 40, 183n68
Lunt, Alfred (and Lynn Fontanne), 30

MacAdam, Barbara, 151
MacDonald, Rose, 79
MacDowell, Edward, 17, 25
Mahler, David, 179n26
Malina, Judith, 5, 54, 55–56, 57, 61–62, 63–64, 66
Mann, Thomas, 24
Mannes School of Music, 29, 30, 35, 46
Margun Music, 105, 110, 146
Marks, Jackie. *See* Highwater, Jamake
Marsicano, Meryl, 62
Marsicano, Nick, 62
Martino, Donald, 118
Mason, Francis, 151
Masselos, William, 127
Maxfield, Richard, 89
McClean, Gloria, 153, 155, 156
McDonagh, Don, 85–86
McEwen, Louis, 155
Meehan, Nancy, 151
Mekas, Jonas (*Guns of the Trees*), 89–90, 112, 160
Melville, Herman, 87, 100
Mendelssohn, Felix, 17, 25
Menken, Marie, 58. *See also Visual Variations on Noguchi*
Menotti, Gian Carlo, 46
Miller, Arthur, 63
Mills College of Education (New York), 71, 72, 74
Mingus, Charles, 112, 113
Mitchell, Joan, 80
Mitropoulos, Dmitri, 30

Monk, Meredith, 163
Monk, Thelonious, 73
Moorman, Charlotte, 123
Morrison, Adelgatha, 17
Morton, Lawrence, 93
Moses, Michael, 151, 155
Motherwell, Renate Ponsold, 149
Motherwell, Robert, 1, 58, 73, 80, 135, 144, 145, 149
Mozart, Wolfgang Amadeus, 17, 165
Mu'Chi, 101
Munch, Edvard, 35
Museum of Modern Art, 35, 39, 62, 91, 127

Nabokov, Vladimir, 114
National Endowment for the Arts, 118, 121, 149
National Medal of Honor, 149–50
Native Land Foundation, 129, 148
NBC Telephone Hour, 36
New Music Federation of American Composers, 36
New York Philharmonic, 10, 30, 108, 118, 120, 121, 123
New York School, The, 6, 28–29, 45, 57, 90
Nicholls, David, 179n26
Nietzsche, Friedrich, 24, 98
Nin, Anaïs, 5, 80
92nd Street Y, 55, 159
Noguchi, Isamu, 1, 60, 65, 117, 135, 201n12
Northeastern High School (Detroit), 17, 20–23
Northrop, F. S. C., 1, 67, 70–72, 76, 78, 79, 90, 91, 98, 114, 121, 129, 140, 164; *Man, Nature, and God,* 102; *Meeting of East and West, The* (1946/1960), 70, 102, 129; *Philosophical Anthropology and Practical Politics,* 72
Norton, Mary. *See* Dorazio, Mary (née Norton)

Oestreich, James R., 148
O'Gorman, Ned, 86
O'Hara, Frank, 1, 29, 56, 58, 62, 79, 80, 112, 113
Olmstead, Leland H., 20
Olson, Charles, 80
Orchestra of Our Time, 117, 129

Ortega, Sergio, 200n57
Ortiz, Kathy, 151, 155
Orvis, Floran, 124, 140–44, 147
Oyama, Phyllis, 151

Paderewski, Ignacy Jan, 25
Paer, Lewis, 134
Palma, Donald, 134
Pan American Association of Composers, 26, 31
Partch, Harry, 6, 124, 163, 179n27
Paulina Rieloff Gallery, 149
Paul Taylor Dance Company, 94
Perle, George, 98
Perras, John, 77
Persichetti, Vincent, 46
Phillips, John Ransom, 131, 148–49, 151
Picasso, Pablo, 55
Poindexter Gallery, 78
Polish culture, 10–13, 17, 19, 25, 34, 38
Pollock, Jackson, 80
Pound, Ezra, 34, 89
Proust, Marcel, 88

Quan, Linda, 134

Rainer, Yvonne, 163
Raining, Eva, 65
Rameau, Jean Phillipe, 17
Rammel, Hal, 58, 125, 154, 156, 163
Rauschenberg, Robert, 29
Ravel, Maurice, 25
Reagan, Ronald, 136
Reich, Steve, 136
Reimann, Aribert, 201n20
Reinhardt, Ad, 63, 75, 91, 93, 97
Reinhart, Charles, 151
Reynolds, Cynthia, 153, 155
Richards, Eric, 179n26
Richards, M. C., 80
Riegger, Wallingford, 30, 33, 53
Rivers, Larry, 80
Rollings, Nigel, 122
Roosevelt, Franklin Delano, 14
Rorem, Ned, 64, 112, 123–24, 129
Rosenlieb, Todd, 155
Rosenman, Ellen Bayuk, 6
Ross, Alex, 165

Routch, Robert, 124
Rudhyar, Dane, 39
Ruggles, Carl, 43
Rzewski, Frederic, 126

Sabin, Robert, 52, 53, 56, 79
Salieri, Antonio, 165
Salinger, J. D., 76, 88, 90, 91, 192n37
Salzer, Felix, 27, 30, 46
Sandler, Irving, 62, 90, 91
Santoro, Gene, 113
Sartre, Jean-Paul, 141
Satie, Erik, 47, 66, 78, 195n51
Scarlatti, Domenico, 25
Schaeffer, Pierre, 64, 190n9
Schenker, Heinrich, 46
Schoenberg, Arnold, 39, 88, 103
Schubert, Franz, 23, 30, 130, 139, 194n27
Schuller, Gunther, 105, 110, 120, 145
Schuman, William, 30, 40, 97, 124, 145
Schumann, Robert, 126
Schwartz, Charles, 77
Schwartz, Delmore, 8
Schwarz, Gerard, 105–6, 118–20, 124, 140, 157
Scripps American Dance Festival Award, 150
Seeger, Pete, 150
Sekula, Sonja, 3
Shakespeare, William, 24, 88
Shields, Alan, 96
Shultis, Christopher, 179n26
Silverman, Stanley, 118
Silverton, Michael, 155
Simons, Netty, 77
Slonimsky, Nicolas, 193n11
Smith, Carlton J., 145
Smith, David, 58
Smith, Leon, 71
Smith, Norman, 124
Smith, Philip, 55
Smyth, Ethel, 3
Solie, Ruth, 3
Sollberger, Harvey, 145
Sorell, Walter, 91, 96
Sperry, Paul, 113
Staltman, Mary, 22
St. Denis, Ruth, 163

Stein, Gertrude, 55, 72, 78, 102, 129, 130
Stephan, Ruth, 112
Sterba, Richard and Editha, 183n67
Sterner, Christina, 153
Stiller, Andrew, 125
Stockhausen, Karlheinz, 70, 97
Stowe, Harriet Beecher, 15
Stravinsky, Igor, 10, 31, 87, 88, 152; *Agon*, 66; *The Flood*, 194n25
Sultan, Grete, 26–27, 30, 32, 33, 35–36, 37, 38, 40, 42, 43, 89, 127
Suzuki, Dean, 110
Swaggart, Jimmy, 142
Swedenborg, Emanuel, 110

Tai, Paul, 7, 179n24
Talma, Louise, 123
Tanabe, Mariko, 151
Tanglewood Festival of Contemporary Music (1976), 120, 121–22, 179n18
Taylor, David, 124, 134, 140
Terry, Walter, 104, 163
Tharin, Catherine, 151, 155
Tharpe, Twyla, 163
Thomas, Dylan, 29, 30, 63
Thome, Joel, 59, 115, 117, 129, 133, 145, 152, 154, 160
Thomson, Virgil, 1, 5, 30, 33, 78, 90, 91, 95–96, 97, 106, 111–12, 115, 119, 121, 129, 145, 164; *American Music Since 1910*, 78, 112; *Sonata da Chiesa*, 97
Thoreau, Henry David, 122
Tick, Judith, 3
Tillard, Françoise, 4
Tircuit, Heuwell, 118
Trigg, William, 148, 158, 159
Trimble, Lester, 112
Tucker, Barbara, 77
Tudor, David, 40, 47, 188n18
Tyler, Parker, 63, 97
Tyranny, "Blue" Gene, 110, 179n26

Unamuno, Miguel de, 139

Van Loen, Alfred, 39
Varèse, Edgard, 1, 27, 29, 30, 33, 34, 35, 39, 59, 88, 114, 117, 127; influence on Dlugoszewski, 4, 31–32, 46–47, 84, 110, 111,

154, 162–63, 178n10, 183n66; *Arcana*, 117; *Density 21.5*, 33; *Ionisation*, 84, 193n11; *Octandre*, 47
Varèse, Louise, 117
Ventura, Anita, 86
Vierk, Lois V, 164, 179n26
Visual Variations on Noguchi, 59–60, 65
Vogelweide, Walther von der, 64

Wagner, Richard, 18
Wagner, Sallie R., 99, 135
Wayne State University, 12, 23–25
WBAI, 97
Weber, Ben, 35, 46, 187n2
Webern, Anton von, 47, 88, 114, 126, 129
Wen-chung, Chou, 123
Whitehead, Alfred North, 98, 130
White Horse Tavern, 28, 63
White Oak Dance Project, 153; White Oak Ensemble, 154

Whitney Museum, 112–13, 127
Wigglesworth, Frank, 43
Williams, William Carlos, 24, 26, 30
Wittgenstein, Ludwig, 98, 121, 130, 140
WNYC, 30, 116, 140
Wolff, Christian, 30, 60, 66, 179n26, 183n67, 184n9
Woolf, Virginia, 6, 67
Wuorinen, Charles, 98
WXYZ, 17

Xenakis, Iannis, 98, 195n51

Yates, Peter, 93, 96
Young, La Monte, 89
Young Writers' Club, 18–19

Zen Buddhism, 57, 59, 60, 88, 95, 112
Zen for Ryoko-in, A, 112
Zimmermann, Alan, 179n26

CALIFORNIA STUDIES IN 20TH-CENTURY MUSIC

Richard Taruskin, General Editor

1. *Revealing Masks: Exotic Influences and Ritualized Performance in Modernist Music Theater,* by W. Anthony Sheppard

2. *Russian Opera and the Symbolist Movement,* by Simon Morrison

3. *German Modernism: Music and the Arts,* by Walter Frisch

4. *New Music, New Allies: American Experimental Music in West Germany from the Zero Hour to Reunification,* by Amy C. Beal

5. *Bartók, Hungary, and the Renewal of Tradition: Case Studies in the Intersection of Modernity and Nationality,* by David E. Schneider

6. *Classic Chic: Music, Fashion, and Modernism,* by Mary E. Davis

7. *Music Divided: Bartók's Legacy in Cold War Culture,* by Danielle Fosler-Lussier

8. *Jewish Identities: Nationalism, Racism, and Utopianism in Twentieth-Century Art Music,* by Klára Móricz

9. *Brecht at the Opera,* by Joy H. Calico

10. *Beautiful Monsters: Imagining the Classic in Musical Media,* by Michael Long

11. *Experimentalism Otherwise: The New York Avant-Garde and Its Limits,* by Benjamin Piekut

12. *Music and the Elusive Revolution: Cultural Politics and Political Culture in France, 1968–1981,* by Eric Drott

13. *Music and Politics in San Francisco: From the 1906 Quake to the Second World War,* by Leta E. Miller

14. *Frontier Figures: American Music and the Mythology of the American West,* by Beth E. Levy

15. *In Search of a Concrete Music,* by Pierre Schaeffer, translated by Christine North and John Dack

16. *The Musical Legacy of Wartime France,* by Leslie A. Sprout

17. *Arnold Schoenberg's* A Survivor from Warsaw *in Postwar Europe,* by Joy H. Calico

18. *Music in America's Cold War Diplomacy,* by Danielle Fosler-Lussier

19. *Making New Music in Cold War Poland: The Warsaw Autumn Festival, 1956–1968,* by Lisa Jakelski

20. *Treatise on Musical Objects: An Essay across Disciplines,* by Pierre Schaeffer, translated by Christine North and John Dack

21. *Nostalgia for the Future: Luigi Nono's Selected Writings and Interviews,* edited by Angela Ida De Benedictis and Veniero Rizzardi

22. *The* Doctor Faustus *Dossier: Arnold Schoenberg, Thomas Mann, and Their Contemporaries, 1930–1951,* edited by E. Randol Schoenberg, with an introduction by Adrian Daub

23. *Stravinsky in the Americas: Transatlantic Tours and Domestic Excursions from Wartime Los Angeles (1925–1945),* by H. Colin Slim, with a foreword by Richard Taruskin

24. *Middlebrow Modernism: Britten's Operas and the Great Divide,* by Christopher Chowrimootoo

25. *A Wayfaring Stranger: Ernst von Dohnányi's American Years, 1949–1960,* by Veronika Kusz, translated by Viktória Kusz and Brian McLean

26. *In Stravinsky's Orbit: Responses to Modernism in Russian Paris,* by Klára Móricz

27. *Zoltan Kodaly's World of Music,* by Anna Dalos

28. *Awangarda: Tradition and Modernity in Postwar Polish Music,* by Lisa Cooper Vest

29. *Magician of Sound: Ravel and the Aesthetics of Illusion,* by Jessie Fillerup
30. *The Art of Appreciation: Music and Middlebrow Culture in Modern Britain,* by Kate Guthrie
31. *Terrible Freedom: The Life and Work of Lucia Dlugoszewski,* by Amy C. Beal

Founded in 1893,
UNIVERSITY OF CALIFORNIA PRESS
publishes bold, progressive books and journals
on topics in the arts, humanities, social sciences,
and natural sciences—with a focus on social
justice issues—that inspire thought and action
among readers worldwide.

The UC PRESS FOUNDATION
raises funds to uphold the press's vital role
as an independent, nonprofit publisher, and
receives philanthropic support from a wide
range of individuals and institutions—and from
committed readers like you. To learn more, visit
ucpress.edu/supportus.

www.ingramcontent.com/pod-product-compliance
Lightning Source LLC
Chambersburg PA
CBHW030531230426
43665CB00010B/843